11/04

Withdrawn

THE MIND AT WORK

THE MIND AT
WORK

*Valuing the Intelligence
of the American Worker*

MIKE ROSE

◊ VIKING ◊

HD
4901
.R67
2004

VIKING
Published by the Penguin Group
Penguin Group (USA) Inc., 375 Hudson Street, New York, New York 10014, U.S.A.
Penguin Books Ltd, 80 Strand, London WC2R 0RL, England
Penguin Books Australia Ltd, 250 Camberwell Road, Camberwell,
Victoria 3124, Australia
Penguin Books Canada Ltd, 10 Alcorn Avenue, Toronto, Ontario, Canada M4V 3B2
Penguin Books India (P) Ltd, 11 Community Centre,
Panchsheel Park, New Delhi–110 017, India
Penguin Group (NZ) Ltd, Cnr Airborne and Rosedale Roads, Albany,
Auckland 1310, New Zealand
Penguin Books (South Africa) (Pty) Ltd, 24 Sturdee Avenue, Rosebank,
Johannesburg 2196, South Africa

Penguin Books Ltd, Registered Offices: 80 Strand, London WC2R 0RL, England

First published in 2004 by Viking Penguin,
a member of Penguin Group (USA) Inc.

10 9 8 7 6 5 4 3 2 1

Grateful acknowledgment is made for permission to reprint excerpts from the following copyrighted works:
    "Partner #6" from *Pioneering: Poems from the Construction Site* by Susan Eisen-
berg, Cornell University Press. Copyright © 1998 by Susan Eisenberg.
    "To Be of Use" from *The Art of Blessing the Day: Poems with a Jewish Theme* by
Marge Piercy, Alfred A. Knopf. Copyright © 1999 by Marge Piercy.

LIBRARY OF CONGRESS CATALOGING-IN-PUBLICATION DATA
Rose, Mike.
    The mind at work : valuing the intelligence of the American worker / Mike Rose.
        p.   cm.
    ISBN 0-670-03282-4
    1. Blue collar workers. 2. Mind and body. 3. Work—Psychological aspects. I. Title.
    HD4901.R67 2004
    331.7'001'9—dc22   2003065760

This book is printed on acid-free paper. ∞

Printed in the United States of America

Designed by Carla Bolte   •   *Set in Scala, with Gill Sans*

For

ROSE EMILY MERAGLIO

and for

FRANK AND JOE

I learned it from them

▲

CONTENTS

INTRODUCTION: MIND AND WORK

I grew up a witness to the intelligence of the waitress in motion, the reflective welder, the strategy of the guy on the assembly line. This, then, is something I know: the thought it takes to do physical work. Such work put food on our table, gave shape to stories of affliction and ability, framed how I saw the world. I come from a family of immigrants who, with two exceptions, did not finish high school, and who worked in blue-collar or service jobs all their lives. I did not do so well in school myself, spent several years in the vocational track, and squeaked my way into a small college on probation—the first in the family to go beyond high school. Measures of intellectual ability and assumptions about it are woven throughout this history. So I've been thinking about this business of intelligence for a long time: the way we decide who's smart and who isn't, the way the work someone does feeds into that judgment, and the effect such judgment has on our sense of who we are and what we can do.

It was tough work that my family did. I would later come to understand the dynamics of occupational status and social class, but I could sense early on how difficult the work was, and that without it, we'd starve. I also saw that people knew things through work. And they used what they learned. This experience was all very specific to me, not abstract, emerging from the lived moments of work I had witnessed, from all sorts of objects and images, from sound and smell, from rhythms of the body. These sensory particulars stay with me, resonant.

There was a table covered with slick plastic in the center of my grandmother's kitchen. Anyone who visited drank a cup of coffee there, wooden chair turned sideways to talk to her as she cooked. All meals were eaten at this table. My uncle Frank, a welder for the Pennsylvania Railroad, has come in from work, soiled denim, the smell of machinist's oil in it, his face smeared with soot. He washes at the kitchen sink, sleeves rolled up, scrubbing his arms, full lather, angling them under the faucet. He settles in at the table; there's a radio at its edge, and he turns it on to hear the evening news. My grandmother sets a large plate of steaming macaroni before him, deep red sauce; there is a bowl of chops, cooked earlier, in the center of the table. Frank's hands are huge, and as he talks to us—a deep voice that can quickly rise in amazement—he tears off a big chunk of Italian bread and begins to eat with a focus and capacity that made its way into the comic tales told about him by his brothers, stories I would acquire through the hearing. After a while, he pushes the chair back, but not too far, unbuttons the top of his trousers, says he's eaten way too much, dear Lord, and reaches for a chop, or for that loaf of bread, and leans in again, a deep pleasure against the bitter cold and exhaustion of the roundhouse.

Frank was a guy who made it a point to know things; he read a lot and inquired until he understood how something worked. It felt good to be with him. I remember him, his well-spoken voice, guiding me through the Railroader's Museum: cutaways of running gear; diagrams and technical information on steam, diesel, and electric locomotives; photos of wooden freight cars, cabooses, the interiors of luxury passenger cars; posed workmen; lots of repair equipment; an operational model railroad. I knew of Frank's many complaints about the railroad: layoffs and erratic scheduling, the brutal hours, the biting cold or sweltering heat, the burns over his arms and legs. But Frank also saw himself as a "railroad man," someone who had made his contribution to this major American industry. Doing a job well mattered. "Work hard," he wrote to his son, away in the army. "No one likes a half-assed man." One of the moments I remember from that day at the museum, a simple but lasting one, is Frank standing before a display case, pointing to some miniature assembly of cable and gear, explaining in detail how it worked, taking his time until I got it.

Many testaments have been written, both in fiction and memoir, about the physical labor of our forebears: from accounts of the prairie farm, the mills, and the mines to tales of immigrant life—the Lower East Side to the agricultural fields of Central and Southern California. One of the most stirring moments in Mario Cuomo's keynote address to the 1984 Democratic National Convention is the memory of his father working long and hard hours in the family grocery store, teaching the young Mario "all I needed to know about faith and hard work by the simple eloquence of his example." Such invocation speaks powerfully to Americans, stirs things deep in our cultural and personal histories. How interesting it is, though, that our testaments to physical work are so often focused on the values such work exhibits rather than on the thought it requires. It is a subtle but pervasive omission. Yet there is a mind at work in dignity, and values are intimately related to thought and action.

It is as though in our cultural iconography we are given the muscled arm, sleeve rolled tight against biceps, but no thought bright behind the eye, no image that links hand and brain. I find myself here wondering about Cuomo's father. I imagine the many decisions he had to make, the alternatives large and small he weighed, the moments when he had to think quickly through his fatigue.

My mother shaped her adult identity in the restaurant business and, all the while I was growing up, worked as a waitress in coffee shops and family-style restaurants. My father and I would some-times visit her at Coffee Dan's, waiting for her shift to end, riding the bus home together, her feet killing her. When she worked the counter and took cash, we would find two stools by the register; when she had the main room, we sat at the back booth where the waitresses took their break. We would pass the time with her once the lunch or dinner rush had faded. There wasn't much for a child to do, the hours stretched out, so I listened to the cooks and wait-resses. They talked about the customers, or the boss, or each other; about the things going on at home with their kids; about how tired they were. And I watched what they did.

I remember particular people, like my mother's coworker Rose Goldstein, a gentle woman whose house across town we visited, and Bobbi, the new hire just out of high school, on whom I had a desperate crush. And there was a cook whose name I've forgotten, but who would sit in the booth on break, smoking, solemn, food splattered all over his white uniform, down to the shoes. At the back booth, you would catch the thick smell of the grill and the whiff of stale food and cigarettes, scraped and dumped. These odors hung in my mother's uniform and hair. When things got busy, there was a heightened clatter of kitchen and dishwasher, and I could feel the rise in the pulse of the place: the cacophony of customers' voices; waitresses weaving in and out, warning "behind you" in a voice both impassive and urgent; all these people eating separately in one big public space.

I remember the restaurant's lingo, remember liking the code of it. Tables were labeled by the number of chairs—and, thus, customers—around them: *deuces, four-tops, six-tops.* Areas of the restaurant had names: the *racetrack* was the speedy front section. Orders were abbreviated for the cook: *fry four on two,* my mother would call out as she clipped a check onto that little rotating wheel. To speak this language gave you a certain authority, signaled know-how.

I have many images of my mother at work, distinct from the other domains of her life: her walking full-tilt with an armload of plates along one arm and two cups of coffee somehow cradled in her other hand; her taking orders, pencil poised over pad; her flopping down in the booth by my father, the whoosh of the cushion; "I'm all in," she'd say, and whisper something quickly to us about a customer. She would stand before a table, her arm stacked with those plates, picking one order off for this person, then another, then another—always seeming to get it right, knowing who got the hamburger, who got the fried shrimp. She'd argue with the cook over a returned order; "he gave me lip," she'd tell us, rushing by. I remember her sitting sideways at the back booth, talking to us, her one hand gripping the outer edge of the table, watching the floor, and noting, in the flow of our conversation, who needed something, who was finishing up, whose order was taking longer to prepare than it should.

What did I come to know about work like Frank's or my mother's, mechanical-industrial or life in the restaurant? Surely, that it was hard, physically taxing, dirty, injurious. I never knew my grandfather—he died of pneumonia before I was born—but I heard, with some frequency, a story about him losing his leg in the railroad stockyards, the same place where Frank worked. This was not the kind of work my parents and uncles and aunts wanted their kids to do. I knew, as well, that work was unsteady; you could lose your job, with disastrous consequences. Hard as it was, railed against as it occasionally was, work was coveted, for it was a stay against poverty. One reason my mother valued waitressing was that she knew she could always find work. I also got the clear sense from observing people in my family or in the neighborhood that having work, though you'd be wiped out at day's end, affected your overall mood, your bearing. The men in the neighborhood who were out of work were unhappily at loose ends, sitting around, listless, time on their hands. My mother bemoaned the physical punishment of her job, but she spoke as well about "being among the public." The phrase carried for her a claim of achievement. The Pennsylvania Railroad had Frank—had much of the town—in its grip, and he cursed it often. But he was, finally, a railroad man— hard work, masculine, with national consequence. The work that my uncle and my mother did affected their sense of who they were, and, though limiting in so many ways, it provided a means of doing something in the world.

Doing something in the world. I couldn't have expressed it this way when I was growing up, but the work I saw connected in my mind with agency and competence—that's what being an adult meant to me, and it was intimately tied to physical work. And, as does any child, I craved competence. Special terminology caught my ear, the idiom of freight trains or food orders, because not everyone could speak it, especially speak it the right way, and it made things happen. Particular movements of the body made things happen, too, in the restaurant or the stockyard. And there was knowledge of tools and devices, wrenches and hacksaws and measures, but the cash register, too, and the whirring blender. Tied to this knowledge were tricks of the trade. And what a kick it was when one of my uncles or a cook or a waitress showed me how to do something a little more effectively, with a little less effort and a little more finesse. Hold it this way. Move it in, like this. See? I became the work's insider, if just for a moment.

I have been a teacher for over thirty years in a wide range of settings: from kindergarten to adult literacy programs, and now in a research university's graduate school of education. Many of the populations I've taught and studied were considered to be educationally at-risk, and questions about intellectual capacity, either implied or explicit, were ever-present. And in a school of education, issues of ability, schooling, and work are part of the conceptual terrain. One thing I've learned from all this is the powerful effect our assumptions about intelligence have on the way people are defined and treated in the classroom, the workplace, and the public sphere. It seems fitting, therefore, to turn with the investigative tools I now have to the work represented by my forebears—factory work, skilled and semiskilled trades, and service occupations—with a focus on the mental processes involved in doing such work, the thought that enables it. To be sure, our view of occupations is shaped by the form of capitalism that has developed in the United States and by the social traditions that attend particular occupations. But running through this economic and cultural history are beliefs about mind. *The Mind at Work*, then, offers an analysis of physical work and intelligence and a reflection on how we might think more clearly and fairly about them.

◻

Labor, as a political and social force, has diminished in power and has less immediate grab on the national imagination. The work that currently captures our fancy involves high technology, electronic media, and "symbolic analysis." Trumpeted as an unprecedented kind of work, such "knowledge work" represents emerging opportunity. It is associated with advanced education, and there is no doubt that work of this type requires high levels of analytic skill. What concerns me, though, is the implication—evident in popular discourse about work—that so-called older types of work, like manufacturing or service work, are, by and large, mindless, "neck down" rather than "neck up." (There is, by the way, a degree of historical amnesia here: each industrial generation heralds the unprecedented intellectual demands of its work.) But, though identified with another era, work of body and hand continues to create the material web of daily life. As with any human achievement, such work merits our understanding; the way we talk about it matters. And the dimension of it that is least discussed and appreciated—and that we can continue to learn from— is the thought it takes to do it well.

A related issue is the way we classify work itself. "Writers on work," notes sociologist Steven Peter Vallas, "routinely employ certain stock categories—'blue-' versus 'white-collar,' 'mental' versus 'manual' labor." Vallas acknowledges that these categories are sometimes useful, but we rely too heavily on them and fail "to observe subtle commonalities between apparently different forms of work." These limiting categories reaffirm longstanding biases about particular occupations and cause us to miss so much: The mental processes that enable service. The aesthetics of physical labor. The complex interplay of the social and the mechanical. The choreography of hand, eye, ear, brain. The everpresence of abstraction, planning, and problem solving in everyday work.

More immediate policy deliberations about work—I write this, for example, during a period of economic downturn and a fragile "jobless recovery"—are focused on specific tangible remedies: economic stimuli, job creation, training programs, and the like. Tied to such discussions are assessments of the state of the workforce, the number unemployed, gross measures of skill level, breakouts by race and gender. And there is, as well, a broader assessment of the workforce that will be a central concern of this book: the general sense of what workers can do, their competence, their intellectual capacity. Such appraisals may well include specific measures—for example, high school graduation as an indicator of literacy and numeracy—but there is also a psychological and cultural dimension to this reckoning, just as there is, at least in some schools of thought, to assessments of the economy. Consider, then, an observation by labor journalist John P. Hoerr: "Since the early days of industrialization, a peculiar notion has gained ascendancy in the United States: that wage workers and their representatives lacked the competence to handle complex issues and problems that required abstract knowledge and analytical ability." This sense of deficiency is in our cultural bones, and it affects, and distorts, the specific economic responses we develop, from education and job training to the way work is organized.

The nation is currently engaged in a discussion about the training of the workforce and about a range of educational experiments involving the integration of the academic and vocational curriculum and the transition from school to work. Yet the educational literature on these issues tends to be pretty thin on any close analysis of the cognitive dimension of physical work. This absence, I think, is rooted in the reductive notions the society carries about such work and the people who do it, notions that prove to be especially troubling as we try to rethink the connection between the schoolhouse and the workplace.

I also believe that there are important social issues here. Judgments about intelligence carry great weight in our culture, and one of the ways we judge each other's intelligence is through the work we do. There are many distinctions that can be made among types of work, distinctions related to income, autonomy, cleanliness, physical risk, and so on. These have a harshly real material meaning, but carry symbolic meaning as well. There's a moral and characterological aura to occupational autonomy, income, cleanliness, leading us to slip from qualities of the work to qualities of the worker. This kind of generalizing, this slippage of assumptions, runs through our cultural history, from post–Revolutionary War mechanics who were portrayed as illiterate and incapable of participating in government to the autoworkers I heard labeled by one supervisor as "a bunch of dummies." These generalizations about mind and work are intimately tied to the dynamics of social class and affect the way we think about each other and ourselves. One of the more striking things writer Barbara Ehrenreich found as she worked a series of low-wage jobs to write *Nickel and Dimed* was how invisible she became. The way work gets defined and the attributions we make about it affect more than occupational rank and income; these attributions color the kind of social and civic life we can imagine.

▢

Running through the upcoming chapters are several key terms, terms with such broad sweep, used in so many ways, that, as I begin to preview this book's contents, some defining is in order.

First, *intelligence,* and the broader term *cognition.* Cognition refers to those mental processes involving perception, attention, memory, knowing, judging. These processes will be displayed throughout the work we're considering as the waitress prioritizes tasks during rush hour or the electrician troubleshoots a faulty circuit. Some researchers study cognition in laboratory settings and others in natural contexts. I will discuss more about method in the afterword, but here let me say that I draw on both kinds of studies to inform the argument of this book. The portraits of cognition you'll read, though, are for the most part developed from my studies of people at work. The busy restaurant, the job site, and the factory floor each present different tasks to be solved, calling forth different cognitive processes. Also, cognition is, I believe, intimately tied to motives and values, to long-range as well as immediate goals, and to one's life history. As a friend of mine so vividly put it, we're not just a brain in a bottle. We think in a material and social world. So when I can, I provide biographical information for the people we're observing, and I am able to provide much more of that kind of detail in the family sketches that run through these pages. It was, after all, through my family that I first saw work close at hand.

Though a more specific term than cognition, intelligence is a much-debated concept. To get us started, I'll use a composite of the most familiar Western definitions of intelligence: it is the ability to learn and act on the environment, to apply knowledge to new situations, to reason, plan, and solve problems. Such definitions have a pervasive effect on educational policy and occupational classification—so they will prove useful to us, for they are the terms of our public discourse. We need to keep in mind, though, that there are aspects of human mental activity that are not captured in the standard definitions of intelligence. They will be evident, however, in the work settings we'll explore.

Because intelligence is such a loaded term, let me sketch out a little more background and offer my own perspective. The way we think about intelligence in the United States has been shaped over the last century by the psychometric tradition, mental measurement, known to most of us through an intelligence test taken in school or in the military. This tradition has contributed—sometimes through misinterpretation—to a number of interconnected popular beliefs about intelligence: that it is a single and unitary quality (so if you're smart, you're smart across the board); that it's fixed, consistent (and this plays into further beliefs about the degree to which intelligence is inherited); that it can be accurately measured with an instrument like an intelligence test and represented numerically, typically through an IQ score; and that people's success in life, or more broadly, their place in the social order, is a reflection of their intelligence. This book is not the place to unpack the many arguments within education, psychology, anthropology, and cognitive science about these claims. Suffice it to say that they—and other aspects of mental measurement, including the statistical procedures that are central to the field—are hotly contested, and, in fact, have been since the father of the modern intelligence test, Alfred Binet, himself raised concerns about the use and interpretation of his instrument.

It is also important to note that within the West there are powerful research traditions that yield other conceptions of intelligence and other means to assess it. In various ways, these traditions posit, for example, that there are multiple components to intelligence, or even multiple intelligences; that intelligence is variable and dynamic; that social context is crucial to its emergence and display; that creativity, emotion, aesthetic response, and the use of the body—removed from traditional psychometric definitions and tests of intelligence—must be considered as aspects of intelligent behavior. And, finally, it is very important to note that any discussion of intelligence is culture-bound. Some aspects of what we consider intelligence might well overlap with definitions from other cultures, but many cultures posit a range of further or different attributes to intelligence, for example, the ability to live in harmony with others.

It is undisputed that formal education will affect one's score on an intelligence test, since the tests tend to be heavy on verbal and numerical items. The big challenge to test designers, then, is to create at least a few components that, in theory, will not be affected by schooling, for example, identifying the missing element in a visual pattern. Though the success of this endeavor is (yet another) contested issue, it seems pretty clear that it is difficult—some say impossible—to tease out the effects of education (including a familiarity with and investment in tests like these) from the effect of "pure" intelligence. Here's what concerns me, given the spirit of this book. If one does well on an intelligence test, that clearly indicates some kind of cognitive competence. But if one doesn't do well—and, historically, poor performers would include low-income, working people—then the meaning of the score is much less clear. So, we have a measure that works only at the upper end of the scale. To do well tells us something about intelligence—and, usually, schooling—but not to do well provides much less information about intellectual capacity . . . though that poor performance may speak volumes about educational opportunity. My worry is the ease with which poor performance gets interpreted as an accurate measure of intelligence, and the effect that interpretation has on the test-taker, both personally and societally.

This is not a call for a simplified egalitarianism. I am not denying the obvious fact that people come to any pursuit with different interests, talents, knacks for things, motivations, capabilities. Nor am I claiming that all bodies of knowledge and expressions of mind are of the same level of cognitive complexity and social importance. All the cultures I'm familiar with make judgments about competence in the domains that matter to them. (Though ours is more obsessed than any I know with developing measures of the mind and schemes to rank them.) No, the distressing thing is that both in our institutional systems and in our informal talk we tend to label entire categories of work and the people associated with them in ways that generalize, erase cognitive variability, and diminish whole traditions of human activity. Attributions of merit and worth flow throughout the process. We order, we rank, we place at steps upon a ladder rather than appreciating an abundant and varied cognitive terrain.

Skill. Let's begin with the *American Heritage Dictionary.* Skill is "proficiency, facility, or dexterity that is acquired or developed through training or experience." In traditional usage, this proficiency would be related to the use of body or hand, though more recently, the word *skill* has come to apply to a wide range of activities. We talk, for example, of communication skills or general problem-solving skills.

It is important to remember, however, that what gets defined as a skill is historically and culturally determined, and this process is of special significance in labeling kinds of work. The politics and power plays by which particular interest groups get one kind of work categorized as "skilled" and another as "semiskilled" or "unskilled" have significant economic and social consequences. Another historical phenomenon to note here is the increasing role school has played over the past century in developing and certifying skills that, in previous eras, would have been developed within the job setting itself. The value that a skill has is also determined by time and place. In the rhetoric of the "new economy," for example, communication skills or general problem-solving skills or the ability to work in teams are privileged, while more specific mechanical skills—associated with conventional blue-collar work—tend to be perceived as less valuable. All of these processes of definition and the status they confer involve attributions of cognition and intelligence, and thus play into the concerns of this book.

Work. What our society defines as work also changes over time and place (consider the debates over how to classify domestic labor), and what gets classified as work in one setting (styling hair in a salon, repairing cars in a garage) would be labeled a hobby if done in another context. There is a fluid quality to this concept of work. For my purposes, I'll posit that work is purposeful, remunerated effort that provides goods or services for another. The majority of people in our society have to work for some significant portion of their lives. Work, any work, calls forth a range of human abilities, from the classifying of objects to the exerting of will. And work is freighted with meaning and moral judgment, by the society, by ourselves. "Work," writes occupational sociologist Everett Cherrington Hughes, "is one of the things by which [people] are judged, and certainly one of the more significant things by which [we] judge [ourselves]."

People work for a number of reasons, survival foremost among them, but, depending on the person, the stage in his or her life, and the particular work being done, there can be a host of other reasons as well. For some, work provides structure to one's day. It can provide, as it did for my mother, social connection. It provides a means to buy goods and services. The work itself can have its own rewards, from intellectual to aesthetic to physical. It can make one feel a part of something bigger than oneself—as was the case with my uncle Frank and the railroad. And it can contribute to a sense of who one is.

In this book we will meet people who are competent at what they do, experienced, adept, their competence recognized by themselves and others. They will enable us to observe mature practice—and often I will elicit their commentary (and that of others of similar qualification) as one source of insight into expertise. We will also meet people, usually younger, who are just entering a field, though some of them have already begun to identify with it—one high school student speaks of the integrity of working with wood. These less-experienced, even novice, practitioners will enable us to watch competence emerging and provide a developmental perspective on work and the thinking that accompanies it.

I will be looking at examples of proficient work, either in its development or in its mature execution, for my intention is to explore some of the characteristics of common work when it is done well, and to find the right words, the right line of sight to depict the mind that enables that competence. As journalist John Hoerr's observation a few pages back suggests, this is not the way American workers are usually depicted. *The Mind at Work* offers an alternative story.

But what about the times when work is mediocre, sloppy, or downright awful? We've all been on the receiving end of bad production or damaging service. There are multiple reasons for poor work—in any occupation, from hairstyling to surgery—reasons of training, or motivation, or characteristics of the workplace, or the twists and turns of a person's life. Though this book is not a study of occupational efficiency and outcomes, not a study of the quality of work produced by specific occupational groups as a whole, it will present along the way some of the factors that affect the quality of performance, particularly from the perspective of workers themselves.

A good deal of modern work—blue-collar and service work especially—is characterized by working conditions that limit, often severely, the various forms of meaning one might gain from it. Social observers from Adam Smith and Karl Marx on down have described the de-skilling, routinizing, and regulating function of the factory. More recently, the office and the "electronic sweatshop" have been the focus of concern. These conditions are not experienced equally across society; in our country, the poor, immigrants, women, and people of color are disproportionately distributed there. And within those distributions there are further patterns of inequality, experienced, for example, by women or African Americans who have been excluded from entire categories of physical work and channeled into those with the lowest pay and the fewest opportunities for advancement. Such disadvantage runs throughout the history of modern work.

We have to be careful, though, not to reduce the wide range of people who work in hard conditions to a single oppressed mass of humanity. In various ways—even as work threatens body and dignity—people tend to seek agency and meaning within the constraints placed on them. While it is clearly true that many working people would quit if they could, that does not mean that, on average, they cease to assert their presence in and through the workplace. During her investigation of routine and repetitive work, journalist Barbara Garson found ample evidence of boredom, resentment, and sabotage. "But the most dramatic thing I found," she writes, "was quite the opposite of noncooperation. *People passionately want to work. . . .* Whatever creativity goes into sabotage," she continues, "a more amazing ingenuity goes into manufacturing goals and satisfactions on jobs where measurable achievement has been all but rationalized out. . . . Almost everyone wants to feel she is getting something accomplished."

A common theme in the social theory related to modern work concerns its detrimental effect on the consciousness of the worker. How does that theme square with a book on the intelligence found in common work? There is no doubt that a good deal of the work people do is repetitive, dumbed down, and, often, dangerous, and this surely can affect one's mood and sense of prospects. There is also research that demonstrates the negative effects of certain kinds of work on intellectual flexibility, as measured by interview questions and psychological tests. But I think we need to be cautious in assuming extensive and necessary effects of particular kinds of work on the thinking ability of the people who do them. Such analysis can obscure the nuance and variation in individual people's experience of work, as well as real differences in the physical and social environment of individual workplaces. The complexity of working life is thereby reduced. We can pinpoint the harmful effects of modern working conditions—the people in this book certainly do—without positing an automatic diminishment of a worker's awareness and capacity to reason.

⌥

There are other tales to tell about mind and work, and my hope is that the ensuing pages contribute to the telling. In these chapters, I present a range of familiar occupations that involve body and hand, representative of the kinds of work many in America have done throughout the last century and into our own. All the chapters deal in some way with the cognitive dimension of these, and similar, occupations. Chapters 1 through 6 focus on particular kinds of work and the particular people doing them. Though some fundamental cognitive processes are evident throughout these chapters—for example, accessing a knowledge base, attending to the immediate environment, or following steps in a sequence—each chapter will, to some degree, feature certain aspects of mental activity in the workplace. So, for example, the first chapter on waitressing will emphasize the ability to think quickly in dynamic environments like the restaurant, while the fourth chapter on carpentry details some of the cognitive processes enabling that trade: calculating, planning, visual thinking, and so on. However, it's important to note that such emphasis does not mean exclusive treatment; cognition on the job is not so neatly segmented. Collectively, the first six chapters, with their different emphases and contexts, give a sense of the overall richness of the mind at work. Though they also contain individual portraits of people at work, chapters 7, 8, and the conclusion have a somewhat broader sweep. They draw on the themes raised in the preceding chapters to further analyze the consequential distinctions our society makes between kinds of work and the assumptions about intelligence embedded in those distinctions.

In chapters 1, "The Working Life of a Waitress," and 2, "Styling Hair," I examine two types of service, two traditional occupational pathways for working-class and immigrant women. These two kinds of work are typically defined in light of the social and emotional needs they fulfill rather than in terms of the thinking involved in their execution. When we examine the work carefully, however, easy distinctions begin to blur.

In the busy restaurant, physical and emotional need, rituals of service, memory, economy of movement, and the regulation of the flow of work all interact dynamically. As in subsequent chapters, we'll get a sense of such interaction through close observation of the work itself—taking orders, getting food to tables—and, as well, we'll get a sense of the way the structure and traditions of a particular workplace initiate the thought within it. My mother holds a central role in this first chapter. Her story serves as a reminder that work is both grounded on and shapes personal history, and thus reveals motives, desires, values, and one's sense of who one is. A working life is rich in meaning.

The hair salon, like the restaurant, is a public space in which intimate things happen. Hair is invested with great personal and cultural significance, and clients enter the salon with variously articulated needs and desires. It is the stylist's job, through conversation and gesture, technique and aesthetic sense, to realize that desire.

Both of these chapters involve people who are expert practitioners, fluid in their performance, so the focus is on competence fully expressed. In chapters 3 through 5, we shift to a developmental perspective as we consider three of the building trades, observing novice plumbers, carpenters, and electricians in educational settings as they think their way through the challenges of materials and structures, function and force. Observing students allows us to get in close to skill as it develops, to the basic kinesthetic and cognitive moves that emerge over time—a perspective that can help us enhance standard notions of intelligence. If we observe with a belief in the remarkable nature of common work, suspending, to the degree possible, the distinctions we habitually make, what might we come to appreciate? The questions I kept asking myself in these settings were: What is going on here? How is it learned? What enables it to happen? What in this moment does it mean to be smart?

Chapter 3, "The Intelligence of Plumbing," provides the occasion to observe a teacher encouraging a problem-solving cast of mind among his students. His role is particularly important, for the students are in a juvenile justice diversion program and benefit especially from his mentoring style. But the interaction demonstrates, as well, the critical role of knowledgeable others in the development of systematic thinking. Furthermore, the teacher and the plumbing trade provide the opportunity for these young people to display intelligence so often missed, or misunderstood, in the typical classroom. A fundamental goal of this book is to help us think and talk differently about common work and the people who do it. This chapter and the next foreground that goal.

"A Vocabulary of Carpentry," chapter 4, offers an extended stay in a high school wood construction class, which allows us to observe growth in skill and knowledge. When I was defining intelligence a few pages back, I wondered about the many manifestations of intelligence in the workplace that might fall outside our standard measures. As we watch the students in this chapter work with wood over time, we get a sense of some of the phenomena that might be included in a richer cognitive language of work, from the strategic use of tool and body, to the making of judgments from the feel of things, to the intricate interplay of the verbal and the technical in planning tasks and solving problems.

In chapter 5, "Reflective Technique: Electrical Wiring and Construction," we again watch people learning a trade—in this case, the electrician's—to consider some long-standing distinctions made in the West about human activity. Since Classical Greece, Western culture has tended to oppose technical skill to reflection, applied or practical pursuits to theoretical or "pure" inquiry, the physical to the conceptual. These distinctions are not benign categories, are not neutral; in many contexts they carry significant differences in status and worth. As we get in close to students doing their work, however, we see how complicated these distinctions are: the technical gives rise to reflection, the physical and conceptual blend, and aesthetics and ethics emerge continually from practical activity.

With chapter 6, "Two Lives: A Welder and a Foreman," we return to expert performance, but considered across the life span: a woman at midpoint in her career, a welder and a teacher of welding; and another of my uncles, a man who retired from the auto industry, having moved from assembly line to supervision. Both have gained multiple kinds of knowledge from their work. The chapter sketches their career trajectories, but with an eye toward the meaning work has had in their lives and the play of mind in that work. Cognitive biographies.

Chapter 7, "Rethinking Hand and Brain," extends a theme running through the book: the liabilities of the body-mind, hand-brain dichotomy in our everyday discourse about work. This chapter provides the occasion to further analyze and unsettle the dichotomy through a reconsideration of a familiar portrait of an early-twentieth-century laborer; a comparative discussion of three kinds of higher-status professional work, including surgery and teaching; and a brief treatment of the process of occupational classification itself. Each of these sections encourages a reimagining of consequential occupational distinctions, and with that reimagining, a different line of sight on widely held beliefs about physical work.

In chapter 8, "Hand and Brain in School: The Paradox of Vocational Education," we consider in more depth the negative institutional effects of one of the family of hand-brain distinctions—the separation of the vocational course of study from the academic in our schools. For close to a century, the academic-vocational divide has defined the high school experience for many young people. Here we consider the history and internal contradictions of vocational education, and the way it has undercut the cognitive possibilities of common work and of those who do it. We also consider current attempts at reform and, with them, basic questions about mind, work, and schooling in a democratic society.

The conclusion, "Working Life," attempts a summing up of

what those who populate this book have taught us about the mind at work, a synthesis of the book's themes and portraits with an eye toward a fuller and more fitting representation of the intelligence that sustains us day after day.

We live in a time of much talk and judgment about intelligence. Some critics say we are obsessed with it to our detriment, from the way intellectual flash blinded us to the many weaknesses of the dot-com and Enron-style bubbles to the urgency with which we hurry our children through ever-higher levels of scholastic achievement. For all that, we operate with a fairly restricted notion of intelligence, one pretty much identified with the particular verbal and quantitative measures of the schoolhouse and the IQ test. And thus we undervalue, or can miss entirely, the many displays of what the mind does every day, all the time, right under our noses. It is not my intention to take anything away from the accomplishments of those whom the culture certifies as intelligent, but rather to widen our gaze enough to catch the presence of mind up and down the ladder of occupational status.

My purpose in writing the book, then, is to provide an alternative lens on everyday work, to aid us in seeing the commonplace with greater precision. I believe that such a change in perception could contribute to a more accurate portrayal of the full world of work, and could help us think more effectively and humanely about education, job training, and the conditions in which so many people make a living.

THE MIND AT WORK

THE WORKING LIFE OF A WAITRESS

Several years ago, I sat down at my mother's kitchen table with a tape recorder and began a series of interviews with her about her work. She had not been able to do any kind of physical work for quite some time, six or seven years, and in the last one or two had gotten very ill, increasingly limited in what she could do. These interviews became the occasion, then, for the two of us to reminisce about her work in the restaurant and for her to tell me, in as much detail as she could summon, about the way she executed it. We talked about the relationships among boss, cook, and waitress; about the importance of regular customers; about her motives for working and what—in addition to income—she got out of it; about the physical punishment of waiting on tables; about the complex emotional field of the restaurant.

I was particularly curious about the thinking involved in doing a waitress's work well. How did she remember all those orders? How did she organize the many tasks that emerged minute by minute? How did she decide what to do first? How, in fact, did she learn how to do these things? As we talked, she would use the kitchen table, cluttered with pill bottles and letters, as an imaginary four-top. She and I would sketch out the floor plan or counter space of Norm's or of Coffee Dan's. She would get up, steadying herself on the back of my chair, and demonstrate how she placed all those plates along her arm. Her memory for the particulars appeared sharp, and her demonstrations were precise. There were times now, the mornings especially, when she seemed so frail and not altogether there—in addition to her weakness, her many medications made her *stonato*, out of sorts, foggy—but the talk about her life in the restaurant vitalized her, a reliving of lost capacity, bittersweet, but sure in its knowledge. She had done this work for over thirty-five years.

Since the interviews with my mother, I have observed and interviewed six other waitresses, from a range of restaurants, using a similar set of questions. I've also been reading whatever popular and scholarly literature I could find on waitressing: from journalistic accounts and training material written in the 1920s and 1930s, to labor histories, to sociological research on the social and emotional dimensions of waitressing, to a handful of cognitive psychological studies of the memory capacity of waiters and waitresses. In synthesizing these interviews and literature, I found correspondence with my mother's account as well as some interesting points of divergence, which I pursued with further interviews or reading, using one source of information to open up the other.

With the exception of those psychological studies of memory, most of what has been written about waitressing focuses on the social aspects of the work—admittedly a vivid story. And, interestingly, as waitress unions developed through the last century and sought to define their occupation, they did so—reflecting the times—primarily in terms of its social abilities, nurturing and caring. What I came to appreciate, though, was the significance of the waitress's ability to process information, to think on her feet. There is the perception in both policy circles and the public mind that waitress work involves little intelligence and is among, in one writer's words, "the least skilled lower class occupations." Gender bias is likely at play here; occupations populated by women have historically been seen as requiring less intelligence. But I think there is something else going on—not unrelated to gender, or to class—and it applies to a lot of service work. The intelligence of the work, the thought that makes it possible, is so embedded in social interaction, routines of service, and emotional dynamics that it goes unacknowledged. The skill of the work, as labor historian Dorothy Sue Cobble puts it, is "rendered invisible." What follows, then, is both an homage to a particular waitress and an attempt to represent the intersecting cognitive and social demands of the work itself.

□

One of the truest things I know about my mother and her work in the restaurant is how central that work was to her sense of self and engagement with the world. What I also know from our shared experience is that her choice of work and the meaning she ascribed to it was shaped by the course of her own life history and the web of social and economic forces surrounding it. My mother didn't choose or execute her work in a vacuum—none of us do. Let me begin, then, with a brief overview of my mother's working life—a life initially defined by the immigrant experience, poverty, and the Great Depression.

Rose Emily Meraglio came to the United States from southern Italy as a little girl in the early 1920s and settled with her family in Altoona, Pennsylvania. Her father worked as a laborer for the Pennsylvania Railroad (and would eventually leave the yards disabled). Her mother raised seven children, took in boarders, made illegal wine and beer, and did whatever else she could to enable the family to survive. Rose was taken out of school in the seventh grade to help raise her three younger brothers and to assist with the tending of the boarders: cooking, cleaning, laundering. She did this work well into her teens, eventually taking a job in a garment factory and, briefly, in a local Italian restaurant, a job that wouldn't last, for "not a soul came in there." This early work at home and beyond was surrounded by profound economic need—and a sense of financial vulnerability would remain with my mother for the rest of her life.

The next phase of my mother's economic history came with her marriage to my father, Tommy Rose: the two opened and ran an Italian restaurant in downtown Altoona, open twenty-four hours a day to cater to the round-the-clock schedule of the Pennsylvania Railroad, the core of the city's economy. Self-described as a "raggedy" and "shy" girl, Rose developed quickly from private household labors and routinized factory work to a young woman in a public role, laden with new, often unpredictable, responsibilities: from cooking, hiring help, and ordering supplies to hostessing, waiting on tables, and tending the register. She would sometimes work fifteen to seventeen hours a day, for she had to remedy whatever mishaps arose. Here's a not atypical entry in a daily journal she kept during those years:

Mrs. Benner walked out on account of Mrs. Kauffman. So here I am alone cooking. June didn't show up either . . . I'm so tired.

But along with the accounts of exhaustion and anxiety, there is also testament to the fulfillment this new life brought:

On this day, I'm two years in business. I love it.

For all its tribulations, the restaurant contrasted with the lonely oppressiveness of her earlier labors, provided the conditions to gain knowledge about the restaurant business through immersion in it, and enabled my mother to learn how to "be with the public."

Though financially uneven, the restaurant did well enough through World War II and just after. But as the Pennsylvania Railroad—along with the railroad industry generally—began its first stage of decline, closing shops, laying people off (my uncle Frank among them), the Rose Spaghetti House failed, ending in bankruptcy. This was 1951. Over the next year, my parents would move to Los Angeles in search of opportunity and a warmer climate for my father, whose health was failing. They had little money and no connections whatsoever; friends and family were twenty-five hundred miles away, a lament I often heard. I was seven. My father couldn't work. So my mother went in search of the kind of work her limited formal education and her experience with the restaurant made possible, work she would continue until 1979, when illness forced her into retirement at sixty-four.

At first she waitressed in a series of coffee shops in downtown L.A., the largest stretch at Coffee Dan's on heavily trafficked Broadway. Then she moved to Norm's, a "family-style" chain, working for nearly a decade at the shop on Sunset and Vermont, by major medical facilities and corporate offices, like that for Prudential. She spent her last ten years at the Norm's in Torrance, amid a more lower-middle class, local merchant, and retirement clientele. During her time at Coffee Dan's and Norm's Sunset, my father would slip into grave illness and, for the last years of his life, be bedridden. I proceeded through elementary and high school. Mustering what immediate help she could, she struggled to balance work, caretaking, and child rearing. This period, roughly from 1952 to the early sixties, was another period of severe hardship. As my mother put it simply: "Dad was ill, and you were little. . . . I *had* to get work."

My father died in 1961. Eventually my mother would meet and marry a man who was a truck driver with the city, a job with stable wages and benefits. They bought a house in Torrance—a nicer house and safer—and she began her final ten years of waitressing at the Norm's nearby. This was a decade of economically better times. Even after she had to quit waitressing, my stepfather's employment carried them through comfortably. But my mother's inactivity during these early years of her retirement brings to the fore the centrality of physical work to her sense of who she is. For all the strain of waitressing, the work provided her with a way to feel useful, to engage her mind, and to be in the flow of things. When in the mid-1980s a neighbor got her a job as a noon aide at a local elementary school, she was revitalized. Her primary responsibility was to seat children for lunch and assist in clearing their tables. The job provided a few hours of minimum wage and, of course, no tips—it was barely a postscript to her economic life—but it held great value for her because of its mix of utility and nurturance. And it thrust her back into life's hustle. And it called on some of her waitressing skills. Though work for my mother was always driven by economic need, it was driven by a blend of other needs as well: cognitive, social, existential.

With this biography as backdrop, let me begin analyzing the work my mother did. Each of the restaurants that employed her had its own character and history, of course, but there are certain regularities to them—and to the many thousands like them—that can be abstracted and can help us understand the particular demands of waitressing.

□

On the face of it, a restaurant is a structured environment. The physical layout guides movement and behavior, and the various conventions associated with dining out are well known, to customer and waitress alike. But when analyzed in terms of the interrelated demands of the work itself, the environment, particularly at peak hours, becomes more complex, with an unpredictable quality to it.

Consider the restaurant in terms of multiple streams of time and motion. Customers enter with expectations: they will be seated without much delay and, once seated, a series of events will unfold along a familiar time line, from ordering through salad, entrée, dessert, delivery of the check. Their satisfaction—physical and emotional—is affected by the manner in which these expectations are met. But customers are entering the restaurant at different times, each with his or her own schedule, so tables (or places at the counter) proceed through meals at different paces. This staggering of customers facilitates the flow of trade but also increases the cognitive demands on the waitress: what she must attend to, keep in mind, prioritize. This situation intensifies during peak hours, for the number of customers expected can be estimated, but not known—coffee shops and family-style restaurants typically do not take reservations. If the numbers swell beyond capacity or an employee calls in sick or is late or quits, then, as the younger waitresses I interviewed vividly put it, you're "slammed," abruptly pushed to the limits of physical and mental performance.

Another timetable kicks in as soon as an order is placed with the cook. Different items have different prep times, and once the item is prepared, there is a limited amount of time—pretty restricted for hot items—during which it can be served. As well, the serving area needs to be cleared quickly so that the cook can deliver further items. The waitress, therefore, is aware of the kitchen as she moves among her customers.

Both waitress and management work by the clock. Profit is related to time; the quicker the turnover, the more revenue for the owner—and the greater the number of tips. There can be exceptions to this principle for the waitress—but not the management—for example, the regulars who may hold a table or stool longer but tip more. Still, generally, the waitress, like her manager, is ever mindful of clearing a plate, closing out a tab, moving the process along.

Imagine these streams of time and motion as co-occurring and related but not synchronous. Any given customer may hem and haw over an order, or want a refill while the waitress is occupied, or send an item back. The cook may deliver a waitress's hot dish while she is in the middle of taking an order and is being summoned by two other customers. Tables may be filled with variously contented customers while the manager feels the press of new customers gathering inside the door.

One more observation about this environment. No matter how efficiently designed the physical layout of the restaurant—let's say that coffeepots, water, soft drinks, cups, glasses, and ice are all located in the same area—the waitress's motion will be punctuated by the continual but irregular demands made of her. For example, all requests for coffee do not come at the same time or in regular intervals. So one request comes during an order, and another as she's rushing back to get extra mayonnaise, and another as she's clearing a table. The waitress must learn how to move efficiently through a vibrant environment that, for all its structural regularities, is dynamically irregular. A basic goal, then, is to manage irregularity and create an economy of movement. And she does this through effective use of body and mind. The work calls for strength and stamina; for memory capacity and strategy; for heightened attention, both to overall layout and to specific areas and items; for the ability to take stock, prioritize tasks, cluster them, and make decisions on the fly. I'll consider each of these qualities in further detail, beginning with physical prowess.

❑

What bodily skill does a waitress need? She must be able to balance and carry multiple items, using the hand, forearm, and biceps, creating stability by locking arms to torso and positioning the back. Then she moves, fast, in bursts, navigating tables, customers, other help. And since this occurs in a public space, it must be done with a certain poise. As waitress and writer Lin Rolens nicely puts it: "You learn a walk that gets you places quickly without looking like you are running. . . . This requires developing a walk that is all business from the waist down, but looks fairly relaxed from the waist up." With time and practice, all this becomes routine, automatic. But early in a career, the waitress will undoubtedly be conscious of various aspects of this physical performance, have to think about it, monitor herself.

My mother gets up slowly from the kitchen table and walks over to the sink where plates are drying on a rack. She demonstrates. She turns her right hand palm up, creating a wider surface on her forearm, and begins placing plates, large and small, from biceps to fingertips, layering them so that the bottom of one plate rests on the edge of another. "You don't dare let a plate touch the food," she explains, "and it's got to be balanced, steady." Then with her left hand, she lays out two coffee cups and two saucers. She kind of pinches the saucers between her fingers and slips her index finger through the handles of the two cups. "The coffee splashes from one side to another if you're not careful. It takes practice. You just can't do it all at one time."

I ask her, then, how she learned to do it. Beginning with her own restaurant, "you watch the other waitresses, what they do." She was "cautious" at first, starting with two plates, being deliberate. Then she began adding plates, responding to the demands of the faster pace of the restaurants in Los Angeles. "Norm's was much busier. So you had to stack as many plates as you possibly could." And, with continued practice in these busy settings, you get to where "you don't even have to think about it." I'm struck by the similarity between my mother's description and the studies I've read on the role of cognition in the development of athletic skill. My mother mixed observation and practice, got some pointers from coworkers, tricks of the trade, monitored her performance, and developed competence. As she achieved mastery, her mind was cleared for other tasks—such as remembering orders.

◻

To be a good waitress, my mother says emphatically, "you have to have one hell of a good memory." Her observation is supported by a small body of psychological research demonstrating that the competent waiter and waitress have techniques that enable them to override the normal limits on human "short-term" or "working" memory. Though there are some differences in the results of the studies, they point to four commonalities: The waiter and waitress know things about food and drink—ingredients, appearance, typical combinations—and this knowledge from "long-term" memory plays continually into their ability to remember orders. Furthermore, they have developed various visual, spatial, and linguistic techniques to aid memory: abbreviating items, grouping them in categories, repeating orders, utilizing customer appearance and location. The routines and physical layout of the restaurant also contribute to remembering orders. And, finally, though not strictly a characteristic of memory—as defined and studied in the psychologist's laboratory—the waiter's and waitress's memory is profoundly goal-directed: to make their work efficient and to enhance their tips. My mother attests to each of these elements.

As she stood before a table, taking orders, sometimes repeating them back while writing them out, sometimes not, making small talk, my mother would "more or less make a picture in my mind" of the person giving her the order, what that person ordered, and where around a table (or at a counter) he or she was located. Though, surely, there was variation in the way my mother did this, her picture could include dress and physical appearance: items of clothing—a red blouse, a splashy tie—and physical features like a birthmark or an unusually shaped nose. Broad social markers such as gender, race, age, body type, and weight also aided in memorization. ("Of course, a child's plate, you can always tell" where that will go, my mother laughingly notes.) My mother's beliefs and biases about these markers could play into the construction of the picture.

The layout of the tables (or the stools at the counter) and people's location at them enabled my mother to store and recall information about orders in a number of ways. A customer's specific position (by the window or closest to her) mattered, especially if it were somehow unusual—let's say that a woman pulls a fifth chair to the edge of a four-top. Relative location also figures in, aided by other characteristics of the person or the order. My mother and I are sitting at the kitchen table, which she uses to illustrate: "The one sitting at the [fifth] chair, she ordered this, *this* is what she ordered, and the next person over [my mother points to the next chair clockwise], that's another lady, and *that's* what she wants." Notice that my mother seems to perform some basic cognitive operations on the spatial information, something noted in the studies of waiters and waitresses. She mentions deviation, sequence, similarity, and contrast. Again, my mother points to an imaginary customer at our table: "I remember, he ordered the hamburger [she moves her gaze to the next chair], but she didn't want a hamburger, she wanted something else." So specific location as well as overall configuration matters.

Sometimes, it's a social expectation that is salient and an aid to memory. For example, cocktail waitresses make distinctions between the drinks men and women typically order, and other waitresses I interviewed spoke of these gender distinctions as well. My mother describes a couple ordering. The man orders a T-bone steak, and the woman "would order something smaller, so naturally you're gonna remember that." And if an order violates expectation—

the woman orders the steak, the man a chef's salad—that will stand out, the memorable deviation.

Some items and the routines associated with them enable the use of external memory aids. My mother describes a six-top at breakfast with orders of ham and eggs, steak and eggs, and hotcakes. As soon as she takes the order she, as a part of her route to the kitchen and back to other tables, sets a little container of syrup in front of the customer who ordered hotcakes. The aid is particularly helpful in a situation like this because "a six-top is especially hard, and sometimes you have to ask the customers who gets what." The container of syrup, then, lightens the load by one item.

Finally, a customer's attitude, the way he or she interacts with the waitress, contributes to her recall of the order. My mother comments on "how a customer would say something—you remember this dish is on the second table because so and so acted this way." She especially notes if "somebody is giving me a rough time." Of course, a particularly abrasive customer would stick in one's mind, but this raises an interesting broader issue: the way one's personal history and social position, the *feelings* related to these, play into cognition on the job.

One of the things that strikes me about my mother's report is the number of techniques it contains, the mix of strategies and processes: imagistic, spatial, verbal, and the role of emotion. Such complexity seems necessary when one is hurriedly tending to seven to nine tables, with two to six people at each. As my mother puts it: "Even though you're very busy, you're *extremely* busy . . . you're still, in your mind, you have a picture . . . you use all these [strategies], and one thing triggers something else." The strategies are interactive and complementary, and they enable us to get a sense of how much and what kind of work is going on in the working memory of a waitress during peak hours in a family-style restaurant.

⟁

Remembering an array of orders, then, takes place in a rush of activity that demands attention to the environment, organizing and sequencing tasks that emerge in the stream of that activity, and occasional problem solving on the fly. My mother's interviews contain more than ten references to the pace and conflicting demands of waitressing. She describes a setting where an obnoxious regular is tapping the side of his coffee cup with a spoon while she is taking an order. The cook rings her bell indicating another order is ready, and a few seconds later the manager seats two new parties at two of her tables that have just cleared. And, oh, as she is rushing back to the kitchen, one customer asks to modify an order, another signals for more coffee, and a third requests a new fork to replace one dropped on the floor. "Your mind is going so fast," she says, "thinking what to do first, where to go first . . . which is the best thing to do . . . which is the quickest." She is describing multiple demands on cognition—and the challenge is not a purely cognitive one.

There is a powerful affective component to all this, one with economic consequences. The requests made of the waitress have emotional weight to them. Customers get grumpy, dissatisfied if they have to wait too long or if their request is bungled or forgotten. The relationship with the cook is fraught with tension—orders need to be picked up quickly and returns handled diplomatically— and the manager is continually urging the movement of customers through a waitress's station. As my mother puts it, you attend to your orders or "the cook will yell at you"; you try to get customers their checks quickly, "because you'll get hell from the manager." The waitress's assessment of the emotional—blended with the economic—consequences of her decisions and actions plays back into the way she thinks through the demands of the moment.

One more thing. Depending on the restaurant, the flow of work can be facilitated (or impeded) by the arrangements and negotiations, mostly informal, made among the waitresses themselves and among the waitresses and those who bus the tables. These negotiations involve, at the least, the clearing of plates and glassware, assisting each other at rush hour, compensating for absent staff, and transitioning between shifts.

What do we know about the cognitive processes the waitress uses to bring some control to these multiple and conflicting demands? A good place to begin is with the psychological research on attention.

Attention is described in terms of its selectivity, a focusing on particular aspects of the environment; of the sustaining of that selective focus, a concentration as well as a vigilance for similar anticipated events or objects; and of the ability to control and coordinate the focus. In expert performance, these processes may become more refined and automatic. As one researcher puts it, attention serves "the purpose of allowing for and maintaining goal-directed behavior in the face of multiple, competing distractions."

There are periods in the waitress's day, lulls in activity, when she can stop and survey her station. My mother talks about a pause, standing back where she can "keep an eye on the register and all the way down the counter." But often the waitress is attending to things while on the move. Every waitress I interviewed commented on the necessity of attending in transit to requests, empty cups, plates moved to the edge of the table. As one waitress explained: "As you walk, every time you cross the restaurant, you're never doing just a single task. You're always looking at the big picture and picking up things along the way." This calls for a certain combination of motor skill and vigilance, captured in this passage where my mother describes her peripheral attention as she's delivering an order:

You look straight ahead to where you're going to take your food. You can't just look completely to the side, carrying all those plates— you could lose your sense of balance. As you're going out of the kitchen, you more or less take little glances to the side.

This vigilance—from a stationary point or while in motion—is not only a matter of perceptual acuity but also involves working memory and knowledge of the restaurant, knowledge of food preparation and of typical routines. My mother reveals this mix of memory, knowledge, and attention in her monitoring of the status of her customers' orders: "You're keeping an eye on who is not served yet. If it's been too long, you go check on the kitchen yourself." She recalls who ordered what and when and knows roughly how long a specific item should take to prepare, given the time of day. As she quickly checks her tables, she's attuned to a possible error in preparation.

Cognitive scientist David LaBerge uses *mindfulness* as a synonym for *attention*, and though the dictionary defines mindfulness somewhat sparely as being aware or heedful, the word connotes something more, something that, I think, suits this discussion of waitressing and attention. Mindfulness, first of all, implies intelligence, a mind knowledgeable and alert. The word also connotes a heightened state and a comprehensiveness, an apprehension of the "big picture," mentioned earlier, and, as well, a cueing toward particulars, and a vigilance for aberration—as when my mother monitors those delayed orders.

I want to return to that harried moment my mother describes where the regular is tapping his coffee cup, the cook is ringing the bell, and so on. A waitress could attend to all this clatter, and know what it means, and yet not know what to do next. How does she decide what her next move should be?

The answer is a multilayered one and involves some of what

we've already seen. First, the waitress's response will be driven by several interrelated high-level goals: to satisfy customers (and thus boost income), to maximize efficiency and minimize effort, and to manage conflict. All the waitresses I interviewed referred in some way to this cluster of goals. My mother speaks of "making every move count" and how "you think quick what you have to do first . . . in order to please people." Another waitress asks, "How can I maximize my effort in that moment?" Yet another emphasizes the value of controlling fatigue by "working smart." These goals will serve to organize the waitress's activity.

Second, the waitress's response is shaped by various kinds of knowledge of the restaurant: knowledge of the menu, of preparation times, of the layout of the place. Included here is a knowledge of emotional dynamics, both a folk psychology about dining out and the characteristics of particular customers. My mother, twenty years after retirement, can recount the quirks and traits of her regulars. As one veteran waitress puts it: "Everybody has their own personality. That's another level of learning . . . you've got to learn this way of working with people."

Third, the high-level goals and knowledge of the restaurant give rise to more specific action rules—waitressing rules of thumb—that, depending on the context, could aid in sequencing one's response. All the waitresses I interviewed, for example, mention the importance of attending to—even if just to acknowledge—newly seated customers. ("The big part of this business is not to ignore anybody.") They also stress the importance of picking up orders—especially hot ones—quickly. Another rule of thumb, applicable during rush hour, is to tally and deliver checks in a timely manner. And yet another is to consider the emotional consequences of action—which calls for an ongoing assessment of character and feeling. Is the cook especially touchy today? Do you have a particularly demanding customer? My mother expresses this emotional calculus when she advises "use your own mind and ask [of your-self] which customer will complain and which won't." Given an environment of multiple demands, these rules of thumb could guide one, for example, to attend to a new customer and serve a hot order—and forestall the circuit through the station to refill coffee. Refills would, in the moment, move lower in priority.

What is striking, though, is the degree to which the expert waitress relies on a broad strategy that makes many either-or decisions moot. And this brings us to the fourth element in the waitress's response to multiple demands. She organizes tasks by type or location. She combines tasks in ways that greatly economize movement, that make activity, in my mother's words, "smooth." As one waitress puts it, she is always asking "which pieces of what I need to do fit together best." Though some prioritizing of tasks— guided by rules of thumb—does occur, the more common move (noted as a mark of experience by several of the waitresses) is to quickly see what tasks can be grouped and executed with least effort.

This leads to a fifth characteristic: the way restaurant routines aid in this organizing of tasks. My mother and the other waitresses I interviewed all refer in some way to a circuit through one's station that is watchful and that takes advantage of the restaurant's physical layout. As one waitress explains it:

> I always think of it as kind of a circle, because there's the tables, there's the bar, there's the coffee station, and it kind of becomes a flow of organizing what can be in one full circle, how many tasks can be accomplished, as opposed to back and forth, back and forth. I think the waitresses who get going back and forth are the ones who get crazy with four tables.

This description resonates with the earlier discussion of attention— the blend of anticipation, vigilance, and motor skill—but in a way that underscores the dynamic interaction of the waitress's ability and the structure and conventions of the restaurant.

Perhaps the thing that most impressed me in all this—and it emerged in every interview—is the claim the waitresses made that they work best when the restaurant is busy. On the face of it, this doesn't make sense. I would imagine that one could remember three or four orders with more accuracy than six or seven, that one could handle refills easier with a half-full station. These numbers would result in a more relaxed pace but, the waitresses claim, not in more skillful performance. In fact, my mother insists she could never have developed her level of skill in slower restaurants. "You're not as alert . . . not thinking that quick"; you're not anticipating orders; "you're making a couple of trips" rather than a single efficient one. "In a slow place, you think slower." One waitress notes the feeling of working "like a well-oiled machine" during rush hour. Another says that "when it gets the craziest, that's when I turn on. I'm even better than when it's dead."

Of course, increased volume of trade can lead to disaster as well—if, for example, a waitress calls in sick or a critical piece of equipment fails. Every waitress tells those horror stories. But it seems that, barring the unusual mishap, the busy restaurant can lead to maximum performance. One's physiology responds—my mother talks about her "adrenaline going faster"—and there is a heightened readiness and reaction. And the increased flow of trade itself provides a variety of demands that call forth, that require the skillful response, the necessary fluid integration of attending, memory, organization of tasks, and strategic use of routine. This is not to deny the exhaustion, even the punishment, of the work, but it is telling how my mother and the other waitresses all comment on the satisfaction that they feel when they perform well under stress. Several use language similar to that of the currently celebrated "flow" experience, felt during those times when a person responds successfully to significant challenges from the environ-ment. "There's a sense of accomplishment in just the mechanics of it," says one waitress, "just knowing that . . . I'm handling it all."

☐

Remembering orders, being vigilant, and regulating the flow of work all play out in an emotional field. "Eating is the most intimate act," writes Lin Rolens, "we are encouraged to perform in public." And Dorothy Sue Cobble, who has studied waitress unions, ob-serves that waitresses "are responding to hungers of many kinds." This emotional field has economic consequences. The very mean-ing of service is defined within it. To understand and appreciate more fully the thought behind waitressing, therefore, we need to ponder the many layers of what "service" means in the waitress-customer encounter.

To begin with, this encounter calls forth historically shaped con-ventions for the serving of food that are associated with the house servant. In Frances Donovan's 1920 account of waitressing, *The Woman Who Waits*, published during the first stage of the feminiza-tion of food service, there is explicit treatment of the association of maid and waitress—and of the waitress's desire to distinguish her work from that of a housemaid. But the association remained (my mother's uniforms, down to the modified caps, resembled stereo-typed maid's apparel) and is reflected in a number of routines of service: from modes of address, to the sequence of questions about the order, to customs for serving and clearing food. ("[D]ishes are placed on the table without noise," notes a 1932 educational tract on waitressing, ". . . the hand must be trained to slip dishes into place very close to the table rather than bring them down directly from a height.") Conventions and symbols change over time, and vary by the type of restaurant, but waitressing continues to involve the acquisition of customs of service—and one's accommodation to them. The residue of the servant's role rankles the women I spoke with, and they resist it in a number of ways: from covert criticism and ridicule of haughty behavior (my mother's typical response) to direct rebuke and declaration of status, letting customers know when they've crossed the line. One means by which the waitress expresses agency is through her use of skill and strategy to regulate the flow of work. "The customer has the illusion that they're in charge," observes one of the waitresses I interviewed, "but they're not." It's the waitress who must "get command of her tables," who is "the commander in chief of her section." This waitress still performs the customs of service, but within routines of practice that she controls.

The encounter between customer and waitress potentially gives rise to a further range of emotions and social scripts, in addition to that of server and served. On any given shift, a stream of customers enters with needs that vary from the physiological—and the emotions that attend hunger—to the desire for public intimacy. And the waitress, depending on the type of restaurant, her reading of the situation, and her own history and motives, may fulfill, modulate, or limit those needs and desires. There has been a fair amount of sociological study of the emotional dimension of waitressing and similar occupations, and this research tends toward two broad-scale findings.

The first is that providing service requires "emotion management" or what sociologist Arlie Russell Hochschild has termed "emotional labor." Regardless of what the waitress actually feels, the interaction with the customer requires that she display emotion that is dictated by the social and economic demands of the restaurant. My mother illustrates such emotional labor through her account of a churlish regular, a man who was always sending his steak back to the cook: "You've got to make an effort to try and please him, even though you can just kill him." Generalizing to all difficult customers, she advises: "Just try the best you can to be nice to them. Even if they're rude to you, you still smile and just go on, because that's your living."

The second finding is that the roles afforded to the waitress in her encounter with the customer play out within stereotypic gender scripts: the waitress becomes servant, mother, daughter, friend, or sexual object. The house uniform and policy, customs of service, and other restaurant traditions contribute to this construction of gender-in-the-moment, as do broader expectations from the culture at large. Though I surely wouldn't have understood her behavior in these terms, I recall the sense I had watching my mother work that she smiled and laughed more than when at home, a quick, not-quite-true laugh, flirtatious, with a touch on the arm or shoulder, a focused vivacity. As she summed it all up while we were sitting at her table, "You've got to be damned good, damned fast, and you've got to make people like you."

The social dynamics of the service encounter affect the tip, a critical economic consideration, given that the base pay in most restaurants is terribly low. The wage structure forces a reliance on gratuity, so the successful waitress soon learns how to play the dynamics to maximize her income. There is actually a fair-sized social-psychological literature on the factors that influence tipping. The shrewd waitress, for example, suggests items—appetizers, desserts, more drinks—that will increase the bill, and thus the size of her potential tip. She can also increase her tip by smiling, by touching the customer on the hand or shoulder, or by squatting or kneeling to get closer to eye level. This literature parses out the social skills and gestures learned in the context of restaurant work, the devices that can increase the amount of money customers leave on the table.

The reward is an economic one, but it is also one fraught with symbolism—at the least, a reminder of servant status—so the reward structure includes emotional factors as well. Customers, Lin Rolens observes, "tip in every spirit imaginable," from a display of status, to an expression of gratitude, to an overture of friendship, to a sexualized gesture. My mother and the waitresses I interviewed and read about express a wide range of feeling about tipping. There's eager anticipation ("You're thinking, 'Oh boy, I'm gonna hurry up and clear that table off . . . because that's a good tipper' ") and satisfaction ("It's fun to have a good night . . . all that cash in your pocket . . . it's a very immediate reward"). There's anger: "Something that really pisses me off is when people stiff the waitress because something happened in the kitchen." And there's a sense of injustice leading to action. Anthropologist Greta Pauff Paules writes of a waitress who "followed two male customers out of a restaurant calling, 'Excuse me! You forgot this!' and holding up the coins they had left as a tip."

Though this field of customer-waitress emotion is shaped by the historical residue of servitude and by stereotyped gender roles, the waitress attempts to control it to her economic and emotional advantage. She does this by the way she defines the situation, by her manipulation of role and routine ("[P]lay the people and the tips will follow," says one waitress interviewed by Lin Rolens), and by judgments that enable her to attribute a low tip to a customer's personal situation, character, or ignorance. These judgments and attributions are part of the restaurant's folk wisdom, played out continually in the talk among waitresses that customers don't hear.

The service encounter provides the tips that enable the waitress to make a living, but in concert with the financial need, other needs of hers, depending on the waitress, can be met as well. Some waitresses gain satisfaction from contributing to a customer's enjoyment: "You supply nurturing and sustenance, the things that make life pleasurable." Some respond to the hustle and stimulation of a busy restaurant, the sense of being in the middle of things. (This was a big one for my mother, and its loss has been difficult for her.) Some like the attention ("the spotlight's on you") and the safe flirtation. Some comment on the pleasure of the brief human interaction: "Though we'll never get to know each other, there's a really nice feeling that goes back and forth." Some waitresses comment on the feeling of independence the job affords; anthropologist Paules characterizes the waitress as a private entrepreneur. And some gain satisfaction from the display of their skill ("I get to show off my memory") and, as we saw, gain a feeling of competence by performing the job well.

Though perhaps obvious, it is worth stating that this array of feeling—like the cognitive processes detailed earlier—is situated in the restaurant; the various feelings are legitimized and shaped by the waitress-customer association. My mother developed a number of friendly relations with her regular clientele. But when I asked her to perform a thought experiment and imagine how those relationships might have changed if tipping were outlawed, she gave sharp expression to the situational nature of the restaurant friendship. "If you know they're gonna tip you, well, then you talk about your flowers, or you have a son, or you have a daughter, or whatever. But if you know they're not gonna tip, you'd be disinterested." My mother got to know some of her regulars pretty well, would talk about their problems at home, worry over them, yet, at heart, the connection to their lives was restaurant-based, for everyone involved.

Waitress-customer interaction, then, is shaped by history and gender. It involves a good deal of economically motivated emotion management and interpersonal manipulation, all centered around the tip, which, itself, is laden with symbolism and feeling. The waitress-customer encounter also provides the occasion for the fulfillment of other needs that are not directly economic, though that fulfillment is embedded in an economic context and defined and bounded by life in the restaurant.

As I talk to my mother and to other waitresses, I'm struck by the way cognitive processes and emotional dynamics are interwoven. Memory, for example, draws on emotional material to aid in storage and recall. Customs of service and social display incorporate the cognitive, certainly in one's reading of people, one's social savvy, and one's folk knowledge of the ways of the restaurant, but also in the very particulars of routine that create the experience of service. One waitress comments on her ability to recall little details about her regulars' typical orders—that they don't like pepper or they like extra horseradish—and, as well, comments on her vigilance: "Attention to detail . . . keeping water glasses full, keeping extra stuff off the table, just the little things that make it a more pleasant sensory experience . . . that's why I like it so much . . . that I'm a contributing factor in somebody having a good meal." Memory, attention, the creation of service, and a waitress's personal satisfaction are all of a piece in the busy restaurant.

◻

The interview for the day is completed; I turn off the tape recorder and gather up my notes. My mother rearranges a few things— paper napkins, salt and pepper shakers, some letters—on the cluttered table. "You know," she muses, folding the napkins, "you learn a lot as a waitress. You work like hell. But you learn a lot." There's a small television set to the side, by the wall, propped up for her by my stepfather. She reaches over and turns it on, clicking through the channels: a rerun of *The Beverly Hillbillies*, a basketball game ("blah"), a base-thumping Ironman competition ("Boy, I couldn't do that"), a PBS documentary on the building of some huge suspension bridge. Is it the Brooklyn Bridge? She stops at this. There are historical photographs of workers—excavating, welding, a remarkable shot of four men sitting in a net of cables high in the air. The men look southern European, possibly Greek or Italian, like so many of the men in the old photographs I have of Altoona. "This is interesting," she says, "they should show more things like this." She keeps watching, and we talk over the images about work and those immigrants of my grandfather's generation.

Her work in the restaurant business—and physical work in general—meant many things to my mother, and even though she is now infirm, work continues to shape her memory and desire, influence her values and identity.

Many of our depictions of physical and service work—popular accounts but more than a few scholarly treatments as well—tend toward the one-dimensional. Work is seen as ennobling or dehumanizing; it is the occasion for opportunity or exploitation; it functions as an arena for identity development or class consciousness. Work is considered in terms of organizational structure or production systems; or of statistical indicators of occupational and employment trends. To be sure, each focus can have its analytical benefit. But one of the things the writing of this book has made clear to me is how difficult it is—given our standard "story lines" for work and the constraints of our disciplinary lenses—to capture the complex meaning work has in the lives of people like Rose Emily Rose. Let me try to tease out the layers of significance restaurant work had for her. They are interrelated, at times contradictory, of a piece in her experience of waitressing.

Through waitressing, my mother generated income, supported a family, kept poverty at bay. The income was low and variable, but, as she saw it, given her limited education and her early work history, she couldn't make better money elsewhere. Also, her income was somewhat under her control: by the hours she was willing to work and the effort she put forth, she could increase her tips.

Though economically dependent on the generosity of others, she had developed, and could continue to develop, the physical, mental, and social skills to influence that generosity.

My mother's work was physically punishing, particularly over the long haul. She pushed herself to exhaustion; her feet were a wreck; her legs increasingly varicose; her fingers and spine, in later years, arthritic.

The work required that she tolerate rude behavior and insult, smile when hurt or angry. Though she did not see herself as a servant, she was economically beholden to others, and, in some ways—particularly in public display—had to be emotionally subservient. Yet, although she certainly could feel the sting of insult, my mother also saw "meanness" and "ignorance" as part of the work, and that provided for her a degree of emotional distance. The rude or demanding customer could be observed, interpreted, described to peers, quietly cursed—and could be manipulated to financial advantage. Explaining how she would be nice to a troublesome customer, she adds: "And, then, what happens is he becomes *your* customer! Even though there are other tables that are empty, he'll wait for your booth."

Work for my mother was a highly individualistic enterprise, to be coveted and protected. She would coordinate effort in the moment with busboys and waitresses in adjoining sections. And she made several good friends at work; they would visit our house and provided a sympathetic ear for restaurant complaints. But much of my mother's interaction with other waitresses—both by my recollection and by her interviews—was competitive. Though she considered Norm's "a good restaurant," I can't recall any expression of attachment to the company; and though much of the time she worked in Los Angeles was a period of union activity, my mother was barely involved in her local. I realize now how isolated she must have felt: thousands of miles from family; responsible for a sick husband and a child; vigilant for incursions, even treachery, from coworkers; not connected to a union or to any civic, social, or church group. And, given her coming-of-age in the Depression and the later waning of the Pennsylvania Railroad, she was always worried about the security of her employment. My mother possessed a strong, if desperate, sense of self-reliance and an in-her-bones belief in the value of hard work that mixed inextricably with a fear that work would disappear.

A restaurant owner I know told me that the business "attracts people who want to step outside of their own lives. There aren't many professions that require you to stay so focused. You don't have time to think about anything else, and that gives you a rush, and you make money." Who knows to what degree this observation holds true across the restaurant population, but it resonates with a theme in my mother's interviews. I asked her, for example, if there was any reason, beyond the economic one, to want a full house. "When we're busy," she answered, "the time goes so fast. You're so tired, but it's better to be real busy than not busy, because then you'll have time on your hands, you'll have an idle mind." This is a somewhat different expression of the flow experience mentioned earlier. I suspect that the strongest protection my mother had against her pressing fear of destitution was to be consumed on the restaurant floor, attentive to cues from the environment, executing routines, her mind filled with orders, working at peak performance, the tips appearing and appearing by the empty plates, scattered between cups and glasses.

Waitressing enabled my mother "to be among the public." This phrase carried a certain pride for her, as it reflected a social facility that the once-shy girl had to develop. The work provided the opportunity for a low-responsibility social exchange—"I like that part. I like to be with people, associated with people"—that must have been pleasant for someone with so many cares at home. (This

casual sociability has traditionally been more afforded to male occupational roles.) To be among the public was also a sign of attain-
ment: it was not the kind of solitary labor she had known as a girl,
and it brought her into contact with a range of people whose occupations she admired. There's paradox here, but the logic goes like
this: yes, you are serving the doctor or the businessman, but it's
your ability that makes everything work right; you are instrumental
in creating their satisfaction. As she is fond of saying, not everyone
can do that.

The restaurant, then, provided the setting for Rose to display a
well-developed set of physical, social, and cognitive skills. It was
her arena of competence. Balancing all those plates on your right
arm and carrying two cups of coffee in your left hand "is damned
hard to do." Remembering your orders during rush hour and getting them served "gives you a feeling of satisfaction."

And the restaurant provided a context for other kinds of learning. Educational researchers are increasingly studying learning in
nonschool settings—workplace programs, social and civic clubs—
but still very much unexplored is the learning that occurs in
everyday, informal social exchange. Given the restrictions of my
mother's formal education, her personal predilections (she did not,
for example, read for pleasure), and all the demands on her life,
she had limited time and means to gain information and learn
new things. Yet, to this day, she possesses an alert curiosity. The
educational medium available to her was the exchange with her
customers, regulars particularly. ("How else can I learn about people?" asks Dolores Dante, the waitress Studs Terkel interviewed for
Working. "How else does the world come to me?") Through the
waitress-customer interaction, she acquired knowledge about a
range of everyday activities—gardening, cooking, home remedies—
and, as well, fed a curiosity that my mother had for as long as I can
remember for topics related to medicine, psychology, and human

relations: "There isn't a day that goes by in the restaurant that you don't learn something." Some of what she learned was a fact or a procedure (for example, on planting roses), and some was more experiential and relational. The restaurant became a kind of informal laboratory for her to observe behavior and think through questions of human motivation. This aspect of waitressing engaged her; "you learn a lot, and it interests me."

Waitressing contributed to the development of my mother's identity. In that 1920 account of waitressing mentioned earlier, Frances Donovan bears witness to the social transformations involving young women from the farm and from urban working-class and immigrant backgrounds, women seeking pathways out of "the restraints put upon [them] by the members of the group from which [they] came." Given the recent studies of waitressing as an occupation embodying stereotyped gender roles, it's interesting to note that historically the work provided the occasion for a certain liberation from constraint and an opportunity for a working-class woman to, as Donovan put it, "set up new standards for herself." Approximately two decades later, my mother would enter the restaurant business, and, for all its hardships, it enabled her to begin to think of herself in a different way, to become relatively independent, to develop a set of skills, and to engage a wider social field than would have been possible in her mother's house or in the surrounding immigrant Italian community.

❑

Talking with my mother about waitressing, and letting that talk generate talk with others, younger, of a different era, getting a sense of the history and sweep of the work, provides for me an opportunity to more fully appreciate the hard but meaningful working life my mother created out of terrible circumstances.

As I leave the kitchen table, to return again—these days, this is where my mother and I most often talk—one thought, then another begin taking shape and will play out as I go back to notes from other settings, other observations. I'm struck by the fact that particular kinds of work can be defined and perceived in ways that mask the range of human abilities that make the work possible. And I'm struck by the intelligence manifest in making choices within constraint. And I'm struck, quite struck, by the way we try to shape our lives and gain a little control by the work we do.

STYLING HAIR

Vanessa works in a trendy salon but also cuts hair in her apartment—for a few friends and friends of friends. Her client Lynn sits in a small barber's chair by the window, the place where you'd imagine a breakfast table, a mirror leaning against the wall in front of her. On the floor by the mirror there is a small bowl for Vanessa's dog and a vase with three yellow flowers. Vanessa stands behind Lynn, asking her questions about her hair, chitchatting a little. She keeps her eyes on Lynn's hair as she moves her fingers through it, lifting up, then pulling down one section, then another, then gesturing with her hands around the hair, indicating shape and movement. "How did you like the last haircut?" she asks. How did it handle? Was it easy to manage? What's bugging you now? Does it feel heavy up front? Lynn answers these questions, describing what she wants, relying on adjectives that have more to do with feeling than shape. She wants the cut "freshened," wants it "sassy."

A pair of scissors, a comb, and a round hand mirror sit on the stove, to Vanessa's side. She reaches for the scissors and begins. She starts at the crown and moves around Lynn's head, picking a strand of hair, pulling it down gently along Lynn's face, eyeballing it, then elevating it, cutting into it, "point cutting," she calls it, not a "blunt" cut, her scissors angling into the hair, layering it, "giving it a softer look."

Vanessa likes to cut hair dry—at least hair like Lynn's, baby-fine, short—because she "can see what it's doing immediately . . . where it's heavy, where it needs to be cut into." ("You can comb hair and cut it," she explains, "only to have it move into a different shape than the one you just cut.") When she does cut hair wet, because a particular style demands it, she "can't wait to dry it and then go in and do *my* work. . . . The initial shape might be there, but the whole interior can change. Eighty percent of the haircut is after you dry it."

As Vanessa continues, cutting, comparing one length of hair to another, her gaze circling her client's head, she tells me more about her work. Though she can do "technical, precise" cuts, like a graduated bob (a bob tapered at the nape of the neck), she most likes to cut "freehand," as she is doing now, a more "flowing" cut, and flowing process. "I don't like authority," she laughs, "so I love cutting this way." Even with that graduated bob, she adds, after it's dry, she'll "go in and add my own touch, a signature."

Vanessa certainly has an idea of how a haircut should look, an idea based on the characteristics of the hair she's cutting and the client's desires, discerned from those opening questions, and, if the client's a regular, from their history together. And she is methodical. But she does not plan her cut in advance to the degree that some stylists do; cognitive psychologists would characterize her planning style as incremental or opportunistic. As the cut progresses, she observes what the hair is doing, how it's falling and moving, and reacts to that. "I do a lot of visual when I cut." And, in fact, about two-thirds of the way through Lynn's haircut, Vanessa exclaims, "Oh, this is starting to look really cute!" Moments like this are pivotal to Vanessa, aesthetically and motivationally. It excites her, is the art of it all, to use her skill in a way that is responsive to, interactive with, the medium of hair, watching the cut emerge, shaping it incrementally, guided by her aesthetic sense and enabled by her repertoire of techniques. Lynn is pleased with the outcome. It *is* a "sassy" cut. "Vanessa understands hair like mine."

Come with me to a salon about a mile from Vanessa's apartment where another experienced hairstylist named Sharon is working on a client with hair not unlike Lynn's, short, fine. It's pretty much a younger crowd on this day, familiar, friendly. Over the speakers comes a mix of techno, acid jazz, and house music; there's an ambient fragrance of shampoo, then the harsher whiff of coloring agents. Mirrors everywhere, mirrors and bright art, high ceiling, greenish blue pipes running across it.

Sharon begins with questions and gestures similar to Vanessa's. She takes her client over to be shampooed, then begins to cut, section by section, talking to her client in the mirror. Sharon considers all the same variables as Vanessa—characteristics of the hair and face, the client's desires—but plans more deliberately:

> You've got to add up all these pieces of the puzzle, and then at the end you've got to come up with a thought, OK, it's gotta be this length, it's gotta be layered here, it's got to be textured there, it can have a fringe, it can't have a fringe, you know, so the thought process goes. . . . It's not like we just start cutting. By the time I take my client to the shampoo bowl, after the consultation, I already have a little road map as to how I'm going to cut this haircut.

To be sure, Sharon, like Vanessa, responds to the emerging cut—she's not locked into her plan—and does further work once she dries the hair, watching how it falls, moves. And, as noted, Vanessa is not without method. But there is a difference here, and the interesting thing is that each approach is integrated into each stylist's practice and both yield effective results. I'll say more about the details of practice momentarily, but, first, let us consider the broader occupational picture of the work Sharon and Vanessa do.

⌁

Though both men and women cut and style women's hair, it is, like waiting tables, primarily a woman's profession—roughly 90 percent of hairstylists in the United States are female. Working with hair has for well over a century provided income for large numbers of American women, many of whom have immigrated here or who were born into the working or lower-middle classes, women constrained by limited financial or educational resources, racial or gender bias, or local norms of domesticity. And in some communities, working with hair has provided a pathway to a solidly middle-class life—this occupational entrée, for example, was central to the appeal made to prospective agents and practitioners by Madame C. J. Walker, an extraordinarily successful early-twentieth-century developer of African American hair products.

Currently, the 854,000 hairdressers and cosmetologists in the United States (772,000 are female) work in a wide range of settings: from their homes; or small neighborhood shops; or specialty salons (with an emphasis on braiding, for example); or multiservice salons (some cut-rate with quick turnaround, others with established stylists and more personal attention); or upscale urban salons, trendy, expensive—Sharon works in one of these. A small percentage work in unusual settings: from movie studios to prisons. And there are a significant number of women who don't get tallied in the compilation of labor statistics, women who work in the informal economy, who may not be licensed and who, by choice or because of economic or social barriers, may have less school-based training. They work out of homes or small shops, cutting or styling hair, braiding or beading or weaving it, learning their craft from family members, friends, or other social networks.

Clearly with such numbers and such a diversity of backgrounds and training, there is, among those who work with hair, a wide range of skill, special competencies, cultural and aesthetic ideals, beliefs about the work, modes of practice, and occupational engagement and success. The stylists I studied for this chapter in one way or another took the traditional pathway into the career; they trained in beauty colleges, community colleges, occupational centers, or salons certified to teach. Thus, they have completed a one- to two-year course of study that includes written exams and two to four thousand hours of hands-on work; they have passed state boards; and they have all further developed their practice in salons. Though it would be a mistake to assume that the physical, cognitive, and communication skills we'll be considering do not develop in less formal contexts, these skills have been affected by this relatively standardized program of training. One more thing to note about my representation of these skills: Though both men and women visit hairstylists, all the stylists I interviewed agreed that, on average, working with women's hair calls for the display of a broader range of competencies, so I'll focus this chapter on work with women clients—though, clearly, the skills displayed apply to the cutting and styling of men's hair as well. Finally, there is this: Not everyone who works with hair is equally proficient at all aspects of the profession. Vanessa, for example, is not drawn to color work, and concentrates on cutting and styling. Neither Vanessa nor Sharon does the elaborate styles associated with weddings. And neither braids hair, which has its own long history and set of techniques.

Let us now return to the details of practice, giving closer consideration to what Sharon calls the pieces of the puzzle.

◻

When I began studying hairstyling, I performed an informal experiment. I showed pictures of women's hairstyles that were centuries old—and thus at least a bit unfamiliar—to several hairstylists and to several nonstylists and asked them to say whatever came to mind. The results were predictable, but, I think, still illustrative: the stylists' comments were heavy on analysis and technique. The nonstylists certainly knew things about hair, and did make occasional comments about techniques that could yield the style in the picture, but they tended to comment on the look of the style, made general historical observations, and generated stories to accompany the picture. The hairstylists also made evaluative and aesthetic comments ("very pretty," "glamorous," "I love the art of this") and generated a tale or two, but much of what they said concerned technique, referring to the "art" or "challenge" of the style, labeling and categorizing aspects of it (finger waves, banana curls, pin curls), speculating as to how an effect was achieved ("you could tease the hair close to the scalp, or pin curl it first, then tease it"). Their commentary provides a nice illustration of the way work informs cognitive response. The stylist considers the face and head spatially, in terms of shape and proportion, and as a kind of working surface—the eye and ear, for example, the tip of the nose, the lip line become markers, guides. And hair is transformed into a rich aesthetic field—shape, color, movement, possible adornment—perceived through a lens of knowledge and craft, the overriding question being: What can I do to get that look?

So when Vanessa and Sharon are consulting with their clients and examining their hair—and this is of particular importance if the client is new—they are considering the client's face and her bone structure, and, if coloring will be involved, skin tone and eye color. The stylist is assessing the characteristics and condition of the client's hair: how dense it is, its texture (coarse, medium, fine), the wave pattern (straight, wavy, curly), and frequently there's variation with the same client, wavy on some parts of the scalp and relatively straight on others. Additionally, there is the porosity and elasticity of the hair, characteristics that can be affected by the client's history of hair treatments—coloring, perming, relaxing, styling—and this assessment can involve tests performed on strands of the client's hair. The stylist is also getting a sense through conversation and the look of things as to how the client manages her hair on her own, which could affect the stylist's decision as to how to cut, treat, and style the hair. All of this becomes baseline data, the presenting information.

While this assessment is proceeding the client is making a request. In some fashion, through pictures, or references to particular people, or descriptions that can range from the precise to the ethereal ("I want something light and summery," said one woman), the client is trying to convey a cut, a style, or, not uncommonly, a feeling she wants. The hairstylist must incorporate the client's baseline data into the process of arriving at a solution to the request. We've already gotten a sense from Vanessa and Sharon as to how the preferred way to formulate a solution might vary from stylist to stylist, but regardless of differences in planning and problem solving, the stylist will be drawing on a repertoire of cuts and styles and a range of techniques to achieve them. This repertoire is acquired through training, experience, observation, classes, and, over time, the competent stylist develops the ability to vary and combine basic cuts and styles and to enhance and individualize them. (Recall Vanessa's statement about adding her "own touch" to a graduated bob.) What strikes me is the number of variables involved. "If you cut the same haircut on curly, wavy, or straight hair," notes Sharon, "it would look totally different each time." To further complicate things, the variables interact: both texture and porosity, for example, affect the way a coloring agent takes in the hair, and the color of the hair will combine with texture and the shape of the cut to affect the final appearance of the hair, the way light plays off it, its sheen and movement.

We have been considering a range of kinds of knowledge—

knowledge of the properties of hair and knowledge of form and design—and the development of an aesthetic sense from them. But, of course, the hands and the tools they manipulate are the instruments of the cut. So let us now focus on the manual techniques of cutting and styling.

The more expert the stylist, the more fluent and unnoticed is her or his manual skill. The stylist moves about the head, slips in and out of conversation, catches the eye of the client in the mirror. There is a lot of touching, handling the hair, some adjusting of the client's head—hands, comb, and scissors engaging the hair, a fluid, attentive performance. But if you watch the hands closely, or attend an introductory-level course, or page through a standard textbook on hairdressing—if you devise a way to regard the manual skill here—then you begin to see the finesse. There is, for example, the way the stylist's "holding" hand, with comb tucked under thumb, pinches strands of hair between the index and middle finger, the position and direction of the hand varying by type of cut—and usually within a single cut—and guiding the cut, as when I saw a stylist extend her little finger downward, forming a diagonal guide for her scissors. In addition to hand position and direction, there is the issue of tension, how tightly does one pull the hair from the scalp, for various kinds of hair, particular areas of the hair, and specific styling effects can require different degrees of tension.

The positioning of the hand holding the scissors is crucial as well, as are considerations of where one cuts along the strand, the angle of the cut, and so on. (Recall here Vanessa's point cutting.) Developing control is everything, and in the expert hairstylist you sense a dexterous blending of hand and tool. The delicacy of this blending was highlighted for me during the first few minutes of Lynn's haircut with Vanessa. It seems that Vanessa had lost her favorite scissors during a recent trip overseas, so she was using an old pair. They didn't feel quite right to her—though she had used them well in the past—and she accidentally jabbed Lynn twice, the only time, Lynn said later, that had ever happened.

The point I am making here about finesse in cutting would apply as well to those who are expert at braiding, "locking," or weaving hair—they likewise have developed a set of manual techniques that makes their work skillful and efficient. As one of the salon owners we'll meet momentarily put it, describing a talented braider: "It requires a lot of dexterity and patience; she's working on one small area at a time. She has to be precise in her partings and consistent—no guessing along the way. There's not much room for error."

Depending on the stylist's focus and clientele, her or his tool kit can include several different types of scissors, a range of combs and brushes (round brushes, vent brushes, metal brushes), razors and clippers, a blow-dryer and attachments (a concentrating nozzle, a diffuser), rollers, curling irons, flat irons, and hot combs. I won't go into detail about these instruments, but will note that all that was said above about variation in technique to gain particular effects is true for each of them. The angle at which the stylist holds the hair when blow-drying, for example, the type of brush or comb used, the tension applied, the amount of time, the attachment on the dryer, and the angle at which the dryer itself is held—all this varies by style. One's keen senses and a developed physical rhythm are of related importance. Describing the use of hot irons, a stylist observes: "You can test the iron on a towel or tissue, but your senses will tell you if it's too hot. . . . Then you get a rhythm going, putting the iron in the oven for a count of three, using it, putting it back in, grabbing another one—it demands your attention, even when you're talking." The last few words of the stylist's comment raise an issue that appears throughout this book: how physical routines can become nearly automatic but still involve some level of awareness and monitoring.

Finally, there is the issue of hair products, a bewildering array of shampoos and conditioners, styling aids (mousses, gels, sprays), color technologies, waving and relaxing agents. Through demonstrations, word of mouth, and experience, stylists develop preferences for particular brands, restricting the scope of choice, but, still, the selection of a particular product for a particular person's hair involves a good deal of practical knowledge, analysis, and decision. Even the fairly straightforward use of a product off the shelf requires an acquired touch; hair spray, for example, comes in different "holding strengths" and must be applied, depending on the style, to varying degrees and on some areas more than others. Things quickly get more complex with waving, relaxing, and coloring agents. Coloring, for example, requires some knowledge of pigment, tone, and color theory; an understanding of the basic chemistry of coloring hair; and a mastery of mixing and application procedures—especially in situations where the stylist is correcting a botched dye job. And, again, multiple factors are involved: previous hair treatments, to name one, or texture and porosity. Finally, as always, there's individual variation. As Sharon puts it, "You have to develop an eye for how what's right for one person is not right for the next."

All of this, the stylists I met would quickly remind us, is the "technical," the "mechanical" dimension of what they do. Exceedingly important. One could not do the work without it, and it is clearly a mark of expertise. But the work itself calls for much more. It is the bringing to bear of technique onto human need that the stylists emphasize, the social and aesthetic aspects of the work that can be most challenging ... and most rewarding. It is to this social-aesthetic dimension of styling hair that we now turn.

◻

"When you first get out of beauty school," says one of the stylists I interviewed, "you feel like a zealot, looking at everyone with a kind of vampire vision and thinking about what you want to do to them. But you eventually learn that it's not [your duty] to make them as you think they should be." She gives expression to the strong aesthetic sense many stylists have about hair, often displayed in childhood play and adolescent styling endeavors ("I've always had scissors in my hand," says Vanessa), and refined and focused during their training. And there may be occasions in stylists' lives—depending on their circumstances—where they can continue to engage hair primarily in aesthetic terms, during professional development classes, for example, or even more so at hair shows, where well-known stylists create both avant-garde and wildly ornamental styles. For some stylists, the aesthetic response is hard to compromise, perhaps from youthful zealotry, perhaps from celebrity intoxication, nicely captured in the proclamation of a New York salon director some years ago: "I want to *create* coiffures for a woman, not to have her tell me what she wants."

But all of the stylists I interviewed—from people working in small neighborhood shops to those in trendy and expensive salons—spoke of the importance of determining what the client wants and negotiating one's aesthetics with client need. This would be the case, one stylist explained, if for no other reason than business savvy: you won't satisfy people, won't develop a following, and will soon be out of work. "It's important to *hear* my client," said one veteran stylist. And Sharon insists that "the consultation is the most important moment of the haircut." When I asked a third stylist the one thing she would distill from her experience to pass on to apprentices, she quickly responded: the importance of communication. And yet another stylist, a man who owns his own salon, will not proceed before sitting face-to-face with new clients and finding out as much as he can about them: their occupation, hobbies, tastes, and daily routines.

Earlier, we considered the kinds of diagnostic information gained by the stylist as she or he examines a client's hair, but over the next few pages I would like to further explore this interaction between stylist and client, unpacking some of the cognitive, cultural, and linguistic aspects of a fairly complex act of communication.

The first thing to note is that we humans tend to invest hair with great meaning—and this seems to hold true across history and culture. Right now on my desk I have a discussion of wigs as status markers in ancient Egypt; a drawing of the mythic Rhine maiden Lorelei, whose flowing hair was part of her destructive allure; the seventeenth-century English poet Richard Lovelace's entreaty to Amarantha to dishevel her hair, "let it fly as unconfin'd"; anthropologist Raymond Firth's treatment of hair as a "public symbol"; and a flyer from the California African American Museum announcing the exhibit "Hair in African Art and Culture." In various ways, we signify age, gender, social status, and religious, cultural, and political beliefs through our hair and, in intimate connection, give expression to personal mood and desire. Thus one woman told me that she avoids certain styles, for "that is simply not a Black middle-class thing to do." A second said that her current style makes her feel "a little more put together and grown up." Another observed that for a number of years she had her hair permed, because she wanted to "look ethnic, but always looked like the Breck girl." A fourth said, "I just feel sexier when my hair is done." So when the women who opened this chapter, Lynn and her stylist, Vanessa, describe a cut as "sassy" or ascribe "snap" or "flick" to it, these descriptions have intricately symbolic meaning.

Now, to be sure, not every haircut is a weighty affair; sometimes a haircut, to reword Freud, is just a haircut. But the important thing for our purposes is that the motives that bring a customer to a stylist can be complex and, as with so many culturally loaded phenomena, not readily accessible. As one stylist curtly puts it: "Don't assume you know what they want, because *they* may not even know what they want."

How, I wondered, does the competent stylist convert an image or feeling held by another human being into some sort of a plan of action? What strategies lead from desire to technique? Here is a sampling of the methods used by the stylists I interviewed.

The stylist asks a series of questions, often, as we saw with Vanessa and Lynn, while picking at the hair, moving one's fingers through it, motioning hands about the head. The client and stylist watch this activity together in the mirror, and the linking of question ("How's the length of the bangs?") to gesture is important, for the gesture specifies the question, grounds it, and generates further collaborative talk—coming, for example, to some agreement about the length and line of the bangs.

Words are crucial here. First, it is important to use a common, nontechnical language. Yet all the stylists agree that common language can give rise to misinterpretation, for we think we share meanings, but don't. One stylist offers the example of clients who say " 'I want an inch off,' and show you two inches with their fingers." "You have to pay attention to the words they use," insists one of the salon owners I interviewed. She points out the frequent misunderstanding of words like *taper,* or the confusion around common color terms: "What people think of as red is not red." So she trains her stylists to zero in on language and ask further clarifying questions, or show pictures, or use color swatches to come to consensus.

When a client's request lacks detail or is more emotive than visually descriptive, another stylist I interviewed presents verbal or visual examples that lie at what she thinks are the limits of acceptability. Thus, she "assesses the parameters" of the request by determining "what's outrageous to them," and then moves progressively in toward an increasingly defined cut.

Sometimes clients bring in pictures or call attention to someone else in the salon. Though there is a difference of opinion among stylists about the usefulness of pictures, some welcome them and even produce their own. Pictures would seem to put stylist and client on firmer ground, and sometimes they do. Two caveats, however. First, as one stylist notes, sometimes the client wants the *feeling* evoked in a picture more than the particulars of the cut itself. Another stylist tells a cautionary tale, drawn from early in her career, about cutting a client's hair to match a model's in a picture, only to have the client recoil at the end. She learned from the experience that a picture needs to spark further questions, to extend, not close down, the consultation. Second, there is the issue discussed earlier in this chapter about variability. "I try not to use too many pictures," a stylist explains, "because no two heads of hair are alike. The client thinks they'll look like the picture." It becomes the stylist's job, then (in fact, is mentioned by several as a mark of professionalism), to explain with words, gestures, or other pictures what's possible, to modify the cut or style, to suggest alternatives. "I tell them in a nice way," one salon owner says, "that your features and her features are different, so let's do something that would be more accommodating to you." This "managing of expectations," as a further stylist puts it, clearly calls for a combination of tact and an aesthetic and technical repertoire.

I've been discussing specific methods (asking questions, using pictures) that stylists use to comprehend what a client wants; let me now consider the broader context of the stylist-client interaction itself. Depending on the nature of the salon, the personalities of the stylist and the client, and the duration of their relationship, the interaction between the two may consist of a good deal of small talk and gossip, but, as well, personal material of some importance. The stylist as confidant, informal counselor. Such a relationship contributes to the client's sense of being cared for, nurtured—thus reflecting the emotional labor of the stylist—and makes the experience, by turns, pleasant, humorous, inspiriting. But it also provides an open channel of information pertinent to the stylist's work. The ongoing conversation between client and stylist fosters an understanding of the client's life, which contributes to the stylist's ability to interpret and enact the client's request, to, as one stylist puts it, "discern what the client is truly asking me to do."

It is telling, I think, that a number of the women I spoke with who are satisfied with their stylists gave high praise to the communicative dimension of the work. The effective stylist "listens," "respects what I want," "cuts it the way I like it," "sees what I mean." A word commonly used—Lynn used it in this chapter's opening vignette—is *understand*, the stylist "understands my hair." By asking questions, defining words, determining parameters, using gestures and visuals, and through the informal conversation of the service encounter, the competent stylist negotiates an understanding of the literal and the symbolic content of a client's request.

◻

I want to introduce three more stylists. Their practice and commentary are reflected in what I've written so far, and they can now help us explore more specifically this business of styling hair, particularly the interaction of the economic, social, and aesthetic dimensions of doing the work.

Shandra is in her midthirties and owns a salon in Los Angeles that caters primarily to an African American clientele. The long, narrow shop has seven chairs, sleek black workstations, arrowhead and philodendron cascading down from ledges and ceiling. "I've been in the business for sixteen years, and I've been a salon owner for going on eight. It's a good business, and I enjoy it." Shandra's voice is mezzo, vibrant. There's an easy professionalism to her manner, and a psychological cast of mind.

> Some stylists have a hard time dealing with other people. They have a hard time with criticism. But you have to be able to accept it and work it out, fix the problem. After a client goes home, they may call you back and say, "You know, that didn't work" or "I thought I wanted it that long, but I think I need a little more layering." You have to be open to that. It's part of the process. It could be that they thought they wanted something, but didn't, or that you didn't hear exactly what they wanted. It comes with the territory. You have two human beings, one trying to render a service, the other trying to let you know what [they want]. You two were on separate sheets of music for a minute, and now you're bringing them together.

Deborah, late thirties, has worked in a number of settings; when I first met her, she was renting space as sole stylist in a tiny shop in a Southern California bedroom community. "I've always liked doing hair. I went to cosmetology school through a regional occupational program when I was eighteen." Deborah gives a sense of her career history, its twists and turns, the early exploitation, long hours, low pay, her bosses cheating her on her wages.

> When you first come out of school, you don't have a clientele, so you work on commission. [The first place I worked] the owners were domineering, and they were cheating us on our checks. [At the second] the owner wanted half of our money. Can you believe it? But then I found a place, a little blue house next to my kid's school, where I rented a room and continued to build a clientele. I loved it.

Olive skin, long black hair, lustrous and curly, Deborah describes herself as a "people person." Earnest, her voice rises often, as if in a question, as her sentences end.

> I'm a hairstylist. It's one of my favorite things to do, to do the cut, the lines, and especially in a really difficult cut, to get the lines perfect and make the hair flow nicely. It's fun. . . . I just like making people happy that way. I love doing hair, just, you know, the whole thing of cutting, styling, being my own boss, the money? People leave my chair happy because of what I did for them. You really don't get that out of too many jobs, you know, that you're gonna affect people like that?

Nancy is in her early fifties and works in an old and well-regarded neighborhood salon in St. Paul. There's a soothing quality to its original wood floors, worn with age. Nancy was an art major in college, and, as one of her clients puts it, she creates beauty all around her.

> I think through my fingers. I like to garden, cook, sew, decorate cakes. I suppose I've always had a strong sense of form, a confidence about it. I went to beauty school because I thought it would be fun to do hair. It's an incredibly portable skill, and at the end of the day, your work is done. It's honest. I really like what I do.

That same client notes that conversation with Nancy tends toward books and movies, politics and ideas. Nancy's been styling hair for thirty-four years, and, as we speak, she tends toward a long view of the work.

> This is a business that is unlike most, there's something very nurturing about it. It is one of the few places in our society where you have permission to touch people. It's so intimate. We humans

have a need for connection. Some salons have gone so far in the opposite direction, they're austere, so above it all. In the shop where I work, we've been through deaths, cancer, weddings. How can someone denigrate that?

Shandra, Deborah, and Nancy, collectively, raise many of the reasons that motivate someone to pursue a career in hairstyling. It is a portable skill, allows a degree of control over one's schedule, has the potential for decent money, is social and less confining than office work and many service jobs. The female stylists I interviewed mention, as well, their personal history with hair: fooling around with their dolls' hair; experimenting with their own and with others' hair; horror stories about haircuts and styles visited upon them; the pleasure of being with older women in the kitchen while hair was being cut or styled, or accompanying them to the beauty shop, the talk, the smells, the look of things. (As young women move into formal training, they face the developmental challenge—captured in Lanita Jacobs-Huey's study of an African American beauty college—of converting personal interest into professional code and bearing.) And all the stylists I interviewed raise, as a significant motivator, the aesthetic dimension of the work. Hair is to them an expressive medium. I think here of a group of apprentices I met in an introductory class on coloring: they were all leaving career paths that were unfulfilling ("If I had to serve one more cup of coffee to an ungrateful customer . . ." said a young man who had been managing a Starbucks) and moving into fields they saw as more creative. "Hair is a three-dimensional art," said one young woman, her own rich brown hair revealing flashes of blonder hues when she gestured.

There are, then, a cluster of reasons to explain why someone would choose this career, and, clearly, any cross-section of stylists would give different weights to each—and, over time, the motives to stay, or leave, can change as well. With Nancy, for example, the importance of the communal aspects of the work has probably increased over time. It is also likely that owning a shop and supervising other stylists has sharpened Shandra's appreciation of the consultation, and, with that, heightened her satisfaction with her own communication skill.

Motives play out in the practice of the craft, so one's working conditions are critical to the further development—or the limiting, even distorting—of one's skill, social competence, and aesthetic sense. Deborah's account of her early jobs is familiar to most stylists—and resonates with the portrayal some twenty-five years ago of the salon in Louise Kapp Howe's classic investigation of female occupational inequity, *Pink Collar Workers*. Though the craft is portable and provides some independence, those who practice it are vulnerable—especially when starting out—to a range of injustices: they are cheated on income, loaded down with menial tasks, pressured to sacrifice quality to quantity. The relations among the stylists—the day-to-day politics of working together—is also mentioned by everyone I interviewed as being critical to job satisfaction, and this relationship can be affected by the way the shop is managed.

The work is physically demanding as well, particularly in shops that stress quantity: all those hours on your feet, or up and down from a stool, the repetitive motion, possible allergies to styling products. And, for some, depending on setting and clientele, the tasks themselves can become flatly routine. As several stylists put it, you don't want your schedule to be just a series of "doing roots"; Nancy, who, as we just read, likes her work, told me that her biggest challenge is "keeping it fresh." And the quality of relationships with one's clients makes a huge difference—thus the effort all stylists put into building a list of regulars. All this leads to an obvious point, but one worth noting, for it applies to all the work covered in this book. The conditions of one's work—as much as the nature of the work itself—are crucial in determining the display and development of competence and directly affect one's job satisfaction. The more enervating and demeaning the conditions, the less opportunity to enhance one's skills, display creativity, and develop satisfying relationships with clients and with fellow stylists.

In a thought-provoking study of power and social class in a Long Island salon—where there was a clear class disparity between stylists and clients—sociologist Debra Gimlin explores the way stylists' knowledge and aesthetic opinion are contested by their clients, thus diminishing the stylists' opportunity to exercise their expertise, reducing them more to the level of service providers only. Without denying the legitimacy of Gimlin's analysis (social class clearly plays into the dynamics of any service encounter), I wonder if there is something further to say about the role of aesthetic negotiation in the meeting of stylist and client—and here I think of Shandra's comments as well as my earlier discussion of the consultation. Certainly, there are plenty of stylists who impose their aesthetic judgment on their clients—frequently to their clients' dismay—and, conversely, there are plenty of clients who frustrate stylists with their resistance. As we saw, however, the stylists I interviewed note that it is a mark of expertise to apply and adjust their aesthetic repertoire to client need, to, as Shandra suggests, harmonize skill and desire. Worth considering here is the Romantic definition of "aesthetic"—the received Western definition—which emphasizes individual and unrestrained expression. But what we have in the salon is an applied aesthetic, aesthetics playing out in a social field. If the stylist's aesthetic is constrained, it is also guided, interactive, fluid, and it is precisely that interactivity (recall those clients' praise of being heard and understood) that leads to client satisfaction. And it is that kind of satisfaction—that immediate response to the display of one's skills—that all the stylists I interviewed cite as being deeply fulfilling. Recall Deborah: "People leave my chair happy because of what I did for them."

Because of what I did for them. I want to consider the social aspect of this social and aesthetic dynamic a moment longer. There is, as Nancy says, an intimacy to the work: the positioning of the client, the touching, the symbolic meaning of hair, the expression of desire, the confidences exchanged. (Interestingly, the role of informal counselor was impressive enough to one group of community mental health researchers that they provided training in counseling techniques to hairstylists.) Yet, as sociologist Gimlin points out, where this relationship exists, it can well be one-directional: the client talks, the stylist listens. At the other end of the spectrum, though, is the kind of social reciprocity described by Nancy (and Shandra told me about closing her salon for a day so that she and her crew could attend a client's out-of-town retirement party). Between these modes of relating, a wide and varied landscape of human connection exists. And, though, as with waitressing, one shouldn't forget the economic base of the relationship, varieties of interaction not strictly economic are possible.

As I spent time with the stylists, I began to understand more about principled action within an economic context. Hairstyling takes place within a twenty-five-billion-dollar beauty industry, that, at the least, fosters the need for products and services, and, in many respects, has created the conditions for a terrible exploitation of desire. As one woman within the industry put it: "Women don't even know what they look like anymore." The stylist's aesthetic values and technical repertoire are shaped to some degree within this industry, and for some observers this is enough reason to be suspect of the stylist's work: it is irredeemably compromised.

What was interesting to me, however, was the way the stylists I studied worked within the industry but worked, as well, to alter its messages to suit their own cultural and aesthetic ideals, their beliefs about their professionalism, and their clients' circumstances. To be sure, there are plenty of stylists out there whose work is dominated by the economic motive and mainstream beauty ideology, happy to push products and costly services. But I was struck by those moments where a stylist, contrary to her own economic self-interest, gave advice or attempted to talk a client out of something that she thought was unnecessary, unattractive, or physically or psychologically unhealthy. True, in some cases, the request could result in a look the stylist doesn't want associated with her name or, worse, in damaged hair—and this would have long-term economic consequences. But at times there was more going on.

Stylists would refuse to wave, relax, or color hair that they determined to be already overtreated. Or would recommend cuts or styles according to their aesthetic judgment rather than by the dollar amount of the service. Or would contest mainstream beauty ideals. They would educate the client, sharing product knowledge and tricks of the trade. They would value a particular cut or style because it requires less maintenance and will last longer. They would bring perspective to what they perceived as excess. "Hair only becomes important," says Nancy, "when it isn't doing what you want it to do." I'm not in any position to say how widespread such moments are, but within my small sample, I observed them with some frequency. They suggest that a stylist's trade can be shaped not only by commercial beauty ideology but by a range of other aesthetic influences, cultural traditions, personal values and beliefs, and conceptions of professional role. "We have a social responsibility," says one stylist. These factors play into the stylist's judgment, and provide an illustration of the way that social and aesthetic values—which are related to knowledge and skill—can be reflected in the service encounter.

One more thing about the aesthetic dimension of styling hair: The stylist needs the opportunity to rejuvenate, find grist for the aesthetic mill; sometimes, one stylist sighs, "the creativity just runs dry." Thus stylists look to colleagues for inspiration, to pick up a trick or two—Deborah finally had to leave that one-chair salon for a more active place because she "was getting stale." Some take professional development classes. "Hair is a science and a mystery," says a man who owns a salon in the South. "There's just so much we don't know, so it keeps me going to learn new things." And many stylists attend hair shows, where aesthetic response is cut loose from customer constraint. As Deborah describes the shows to me: "It's the most amazing thing you've ever seen, hair extensions, sculpture, they'll have women walking around with trees on their heads!" In various ways, then, the stylist recharges and brings new ideas back to the client's chair. Writing about the training of chefs, sociologist Gary Alan Fine has focused on the "occupational aesthetics" of cooking, but, overall, limited attention has been paid to the considerable aesthetic dimension of so much common work. The social science tendency to analyze service encounters in terms of power dynamics—combined with Romantic and individualist notions of aesthetics—may limit our understanding of the many ways aesthetic response is manifested in workplaces like the salon.

❑

There are five of us around the narrow rectangular table in the utility room behind the salon. Sharon, the careful planner we met earlier, is teaching a course on coloring that is part of the salon's apprenticeship program. There is a sink, a refrigerator, a coffeemaker, assorted cups, some brooms, lockers for the staff on one narrow wall, and a long wall of coloring agents arranged by level and hue, one to ten, warm to cold. Sharon stands before the wall of color, talking as she sketches on an upright drawing pad: outlines of hair structure, facts about the chemistry of coloring hair, diagrams of color theory. The science that underlies the stylist's aesthetic choices. The four students at the table assist in the salon, and three of the four have been taking classes at a beauty school or community college cosmetology program. As a group, they know a lot, casually contributing facts about the topics Sharon is covering as well as observations from the salon. They are attentive in an easy way, take notes dutifully, and have a nice manner among themselves, slipping in little jokes and quips amid the attention they give to Sharon. There's a pleasant feeling in these cramped quarters, the kind of chemistry that Sharon—that any teacher—is grateful for.

During one stretch of the two-hour class, Sharon is detailing the structure of the human hair, explaining, as she does so, the process of coloring, the way various products work. One young woman, a forties vamp, leg revealed, tattooed on her arm, ticks off terms and definitions as Sharon is about to write them out. Sharon smiles, poising her pen for the next term and the next. This is the kind of memory and recall central to much of schooling. A bit later, Sharon is discussing the role of ammonia in the developing process, its use in opening the cuticle of the hair shaft, which contributes to the permanence of the resulting color. She begins to explain the problems with ammonia—it's a harsh agent—and here the one man in the group (the fellow who couldn't bear to serve another cup of Starbucks coffee) wonders out loud if you could achieve the same effect by decreasing the level of ammonia but adding heat, which, he recalls, also opens the cuticle. This, Sharon tells me later, "is my most exciting time as a teacher," for her student is not just recalling a fact but is reasoning his way through a problem with it. He is thinking with an orientation toward practice. The facts have moved off the page, so to speak, and into the medium of hair.

After class I ask the young woman with the keen memory what her biggest challenge is at this point in her training. She says that she's at the place where she knows how to handle her scissors and where to hold the hair as she cuts—she's developing the manual techniques of the work. The big challenge now is applying those techniques to real people, actual varied heads of hair, "actually doing it, knowing where to cut when hair changes from straight to wavy, seeing how it'll fall, knowing what it'll look like on different heads." She is making the transition from a focus on technique to an engagement in the work itself. She is incorporating technique into the planning and execution of a cut, responding to problems emerging in the cut, thinking through the scissors in her hand.

THE INTELLIGENCE OF PLUMBING

We are crowded into the kitchen of a small apartment. The tenant, a young woman bouncing a baby on her knee, sits by the back door watching us. Mr. Guthier, Terry, and two other boys are squatting down looking under the sink. The base of the sink is enclosed within a cabinet, so access is restricted. There is an old pan under the curve of the p-trap; it catches one of the leaks Mr. Guthier and his students will fix. A section of the pipe has been replaced, and dried glue of some kind covers the seam in uneven globs. About three-quarters of the pipe, from the sink to the p-trap, is wound in black tape. I am kneeling next to Terry, seventeen, two days' beard, slight nose, a scar across his extended hand. Like the young hairstylists we just met, Terry is at an important point in his development—but for him, an opportunity or a disruption could have huge consequences.

Terry, like most of the boys in this room, is in a special program for young people who have a history of drug abuse and a consequent history with the juvenile justice system. The program enables them, as part of their probation, to finish high school in a curriculum that will provide a general education and entry-level competence in one or more of the construction trades. Though most of the boys have mediocre to poor school records, a number of them take to the program, seeing it as a way out of a bad situation. They throw their considerable energy into the work, running back and forth for supplies, taking stairs two at a time, curling themselves around and under sink cabinets, toilets, the underbellies of old houses. As one boy announces to his classmates after a successful toilet installation: "Hey, this ain't that hard. I could do this for a living."

I met Mr. Guthier and his students during my visits to Metro-Tech, a vocational high school in Phoenix, Arizona, that is making the transition to an integrated academic-vocational curriculum. This particular program is one of a number of efforts these days to create surer pathways from school to work. The emphasis in much of what is said and written about such programs is on the economic benefits to student and society. And there is also a critical literature, skeptical about linking education so closely to the job market. I'll say more about these issues in a subsequent chapter on vocational education, but for now I want to consider a set of issues less discussed in the school-to-work debates, but important to the themes of this book: work as a vehicle for human relation, the importance of adult mentors in the development of competence, and the continual play of intelligence in that relationship and development. Along with the story of Terry and his peers learning a trade, and the story of their rehabilitation, there is a story here about mind and the pivotal role of human connection.

Field experience is essential to Jon Guthier's teaching, and one way he secures such experience for his students is through an arrangement with the city to do free repairs on low-income housing. Repair work, especially on older or less expensive homes and apartments, offers important challenges for young plumbers that they won't get doing new construction. Materials are not always standard; there are unusual structures, nooks, crannies, surprises within the wall; there is often a series of past repairs, layered one over the other, often makeshift. In a sense, such occasions take the students back to a time before codes and prefabrication. They will need to develop a certain resourcefulness and a problem-solving orientation to things.

"What do you make of this, boys?" asks Mr. Guthier, pointing to the taped pipe. "Looks like a mess," says Terry. "Yep," says the teacher. "What do you think we should do with it?" "We gotta replace it," says one boy. "Well, sure," says Mr. Guthier, "but how, where . . . how do we start?"

Jon Guthier is a slight man, about 5'7", 135 pounds, with thin muscled arms, long brown hair, and glasses. At forty-seven, he's worked plenty of construction-related jobs, has been a journeyman plumber and gas fitter for a number of years, and has been teaching for the last twelve. A photograph of him might suggest severity of manner—his features are sharp, angular, and weathered from all those years outdoors—but he has an easygoing way about him, a how's-it-going loquaciousness. The kids call him "Mr. G," or just "G." And they respect him, his concern for them, and his expertise. He's been there, has done the work, knows what he's talking about. So they consult him frequently—he's on the run at a job site from one kid to another—and they take his questions seriously. He poses questions often. When he and a class return to a job site, he'll begin the day by asking the students to go over the problems they had the day before and, as a consequence, to list the things they'll need to do today. When they confront a new job—replacing a toilet, fixing a leak—he asks what they'd do and why. Terry takes his question about that pipe under the sink and suggests they strip the tape to get to the nut attaching the drainpipe to the p-trap. That's reasonable, says Mr. Guthier, and with his right hand guiding their gaze over the entire structure asks the boys to consider what might happen as you take a wrench to that nut, given that other sections of the pipe, p-trap, and wall fixture are glued and, most likely, rusted. Terry gets it: "You've gotta be careful. If that nut won't turn, you might tear something else loose."

The interconnection of the component parts of a structure is an obvious notion. But to grasp the meaning of that interconnection for your own action, and to realize that what you do can extend across different kinds of materials, and can be close by or at some distance—such understanding can give rise to deliberation. A stop-and-think orientation. I recall an experienced plumber, facing a somewhat more complicated situation of this type, telling me, "It's as important to say 'no' [to a possible course of action] as to say 'yes.' You can get yourself in real trouble if you don't think it through."

Mr. Guthier is moving his students toward the comprehension of a house as a complex system of materials, processes, and forces: not an obvious way to think about a building. And his questioning serves a further purpose: to help students become systematic in their approach to repair. The good plumber has a diagnostic frame of mind, evident in a manual that Mr. Guthier uses during classroom instruction. The manual is organized by problems—for example, "a valve or faucet does not completely stop water flow"—that are followed by lists of possible causes. Students are required to consider and test each possibility in turn: a kind of plumber's differential diagnosis. Could it be a bad washer? How about foreign matter—rust, grit—caught in the valve?

To think this way, Mr. Guthier explains to me, you need "to know how a thing is put together," how a device, or a category of devices, works. You may not be familiar with a particular brand of a valve, but if you can determine whether it's a cartridge valve or a compression valve, then you'll know something generally about its components and how they function. Then you're able "to go through these steps in your mind." Given the huge variety of devices and structures you'll encounter in any group of old houses, you need to be able to operate in some systematic way. As they get more adept, these young plumbers may abbreviate the steps, zeroing in on a key feature of the problem rather than ticking off each item on a checklist. But for now I want to dwell on the development of these students' skill and their teacher's desire that they become both knowledgeable about the way things are constructed and systematic in the way they use that knowledge.

In this regard, it would be worth considering how Jon Guthier functions as mentor, as guiding adult, given his students' legal situation. "You feel that sense of urgency in them," he observes, "because even as things go well, something could fall apart right at the end." Though he does have heart-to-heart conversations with these boys about their behavior, the direction of their lives, and particular ethical dilemmas they face, a significant dimension of his mentoring role is played out through the work itself. Some of the teachers I've observed while writing this book tend toward the moral lecture, the lesson-on-life delivered from the front of the classroom. These, as best as I can tell, have little effect—did many of us respond well to them? Yet, as Mr. Guthier pointed out, there is great need here for guidance and structure. "When children feel that adults cannot or will not protect them," writes youth activist Geoffrey Canada in *Fist, Stick, Knife, Gun*, "they devise ways of protecting themselves." Yet, despite their hard-nosed bravado, most of these kids' lives are chaotic. Think, then, of what a guided participation in the work provides: structure and routine, to be sure, and a meaningful connection to an adult, and a sense of helping people out by repairing their homes. There is also, I believe, an ethical dimension to the way Mr. G encourages the young people in his charge toward a skillful and systematic encounter with the material world, toward an understanding that yields agency.

Several days after the students were pondering that taped drainpipe, Terry and a big kid named Ken are replacing a toilet in an old house. Terry has more experience at this task than Ken, so Mr. Guthier tells Ken to do most of the installation and asks Terry to observe and help out.

Installing a toilet is a pretty straightforward procedure, but replacing one, especially in an older house, can have its moments: removing the old toilet, negotiating tight space, fitting a newer model into the existing confines and fittings. One decision that has to be made concerns the flange, the collar that fits over the drainpipe in the floor, and onto which the toilet itself is attached. There's some ambiguity here, but you try to determine how corroded the existing flange is, whether or not it'll hold new bolts, will they be stable?

As soon as the boys remove the old toilet, Mr. Guthier asks them what they think of the flange. There's a quick exchange, then Mr. Guthier hears someone calling him from the kitchen and excuses himself. "I'm not sure," he says, exiting, "but I think you might want to replace it. You don't want to take a chance on a callback."

Ken and Terry settle in, Ken getting down close to the flange, inspecting it. Terry asks, "How's it lookin' to you, Ken?" Ken scrapes at the edge of the flange with a screwdriver. "It looks OK," he answers and cocks his head to get a better take on the edges. Then he slips in two new bolts. "The bolts are going in nice and strong." Pause. "I think we can keep it. Go get G." Terry retrieves Mr. Guthier; the boys explain what they've done and their conclusion. "Well," he says, "you might be right."

Not everything Terry and Ken say during this installation, God knows, surely not everything, is so dialogic and problem-focused. But the installation proceeds effectively, and, at several junctures, is characterized by this kind of thoughtful activity. The boys' decision does not take the easy path of agreement, which suggests that they're appropriating the diagnostic frame of mind modeled by Jon Guthier. They don't simply follow a routine, but vary it purposefully in response to their testing of the materials before them.

As I spend time with these young people, I'm struck by the way that Mr. Guthier's program not only allows them to find a temporary balance within chaos but, as well, becomes a means for them to achieve what they, for a variety of reasons—some beyond their control, some of their own making—could not achieve in the standard classroom. Their work with Jon Guthier exposes and nurtures their intelligence, becomes a measure of what they can do when they put their minds to it. Their teacher realizes acutely the legal and existential fix the boys are in, but addresses it, so to speak, through their engagement with tools and fixtures, water and pipe and surrounding structures.

I find myself thinking, too, of the imperfect bargain here. There is a long tradition in the United States—dating back to nineteenth-century reform schools—of trying to redeem wayward children through the industrial arts. This tradition often brought with it assumptions not only about the moral benefits of physical work but also about the intellectual capacity of working-class, urban youth. Jon Guthier's program, then, is embedded in a complicated history—one he works within, but modifies. It is blue-collar work that is offered to these boys—wealthy kids in trouble would have many more options—but Mr. Guthier takes it seriously and makes it substantial. (Historically, programs of this type frequently involved low-level and limiting tasks.) And from what I could discern of Terry and his peers' point of view, the plumber's trade provides one of the most unambiguous pathways they'd yet seen toward stability.

The huge question—one Jon Guthier frets over—is what will happen to the boys once they complete the program? What social and occupational mechanisms will be in place to forward their development? There's a crucial public policy question here, one frightful to ask in these times of backlash against the less fortunate. What opportunities exist for the kind of technical and human engagement this program provides, and how deeply does the nation believe in its value?

◻

Dwayne, the fellow who announced that he could install toilets for a living, sits amid a group of boys on the bus, headphones on, singing along loudly to a Twista cassette, which, of course, we can't hear, and are left, instead, with Dwayne's assured but not very capable falsetto. Several of the boys around him, Denzell particularly, complain, questioning his talents, but Dwayne, a mix of nonchalance and confrontation, throws it right back, praising the quality of his own voice. Then back to song and complaint. Finally, Mr. Guthier, looking up into the rearview mirror, asks if everyone could please cool it, and they do, at least for a few blocks.

Dwayne will not let you miss him for long. He's boastful, funny, quick-witted, out on you for a response or a cigarette, charming in a boyish, street-smart way. With older men his demeanor shifts—he's still working you, but the quality of the interaction changes—there's more accommodation, and more need and request. Dwayne generates so much activity in the immediate space surrounding him—a flurry of word and gesture—that it's easy to miss, I certainly did, his considerable promise as a tradesperson. Mr. Guthier calls him "a quick study" and thinks he's the most competent student in the class.

If you hang around Dwayne at a job site, you'll witness, more than a few times, an event like this: Dwayne and another boy are finishing the installation of a toilet, and are hooking up the braided hose that brings water from the wall outlet—called an angle stop—to the tank. As they tighten the nuts, Dwayne cradles the hose in a certain way to keep it from twisting and kinking. A few minutes later, Mr. Guthier comes in to remind the boys to be careful that the hose doesn't kink on you—but Dwayne had anticipated that, having already acquired the proper trick of the trade from Mr. G. Here's another: Dwayne is assisting Denzell as he replaces a showerhead. Denzell tightens the head and tries it. It leaks. He tightens it further. The head still leaks. "I bet you don't have the washer in right," suggests Dwayne. Upon disassembly Dwayne turned out to be correct.

Dwayne's advice to Denzell came amid a narrative about a confrontation with some guy at a girl's house, whereupon Dwayne conducted himself mightily, deftly . . . and, then, *bip*—tune out and you'll miss it—there's the hunch about the washer. Settle in with Dwayne long enough, and you begin to see: Dwayne leaning in to inspect a faucet or a flange, feeling carefully with an index finger to confirm what he sees; ticking off, amid chatter, the steps needed to test a fixture; recalling a solution to a similar problem solved in another house, another time.

Dwayne is demonstrating the development of what Jon Guthier calls "a kind of a library" of mechanical knowledge: knowledge of types of devices, how they're put together, how to work with them, processes to follow. This blend of learned facts, experiences, and procedures makes Dwayne capable of functioning without close supervision. The relation of learning and independent action.

To consider action, though, one has to consider factors beyond knowledge alone. To continue with Jon Guthier's metaphor, the tradesperson's library contains more than books; there's a feel and mood to the place, a history, traditions, practices. The skillful tradesperson is defined by what he or she knows, but, as well, by the quality of the work that knowledge yields. Dwayne and two other boys are installing a toilet. They have removed the old unit, and while one is replacing the angle stop on the wall, another is quickly scraping the residue of the previous assembly from the floor. Then they put in a new flange, tap it into place, insert the bolts onto which the new toilet will rest, measure the distance of each bolt from the wall ($13^{1}/_{2}$ inches) to check alignment, place a donut of bowl wax over the flange (this protects against leaking), settle the new toilet onto the bolts, and measure again. These three boys work well together, dividing tasks yet assisting each other, efficient, assured. While they finish the installation, they talk about employment, jobs this training might enable them to get.

The final step is to apply caulking along the base of the toilet. Dwayne cleans up and dries off the floor, then reaches for the caulking gun and begins laying a neat strip of caulk around the porcelain. The caulk smells like pungent bananas—chemical and fruity—and another boy follows Dwayne's trail with a gloved forefinger, narrowing the line. Finished, Dwayne takes a small sponge and further trims the caulking, a thin line now at the base of the toilet. He stands up: "A few good flushes, and we're done." It does look good. Clean and tidy. As the other boys pick up tools and leave to reassemble with Mr. Guthier, I compliment Dwayne, who has fallen quiet. He breaks into a full smile. "Why, thank you very much," he says.

This moment clarifies in my notes like a snapshot. How much comes together to account for it, a developmental integration. The increasing dexterity with tools. Knowledge of plumbing devices and materials. A range of understandings about repair. Tricks of the trade. A systematic approach to problems. And there is the less measurable—but readily evident—sense of workmanship, the cluster of values that, one assumes, leads Dwayne both to check the distance of the toilet to the wall—an action with functional consequences for repair—and to take one more pass at the caulking to reduce it to a visually pleasing line, an aesthetic outcome.

A sense of workmanship is something that Mr. Guthier hopes

for. "I know these boys don't like to handle dirty toilets," he observes one day after we've returned to school, "so there's got to be something there that gives them pride in what they've been able to do." Some of the boys, he continues, "had very rarely been successful at things. Probably it's the first thing they've finished in a long time." If this is true, then one can only imagine the twinge of possibility they feel as they see something they made work, as they gain respect from adults whom they respect, as they begin to imagine—tentatively, anxiously—a different kind of life for themselves, fashioned through hand and brain.

And what might happen, I wonder, if *we* began to experiment with our own thinking about young people like Terry and Dwayne, and, more broadly, about the revelation of mind in the work they're doing. Jon Guthier's unexpected metaphor of the library can help us here and take us beyond the typical discussion of vocational students. How might it productively unsettle our thinking about intelligence, social class, and education to consider the foregoing account in terms of libraries and aesthetics, of differential diagnosis, of conceptualizing, planning, and problem solving, of the intimate connection between respectful human relation and cognitive display? My hope is that such shifts in perception would have consequences for the way we teach Terry and Dwayne, for the subsequent work we create for them, for how we talk to them and about them, and for the words we use to describe what they do.

A VOCABULARY OF CARPENTRY

From the Renaissance through the nineteenth century, mechanics and engineers developed a variety of picture books, charts, and model displays that classified and illustrated basic mechanisms and mechanical movements: gear assemblies, for example, or ratchets, or levers and pullies. (Diderot's *Encyclopedia* contains a number of such illustrations, and we see descendants of them in vocational textbooks and on wall displays in trade school classrooms.) Reading about the history of these mechanical aids, I was curious about the way mechanisms were classified and the role such illustrated classification might play in developing a visual storehouse of devices (think here of Jon Guthier's library). And I was captivated by the names given to these aids: "theaters of machines" and "mechanical alphabet." The mechanical alphabet, especially, got me to think further, beyond the models to the words and metaphors we use, how much we could benefit from a richer alphabet, a vocabulary broad enough to accurately render physical work.

Looking at the old plates, thinking in terms of alphabets, ways to spell and depict, I wonder how many aspects of workplace intelligent behavior are underappreciated, or go unnoticed, because our occupational vocabularies are reductive or because we don't have a category for such behaviors in standard measures of intelligence. What testing vocabulary do we have, for example, to discern the making of judgments from the feel of things, or the strategic use of tool and body, or the rhythmic spacing of tasks, or the coordination of effort and material toward the construction of a complex object?

◻

The display case sits in the back of the workshop like a monument. Lustrous oak, glass shelves and doors, interior lights. Students walk by it, run a hand over it, comment to visitors on its appearance. At the end of every day, they cover it with brown wrapping paper, forming the paper into a protective cowl. At least half of the students in Jerry Devries's wood construction class have worked on the display case over the semester; it is now about a week or two from completion. A time of finishing touches.

Mr. Devries's workshop is one huge room, fifty feet by one hundred. If you started at the display case and slowly walked toward the front of the room, looking about, you'd see wood and metal workstations and old and new power tools: a band saw, a radial arm saw, a circular saw, a jointer, a belt sander as well as an edge-bander, a panel router, and a router controlled by computer. Various vent pipes rise overhead, and yellow air compressor hoses coil down from the ceiling. Against the middle of the west wall sits a large open cabinet with neat rows of chisels and gouges, files, mallets, bit braces, awls, planes, spokeshaves, handsaws. Generation upon generation of woodworker's tools. This is the environment in which skill develops. Along the walls and resting above storage cabinets are models (a house frame, a chest of drawers) and displays of drawer guides, miniature sliding cabinet doors, miter joints, and post and panel assemblies. At the very front of the room you'll find twenty-four student desks along with Mr. Devries's own cluttered desk and podium. There is a blackboard covered with projects and the students assigned to them ("Wall Cabinet: Felipe, Jesus, Gloria"), various sketches of these projects, some dimensions and calculations, and assorted announcements: "Habitat for

Humanity job site visit Aug. 1." The board extends around to a side wall by the door where the lists continue, and there is a space where students write comments drawn from the chatter and events of the day: "To sand or not to sand, that is the question."

Mr. Devries stands behind his podium, inching his index finger down a roster. He is 5'3", a solid man in his midforties with thinning red-brown hair. He is an experienced cabinetmaker who has taught for twenty years, many of them here at John Marshall High School in Northeast Los Angeles. Alternating between comedy and drama as he finishes taking roll, he secures parental permission slips for that visit to the Habitat for Humanity construction site (where the class volunteers their labor) and dispatches with the many microadministrative tasks of the high school teacher. His students, twenty-three boys and one girl, with one exception all Latino, are a mix of sophomores, juniors, and seniors. They sit postured in the angles and half-turns of variable attention, doodling at arm's length, looking, in pairs, through fantasy art magazines, watching Mr. Devries. In the rear corner seat, Louie, the class clown, cracks a fairly audible joke about a guy chewing gum laced with Viagra.

Mr. Devries finishes up, closes his roll book, and with rising voice says, "OK, let's *get to work*." And, in movement that is fluid, almost gentle, the students slide out of repose, up and out of their seats, and stream across the floor to stations around the room: to the worktable by the radial arm saw, to the tool cabinet, to the panel router, to wall racks in the far corner where they don aprons and safety glasses. Within minutes the room is vibrant with the slam of boards laid out to measure, the screech of the circular saw, the acrid smell of blade on wood.

Some of the work the students do maintains the shop itself. They clean machinery, cut and store wood stock, and make simple tools like sanding blocks—the same activity you would have found in a nineteenth-century workshop. This work goes on continually, in between or during the primary projects the students undertake. They can work on individual projects—a table or cabinet or bookcase for their homes—or work in teams on projects that flow into the shop. After so many years of recognized achievement, Jerry Devries's classes get requests from within the school and throughout the district to bid on larger projects: storage cabinets, quantities of podiums, secretaries' stations, computer tables, the majestic display case.

The majority of students, particularly at the sophomore and junior levels, choose the team effort on these larger projects. Mr. Devries will select an older student to supervise, thus providing extended experience in planning and delegating—and with the delegating comes a good deal of teaching, peer to peer. For younger or less-experienced students, the team affords an apprenticing structure in which to further develop the basic skills of woodworking and some guided opportunity to plan, calculate, and think through a project. As you look around the classroom, then, you'll see clusters of four and five students at various workstations, and an occasional lone student measuring, cutting stock, or assembling—though even there, you'll often see someone assisting, for a cooperative spirit pervades the room.

I follow one of the sophomore boys back to the display case. Paul is a handsome kid whose usual dress is a black T-shirt adorned with bright and elaborate fantasy art—cyborgs, aliens, cartoon characters, the sultry, exaggerated women of car detailing—and baggy jeans cut at the cuff to form a floppy cover over running shoes. He smiles, sometimes laughs out loud, at the antics of the older, rambunctious boys—hooting at Louie's Viagra joke—but tends toward a more serious demeanor. He sits sidesaddle in his desk against the west wall, looking out onto his classmates, looking across the room to Jerry Devries. It's common that Paul will be the first at his workstation once Mr. Devries releases the class from the preliminary business of the day. It is this blend of adolescent sociability and focus that caught my eye—this boy who is laughing with everyone else while tying his apron or reaching for a tape measure. He talks readily about the "integrity" of working with wood.

Paul enlists another boy to help him remove the paper covering from the display case. Then he grabs a framing square (an L-shaped metal ruler) off of a nearby table, pulls a stool over to the back of the display case, and begins the task assigned to him by Mr. DeVries. Boards for support still need to be fastened to the back of the case, one along the top and one along the bottom. Paul's job is to draw the lines on the case that will mark the placement of the supports. Paul steps onto the stool, framing square in hand, pencil behind ear. He begins. I watch him for a long time.

Because the framing square is two feet long, Paul has to draw the lines in increments, steadying the framing square against several reference points, checking and double-checking each segment of each line. He has to be sure that each line is so many inches from the top or bottom and that each segment of each line is aligned with the other, and that the twin lines (across the top and across the bottom) are aligned.

Paul is cautious. Every time he slides the framing square from one increment of the line to another, he checks it at several points, his face turned slightly, eye close to the wood. Then he runs his pencil slowly along the rule, pulls his head back, and checks it again. This is a pretty basic task: Paul is using some fundamental measurement arithmetic and gaining practice with the framing square, aligning it on a surface, reading it. But he is also learning something, I think, about attending, summoning one's powers of concentration in the service of precision. We saw the role of attention in the waitress's work. Here we see it in a different context, and in a way that calls forth William James's classic discussion of attention: "Focalization, concentration of consciousness are of its essence." The exact placement of the supports matters, and it is one of the last tasks in the long life of this valued project. Paul focuses his efforts to get it right. I am drawn by his deliberateness, its development manifest in this task.

When we think about problem solving, creativity, acts of the mind, we tend to think of the grand moment, the clarifying insight, the breakthrough, the tough nut cracked. Fair enough. Such moments are worthy of acknowledgment. But I think it is also worth dwelling on the commonplace, ordinary expressions of mind that every day, a thousand times over, enable the work of the world to get done, and that, more than we think, are critical in solving the less common, more dramatic problems that face us. In his study of creativity, *The Mind's Best Work*, psychologist D. N. Perkins argues that creative ability, long studied as exceptional, can also be understood as "exceptional versions of familiar mental operations," such as perception and memory. The notion is valuable here, for it encourages an appreciation of the significance of cognitive processes that, because of their frequency and familiarity, are taken for granted. Such an appreciation might provide one way to develop a vocabulary befitting the mind at work.

The more time I spend in Jerry Devries's workshop, the more I notice the various ways this mix of attention and perception, knowledge of the field, and values plays out in the day-to-day routines of working with wood. Consider, for example, the sharpening of the senses that develops in the woodworking environment. "Use the eyes to test straightness, squareness, and symmetry," writes the author of an early-twentieth-century pedagogical tract, "before applying any other testing instruments." Jerry, like other expert carpenters I observed, is able to estimate length at a glance. He can eyeball a structure for misalignment, an angle that's off, gaps, bows, sags in an assembly. He troubleshoots the cause of problems through the look of things. He has an eye, and a touch, for texture.

He scans for flaws, spotting a place high up on the interior wall of the display case where a screw has barely broken through the wood. This ability has been characterized by several cognitive researchers as *disciplined perception*—and we saw it in another kind of work with the hairstylists. It is disciplined because it emerges from one's training and depends on—and helps constitute—a body of knowledge. And what is perceived is connected to systematic action; here perception has meaning and consequence for assembly and repair.

The woodworker's visual skill is so much a part of the work that it's easy to miss its special quality. Thus it was through a sense less identified with carpentry that the importance of disciplined perception first struck me.

We were at the Habitat for Humanity job site, Jerry and I talking. About fifteen yards away, a group of students was drilling holes in fence posts. Jerry suddenly turned around. "Hey," he yelled, "don't burn the motor out!" The students stopped, and he walked over. "Go slow," he said, and showed them how to handle the drill with more finesse. Earlier that day, another crew of Jerry's students had been cutting stock to length for the fence, and, this time, it was the sound of the saw that caught Jerry's ear. He made his way to the place where the students had set up the power miter box they were using—they had placed the tool on a sheet of plywood that rested on two sawhorses—and he moved the two sawhorses closer together. The weight of the miter box was causing the plywood to bend, and thus the stock that the students were cutting was bowing slightly, causing the saw to grab or bind into the wood. Jerry turned to Louie, of Viagra fame. "What'd I just do?" Louie explained the principle behind the action, using his hands to illustrate. As Jerry walked away, Louie leaned toward me and nodded at his teacher's retreating figure: "Interesting, huh?" Then, louder, for the benefit of his peers, he said, "Devries tactics," a phrase the students use to label one of Mr. Devries's tricks of the trade, adjustments, or techniques.

As I walk around Jerry Devries's classroom or the Habitat for Humanity job site, I too hear a range of sounds: the pounding of hammers, the squeal of power saws, the harsh router. But it's cacophonous, gross distinctions at best. I ask Jerry about the keenness of his ear. He laughs and says that he doesn't think he hears with particular acuity, that, in fact, he sometimes has trouble hearing what his students are saying. But he clearly has developed an ear for the sounds of trouble related to the use of power tools. In the first vignette with the drill, he hears a motor being pushed close to its limits. In the second, he hears something in the sound of the cut that suggests that the saw blade is binding into the wood. His is an ear trained to hear trouble, to perceive it amid all the other sounds of the workplace. This heightened perception enables him to protect against error or damage, and it also has pedagogic value, enabling him to intervene right at a strategic, teachable moment.

As with many work-related abilities, it's hard to trace specifically how this skill develops, other than to say that it develops with experience, over time, and with certain motives and incentives—like protecting tools and teaching their proper use. But though difficult to trace, you can see moments of its development. Paul, whom we just met measuring the display case, is running a piece of stock through the jointer, to plane smooth its edge. He runs the board through three or four times, occasionally leaning back to look under the machine to see the shavings coming off. I ask him why he runs it through multiple times, and he explains that he had determined that it had a bow in the middle. (To check the evenness of the surface of an edge, Mr. Devries had shown the students how to set a board on the flat metal surface of the machine, then hunch down and look to see if any light comes through.) I then ask Paul how he decides on the number of times to put the board through—since he isn't stopping after every pass to perform the light test, and he explains that you can *hear* when the board is even, for the sound will continue without interruption, the blade will not be hitting any gaps in the surface of the wood. Paul seems to be on his way to developing the kind of trained ear that Jerry Devries has, an ear attuned to variation in the sound of a power tool on wood, and the potential meaning that sound may have.

I have been discussing the individual senses, but the integrated use of multiple senses—a long-standing curiosity to psychologists of perception—is also commonplace in the shops I visited. I watched, for example, an auto mechanic use all of his senses but taste while repairing an engine—often using the senses in combination to "give [him] more information" or "to check one against the other." A fascinating variation of this sensory integration is when a tradesperson uses one sense as a substitute for another, as when the plumber Jon Guthier reached up inside a wall to "help [him] see" the condition of the pipes hidden within. Here touch is used as a visualizing mechanism, to interpretive, diagnostic ends.

◻

This focusing of attention and refinement of the senses occurs in the service of assembly and repair, so they are intimately linked to the use of tools. And tools, of course, would be a key element in any vocabulary of work. The development of skill with tools involves, at the least, knowledge of a tool's purpose and function and competent use of the body: grip, stance, leverage, the efficient transfer of force. This attunement of body and tool is less foreign to me than Jerry's and Paul's refined ear. It was during one of my uncle Frank's visits to Los Angeles—the railroad had laid people off again, and he was looking out West for work—that he helped me build a storage box. I was hammering a panel onto the frame when he stopped me, moved my hand down to the base of the handle—I was "choking" it—and showed me how to swing the tool in a way that "let the hammer do the work." What struck me, I remember, was the surprise of the feel: the hammer seemed more powerful and my swing—from shoulder through wrist—increasingly fluid. And I got better at driving a nail.

Looking across Jerry Devries's workshop with a focus on movement, attending to biomechanics, I see a range of physical skill with a variety of tools and tasks: from one of the youngest boys struggling with the saw in a miter box, his strokes wobbly and uneven, to Louie on one knee, his torso turned into the tight space of a cabinet, working a chisel over a flaw in the frame. The biomechanical skills related to carpentry build on and enhance basic sensory, kinesthetic, and cognitive abilities that emerge through natural development, abilities that, themselves, as any neurologist will tell you, are wondrous: the ability to grasp, to pound, to attend to and track an object, to sequence movements. This is the endowment Mr. Devries's students bring with them and that, in his class or (often) earlier in fathers' or grandfathers' workshops, is further developed and channeled toward the skillful use of tools. His students' learning occurs continually and in multiple ways.

They learn how to effectively use their bodies by observing Mr. Devries's demonstrations and the work of their peers. (Paul notes: "You see work going on all around you. You see people making small, small mistakes, and you learn from that.") Students learn through guided practice: Mr. Devries or an older student coaching or physically directing their movement. And they learn through their own trial and error, adjusting their stance and motion via the visual and tactile feedback they get from tool and wood. Just about every photograph I have of Mr. Devries or a student using a tool catches several others looking on, gaze focused on the task. If we were to animate the photos, you'd commonly see those observers move from the periphery to take in hand the file, the nail punch, the bench plane. They would then mimic what they saw, getting the actual feel of it. Another thing you'd see is Mr. Devries or an older student moving into the frame to orally or physically guide the motion of hand and arm. Felipe, one of Mr. Devries's more competent juniors, comes over to the boy struggling with the backsaw in the miter box. Here, he tells him in Spanish, stand like this. And, look, this saw cuts going in, so push it all the way in, move your arm like this, now easy coming back. See?

Felipe's assist reveals something important—but often unsaid—about physical skill: that it's usually integrated with knowledge. His feel for the backsaw is combined with an understanding of how it works. I think of Willie, the expert mechanic in Douglas Harper's *Working Knowledge*, as he advises Harper on his misuse of the hacksaw: "A hacksaw *plays* its way through the metal. . . . If you lay on it too hard it will not cut on a straight line. Take your time—let it play." Willie and Felipe know things about the saws they're using and the materials they're using them on, and that knowledge informs their movement.

And students learn how to use a tool not only on the bench but in constrained space. Thus they learn how to maximize biomechanics, begin to develop the physical savvy that eventually yields the deft touch of the drywaller working overhead or the carpenter starting a nail with one hand. Gloria is standing with one leg inside and one leg outside the frame of a cabinet for the art department. She is attaching small boards under the base—these will protect the frame when it is stood upright—and has to lean out and over to get a clean swing of her hammer. She secures a board with her foot, angling the tip of her shoe in about forty-five degrees. She drives the nails. On the second board, she angles her foot differently, learning from the feel of her first attempt, and drives the nails home.

As with waitressing, many of these moves will become routine, but now, at these freeze-frames of development, we see a conscious attending, mimicking, calibrating of the body. It is commonplace both in vernacular and in the psychological sciences to say that over time these physical skills become automatic, and to be sure, with practice, they require much less attention. But one of the professional carpenters I spoke to had an interesting take on this business of automaticity. He stopped me when I used the word *automatic*. It didn't feel right to him. "Confident," he said, after a moment, thinking out loud. Sure, your hammer strokes and sawing and all that, by now, are proficient, you do it right, you do it once. But there's always some element of awareness to the work, for safety, but also because the task at hand will have its own demands, require its own minor adjustments. This calls to mind one of the conclusions in a recent study of blacksmithing: "Skilled performances [are] conceptually embedded even when immediate events press an agent to react seemingly without thinking." One's physical skills, then, though highly developed, will always be responsive to the environment, calling for a certain circumspection and adaptability. The hammer stroke becomes routinized but not mindless.

Let us now turn from a focus on body and hand to a consideration of tools themselves. Mr. Devries's students are surrounded by tools, both manual and power, and one of the significant things that will happen to these young people over their time with him and beyond is that their knowledge of tools, and the variations within kinds of tools—the crosscut saw, the ripsaw, the backsaw, the coping saw—will increase dramatically. They will be able to recognize these objects, name them, know what each can do—and as we just saw, they will learn how to manipulate them effectively. At the most fundamental level, clear in the human archaeological record, there are about a half-dozen things tools enable us to do, and to do profoundly better than by hand and arm alone: pound, cut, probe, scrape, join. But the variety of methods humankind has developed to perform these basic tasks, responses to emerging needs in assembly and repair, is staggering. Neuropsychologist Richard Gregory makes the nice observation that "tools contain ready-made answers to practical problems." Jerry Devries's students do not have to solve anew the problem of how to make an accurate forty-five-degree cut; they have the miter box and backsaw available, a set of devices that represents many generations of thought as well as advances in metallurgy and toolmaking. Tool as legacy. As Felipe helps that younger student use the miter box, he orients him to a historically embodied set of solved problems, and, in a sense, activates them, yielding the precise cut, the clean angle ready for joining.

Tools not only act on material but with experience become a vehicle for learning about the properties of materials themselves. As well, one learns about force and function, design and structure. Brain, hand, tool, wood become a complex cybernetic system, information flowing back and forth in action. We saw this feedback loop in play as students were learning to use their bodies in concert with tools. And, of course, tools like the tape measure, the framing square, and the spirit level provide data on length, angle, and tilt. Other tools, from the awl (that pointed tool that looks like an ice pick) to the crowbar, can be used inventively to help you determine and effect alignment. And, as Paul explains to me holding up, first, a piece of oak, then pine, different kinds of wood respond in different ways to nail, saw, plane, and sandpaper.

"The hammer," claims carpenter and writer Jeff Taylor, ". . . changes the way you think." The use of tools over time contributes to a bodily, material physics and mechanics, to a rich knowledge of assembly and repair, and to a problem-solving orientation toward the built environment. This knowledge is manifest in the workshop. I sensed it before I could put words to it—and Richard Gregory's observation about tools embodying solutions to problems helped guide my expression. There is intelligence in the surround, poised, so to speak, for purposeful action. For the young person with an interest in woodworking, the shop must feel like a powerful invitation to competence, a pathway to achievement. As I talk to Paul about the nearly completed display case, he comments on its appearance and says how good it feels to see it through to completion. He pauses, and shifts. "As time goes on," he says, gesturing, moving his hand along an imaginary time line, "you get to use tools you haven't used before. There's some tools here I haven't used yet." His eyes get big and he smiles, "like the panel router," and he points across the room to a router on a carriage that glides over a large, retaining frame. "That will enable me to do some new things, and I'm excited. It gives you a good, nice cut."

❑

Paul's comment brings us directly to the topic of power tools, which could be seen to qualify much of what I've written about the development of physical skill. With the advent of steam-powered (and, later, electrically powered) tools, there has been a diminished need for the manual finesse of the preindustrial craftsman. The band saw and jigsaw, for example, can quickly make all sorts of irregular and curved cuts that took much longer, with much more adroit manipulation, when performed by hand. The use of power tools brought with it a degree of de-skilling—and, some would say, a loss of craftsmanship. But what is also true—immediately evident to anyone who tries to use a jig- or band saw—is that power tools require a skill of their own. Also, as the historical record shows, in domains such as furniture making, power tools were integrated into craft traditions and practices, significantly altering the performance of many operations but within the ethos and character of craft work.

Craft traditions are evident in the environment Jerry Devries provides. And there is another, more personal, means of transmission. Some of the students I got to know had people in their families who worked with wood—fathers, uncles, grandfathers—and these students, as youngsters, had spent time in garages and workshops hanging around the older men. "Just seeing what he could do," says one boy, "interested me." Craft traditions were manifest in this work, transmitted and made immediate through bloodlines, through what one group of educational researchers aptly calls a family's "funds of knowledge." When I ask another boy why he's putting shelves in a bookcase with dowels—rather than with more expedient metal fasteners—he credits his grandfather, a master cabinetmaker, and says, "I just like to do it the old way." The use of dowels harkens back to, and honors, days in a grandfather's workshop and, as well, serves as an expression of who this boy wants to be.

I continually witnessed this dynamic relation between old craft and new technology. Felipe had run one of the shelves of the wall cabinet he's building through the edge-bander, a machine that cuts and glues thin strips of decorative laminate along the edges of plywood or particleboard, and as he was inspecting the shelf, he noticed a small bubble of glue rising out of one of the seams. He is a deliberate and cautious worker and is a good teacher of his peers—as we saw in the miter box example. His grandfather and his uncles are cabinetmakers in Mexico, and they do their work by hand, with no power tools. As a boy, he would visit, watch, "help them a little, bring them their tools." But though he grew up around woodworkers, he says he's learned the skills and procedures of the trade primarily through the classes he's taken with Mr. Devries.

When we join Felipe—buzz-cut brown hair, a small stud on the top of each ear—he has the shelf upright on a worktable, holding it with his right hand, a utility knife in his left, cutting in small, restricted motions at the bubble. Felipe moves here with a delicate touch. His face is right up on the seam, so close that the handle of the knife grazes his left cheek. He puts the knife down, taps the edge of the board with a small hammer, picks with thumb and forefinger at the remaining glue, then reaches for the knife and continues to trim the excess, face in close, eye fixed. With no direction from anyone, as a matter of course, it seems, Felipe scans the work of the edge-bander, detects a small flaw that disrupts the smooth line of the edge, and sets out to fix it. With careful and fine movement of the hand and the aid of tools that cut and compress, he continues the work of the edge-bander, completing the aesthetically clean line.

To be sure, the various cutting and routing power tools in Jerry Devries's classroom remove some opportunity to develop hand and eye; they channel and in some ways limit Felipe's growth. Before the edge-bander was invented, a woodworker would have had to cut, align, and glue the laminate on that cabinet shelf, then trim and finish it. As well, the joints that hold the panels of the cabinet together would have been fashioned manually. In his celebration of hand tools, *Tools of the Trade: The Art and Craft of Carpentry*, Jeff Taylor provides eloquent commentary on the sense of craft such work develops: "At a certain point, upon a day, you almost become the work, a moving and cognitive part of the tool in your own hand."

With Taylor in mind, let me offer several interrelated observations based on my time in Jerry Devries's workshop. First, Mr. Devries's curriculum, particularly for those students who work with him over time, includes considerable instruction in the use of hand tools. And there are times when tasks like cutting joints or affixing and trimming laminate must be done by hand: for example where structural constraints are severe or where power tools fail—as when the compressor attached to the edge-bander broke, forcing Felipe and his coworkers to prepare another shelf by hand.

Second, the speed and precision of power tools does ease the work and free up time—important motivations for those early tradespersons who adopted such tools—time that can be spent on the planning and refinement of projects, on assembly, on detail and repair. Electrical tools do not erase the need for thought and care.

Furthermore, power tools, as the students continually tell me, bring their own challenges, their own opportunities to master sequence and procedure and physical skill. As I watch Paul use a table saw (a circular blade that comes up through a slit in the table) to cut one-quarter of an inch off the width of a board, he must first make sure one edge of the board is straight, so he had to plane it by running it through the jointer. Then he must adjust the height and angle of the saw blade, account for the width of the saw blade in his measurements, set the guiding or "rip" fence against the board appropriately, and control the wood through his own stance and movement—possibly with the aid of a push stick. "It's the preparation that's hardest," he says, "remembering all the steps and then doing them right." And once a student is actually operating the tool, further knowledge and finesse are necessary. Felipe is using the band saw to cut a half circle into a panel. The blade on a band saw is narrow and can twist as it curves through the wood. To protect against this—and to assure a smooth cut—Felipe, moving slowly and precisely ("you have to take your time with the band saw"), makes a series of "relief cuts" into the section of the panel that will be cut away, essentially breaking up the curve into smaller units, cutting each in turn.

Finally, though power tools "build the skill into the machine," the effective use of such tools requires, at the least, some degree of that skill: in order to know what the skill should yield, to adjust the machine accordingly, to troubleshoot problems and repair them, and to judge the outcome. Paul and a senior named Ricky are building an L-shaped secretarial workstation. Nine have been ordered, and this is the prototype. Paul has prepared strips of alder molding for the edges of the plywood top, and, upon affixing them, spies a tiny gap where two of the strips meet. It's not sufficient to correct the problem here, for this is the first of nine stations; if the cause of the problem isn't found, it will bedevil subsequent production. Over the next hour, with the more knowledgeable Ricky taking the lead, but with Paul participating fully as apprentice, the boys run through possible problems with the tools that fashioned the molding: perhaps the gauge on the power miter box is faulty; perhaps there is dirt or debris behind the fence on the router table. Or maybe the problem lies not with the molding but with the construction of the frame to which it is affixed. Did they make a mistake when assembling the frame? As they think the problem through, they also display knowledge of the way power tools work and of the physics they embody—as when Ricky discusses the "velocity and friction" of a sanding tool as a reason not to use it to remedy the kind of error they're confronting. This tool talk is coupled with a concern about the durability and appearance of the desk top, displaying, I think, an impressive integration of tool knowledge, troubleshooting, and craft values. And the entire event demonstrates something that we've been seeing in this workshop: a systematic approach to problems that would be useful in other academic and professional settings.

When I describe the above vignettes to expert carpenters, they comment that as the students spend more time with power tools like these, their mastery of procedure will increase as will their feel for the tools, their finesse with them, and their capacity to express themselves through variations in design. As well, considering the wide range of ways one can cut and join, they will begin to make wiser decisions about which kind of saw or router or sander to use, given the materials and task at hand. They'll become adroit at adapting tool to need. It makes me think that someone, following Jeff Taylor's lead, should write a subsequent book on the "art and craft" of the power tool: an attempt to render the knack and judgment required for the router, the jointer, the band saw.

Before I leave this discussion of tool use, I want to consider a seemingly unrelated element of the vocabulary of work operating in Mr. Devries's classroom, one so familiar and ever-present that it frequently escapes mention: talk. Traditional discussions of technology tend, in various ways, to separate the technical and the social—and with the social, the play of language. What is so clear in this workshop setting, though, is the intimate interconnection of tool use, wood construction, and speech. Electrician and poet Susan Eisenberg captures the mix: "[W]ork and talk flowing like/ wire through well-laid pipe."

Here is Jerry Devries showing Felipe and his peers how to make a "layout stick," a long, thin piece of wood that has the measurements of the main components of their cabinet marked and labeled on it. As Mr. Devries demonstrates, he repeats for his students the names of new components (the *mullion* is the center support of the front, or "face," frame of the cabinet); queries them on the functional justification for these components ("You're not gonna make a sixty-eight-inch cabinet without a mullion, why?"); informs them of pertinent codes ("Anything over thirty-six inches requires support"); asks them to think through the mathematical consequences of the interrelation of the cabinet's components ("How will you adjust for the presence of the two-inch mullion?"); voices functional or aesthetic biases ("Some cabinetmakers like a lot of face frame; I don't like as much face frame"); and has Felipe and company think about the physical context of their cabinet ("Is it going up to the height of the ceiling?"). The fashioning of the layout stick is surrounded by statements of fact, questions, opinions. All of Mr. Devries's instruction—before the whole class, in small groups, or individually—involves speech and gesture, and, as we've seen, peer-to-peer instruction is oral and gestural as well.

If we were able to record a day's worth of the more informal talk in Mr. Devries's classroom—or, for that fact, at a typical construction site—we'd get a wide range of types and topics: gossip, banter, commentary on the events of the day, declarations of things hoped for, plans and goals, chronicles of life on the home front. A lot of it would be crude and combative. What interests me, though, is the way this informal talk—as we saw with the hairstylists—functions as an open channel, rich in cognitive possibility; the way information, procedures, and tricks of the trade flow in and out of the banter, fantasy, and dirty jokes.

Mike, one of Mr. Devries's seniors, is showing Paul, who has been eager for this opportunity, how to use the panel router. Another senior, Ruben, takes a break from his work nearby and walks over, sparring lightly with Mike and Paul. The three gab a little, and Mike begins to clamp a small board over the panel he's placed on the frame of the router. Ruben asks what's with the board; Mike says it's to protect the panel and to stabilize it, fool. You don't need to do that, Ruben counters, unless the panel has been edge-banded—the small board will keep the router from stripping off the laminate. No, you do it anyway, says Mike, and the discussion goes back and forth around the panel router, Paul looking on, listening in.

Across the room, Felipe and his crew are working on the wall cabinet. Felipe, Gloria, and Jesus are double-checking the measurements for the cabinet when they run into some confusion about the length of the top panel. Felipe leaves to find Mr. Devries. Gloria and Jesus start exchanging flirtatious jabs, and as they do, they look at the sketches and lists on the table before them. Gloria points to the top panel, and they start calculating with pencil the measurements again, confirming the dimensions written on the plans for themselves.

During another part of the day, Mr. Devries is in the library with two younger students, Ray and Billy, taking measurements for new doors on some storage cabinets. Measuring the dimensions of the doors is a straightforward task, but then Jerry begins to explain how the hinges they use may require that they alter their measurements, for different hinges require different tolerances. So given the kind of hinge currently used in the cabinets, they'll need to adjust their measurement by one-half inch. Ray takes out a sheet of paper and writes this down; Jerry leaves to check in on other students. Billy and Ray take the measurements again, and, in the midst of gossip about school, in a mix of English and Spanish, Billy explains the concept of tolerance, placing his hand at the edge of the door, turning his hand in and out, illustrating the function of the hinge, and explaining the consequences for measurement.

And there are times when talk is not so directly purposeful, but still serves a cognitive function. Ray, Billy, and I are walking back from the library. At some point, it seems, the librarian described to Ray the kind of doors she wanted—ones with ventilating holes along the bottom. As we walk, Ray is telling the story of their encounter and laughing. Ray speaks English pretty well, but still hesitates at times and can't find the right phrasing, particularly with idiomatic speech. "She confused me," he says. "She wanted it like mouse cheese." He laughs, and we do too. "Mouse cheese!" Ray continues and gestures with his right hand by his head as he explains his puzzled reaction to what I assume was her description of the ventilation holes being like Swiss cheese. We talk a few minutes more, until we arrive at the classroom, Ray and Billy still discussing the doors and their function. Ray initiated the conversation to spark a laugh, but also, I think, to clarify things in the safe conversational space created through humor and with his friend Billy, in motion, outside the library. The comic story becomes here a means to gain public consideration and assistance, to turn an event over in one's mind and to think it through in the presence of others. And it is one more reminder of the social and linguistic dimension of fashioning things with tools.

◻

As students take on projects like the display case or the kitchen cabinet, they often find themselves at the current limits of their ability, and it is at those limits that further aspects of carpentry develop, both by instruction and guidance and by assembly itself— through practice, peer interaction, trial and error. Three of these aspects, interrelated ones, are planning the project and sequencing the steps of assembly; conceptualizing and visualizing the project, both incrementally and as finished object; and the use of what I'll call *material mathematics* to facilitate planning and assembly. All the fundamental elements of carpentry discussed earlier—from tool use to talk—are evident in these activities, both enable them and are further developed by them. Our expanded vocabulary of work would have to account for these activities, giving a sense of how they play out in practice.

Let me begin with planning and procedure. "Before a single piece of wood is cut," as Jerry Devries puts it, his students engage in the following planning processes. When a project is conceived or contracted, Mr. Devries breaks his class into small groups (composed of both more- and less-experienced students) and assigns to each a part of the project. In the case of the cabinet, one group has the face frame, another the shelves, another the doors. The groups draw up lists of the materials they think they'll need to make their part and the tools they'll use for preparation. Then the groups come together and write their lists on the chalkboard, and as a class revise them. These generic lists of procedures are compiled and further adapted to the specifics of a project—so for the shelves of Felipe's wall cabinet, you'd see:

Materials and Procedures	*Tools*
Select stock for 2 shelves (maple plywood)	
Ripcut [that is, lengthwise with the grain] to width 17"	circular saw
Crosscut to length 36³/₄"	panel saw

and so on.

In addition to a list of procedures, Jerry provides a general sketch of the project. On the front chalkboard, there is a three-dimensional drawing of a cabinet with some pieces and dimensions labeled. The team working on the cabinet has to adapt the sketch to their project. As the team begins the project, Jerry consults with them on the dimensions of the components. Usually this involves time spent filling out and verifying a list of exact measurements and the development of the layout stick, that handy, at-a-glance ruler. And as planning takes place, someone on the team (usually the more experienced member) fills out a "bill of materials," basically a price list of kinds of wood, dimensions, and expense.

Thus students specify and articulate in written lists and graphic representations the materials they'll need, their dimensions, and their cost; the procedures required to prepare and assemble them; and the way they'll look when assembled, their relation each to the other. Through his assignments, Mr. Devries makes these aspects of carpentry explicit, requiring students to think them through, talk them over. Not all teachers, not to mention apprenticeship arrangements, would initiate beginners in so systematic a fashion.

There are other ways these skills can be learned—in some settings they are acquired primarily through observation and graduated participation—but Jerry Devries's approach does enable us to get some sense of the complexity of these skills and their mastery, a sense of what gets absorbed into the expert's fluid practice.

The first thing to note is just how many sequential steps are involved in the assembly of even a fairly simple structure. There are 125 steps enumerated in Felipe's list of procedures, and these lead only to the basic structure of the cabinet. And each step—crosscut door panels to $31^1/4$"; edge-band the edge of the shelves—is, as we saw, composed of a number of more basic cognitive and biomechanical operations. The number of things to keep in mind—and the proper ordering of them—is, at Felipe's stage of development, overwhelming. (I saw evidence of the cognitive overload when he would, in addressing an item on the list of procedures, forget to do something—like plane an edge—that I saw him do routinely on simpler tasks.) Felipe notes that this cabinet "is the biggest thing I've been in charge of," and that the planning of it and keeping track of the procedures are the hardest aspects of the work. He is only able to do the job at all with a good deal of written and oral support. He follows his list of procedures carefully. My notes are full of moments when Felipe is looking over to his list (or to his sketch of the cabinet), or stopping work to fish the list out of his pocket or backpack. His activity is strongly coupled to these pieces of paper. As well, he draws on his peers when he can, though, because they are less experienced, they provide limited help with this aspect of the work. And, frequently, he consults with Mr. Devries, much of whose time is spent doing just this kind of checking in, verifying, guiding, instructing on the spot. This written and verbal assistance enables Felipe to move forward intellectually and functionally, learning and doing right at the brink of his ability.

As a long line of psychological studies—and our own commonsense experience—suggests, skilled routines develop with practice. ("You develop a sense of anticipation," a retired stonemason tells me. "The idea is to always think ahead, visualize where you'll end up, what you'll need next, and next after that.") As Felipe builds this and further cabinets, he will learn more about their structure and properties, and all the steps of preparation and assembly will become familiar, combined into meaningful units, executed more efficiently. He will need less support from his teacher and from his lists. It's as if his lists become abbreviated and internalized.

As this happens, the time required to complete a cabinet will decrease significantly. Felipe will also be able to think ahead, anticipate subsequent procedures, and keep potential problems in mind. Eventually, the emerging structure of the object he is building will itself aid recall and proper sequencing of behaviors. I watched Felipe and his crew work on a second cabinet about five months after completing the first. They were fairly well along, inserting shelf standards into grooves they had cut into the interior of the side panels. (Standards are the perforated metal strips onto which adjustable shelves are secured.) The exact placement and fastening of the standards is, in Felipe's words, "critical"; driving small nails into them, for example, can cause them to move slightly, leading to misalignment. I observed the installation of the standards in the first cabinet—a lengthy, painstaking affair—and in the second, which went more smoothly. As Felipe and his crew work with the standards for the second cabinet, Jesus, one of the younger boys, says that the first installation was harder, but now, pointing to the side of his head, they remember how to do it. "You get the experience," Felipe adds, "and you know what to do. Once you're building it, you see what's needed. You don't need the list of procedures." At about the midpoint of the construction of the first cabinet, Felipe, with several lists spread before him, bemoaned all this "paperwork," expressing a desire to "have things come back to you" as you do them. Already, it seems, he is moving in that direction, aided by memory, developing routines, and the object he and his coworkers are assembling.

◻

Over time, Felipe will not only master routines of assembly, but, hand in glove, will acquire more knowledge about cabinets (and other wood furnishings), different types, different particulars of form and function, and an understanding of the range of possible configurations of parts to whole. At this point in his education, however, Felipe has built but one small, structurally simple cabinet, and the current, second, cabinet has a number of features the earlier project didn't. His storehouse of knowledge about cabinets, his "cabinet sense," is just developing, and the limits of his knowledge reveal themselves at various points throughout assembly. Like this one.

Felipe is trying to record final figures for all the components of the cabinet—he and his coworkers are eager to begin assembly. He is working with Gloria and Jesus, and he is sketching with them one more three-dimensional representation of the cabinet, using the layout stick, the list of procedures, and the bill of materials. When I come upon him, he is looking back and forth from the bill of materials to the sketch and talking to his peers. He seems puzzled. He asks Gloria to get the first sketch they made of the cabinet. She retrieves it from her backpack and unfolds it. They study it for a moment. He says something to Jesus, then takes a tape and measures—as if to confirm—the length of the cabinet. Sixty-eight inches. Felipe continues this way, double-checking, trying to verify, looking up occasionally to snag Mr. Devries who, however, is helping a group across the room. The source of this vexation, which lasts a good fifteen minutes, is a discrepancy that emerged as Felipe, Jesus, and Gloria were listing final numbers: the length of the sheet of plywood for the bottom of the cabinet—this is found on the bill of materials—is sixty-eight inches. But the length of the top panel—listed on another sheet—is sixty-seven inches. This makes no sense. As Felipe explains it, exhibiting a nice shift from numbers to their structural meaning, the top can't be shorter than the bottom, or the cabinet will look like this: and here he makes an abbreviated triangle in the air with his hands. What's going on?

Finally, Mr. Devries is free, Felipe goes to get him, and they confer. The sketch Felipe has is inadequate, is not detailed enough to reveal that the top panel rests inside notches cut into the top of the side panels. These are called rabbit cuts. Felipe's discomfort resolves quickly into understanding. The bottom panel extends to the very ends of the side panels, but the top will be shorter by a half inch on each side, the dimensions of the rabbit cuts. Thus the mystery of the sixty-eight-inch bottom and the sixty-seven-inch top.

The depictions of the cabinet in Felipe's plans do not provide enough information—through graphics or numbers—to enable him to figure out the discrepancy in measurement between top and bottom. Yet he must rely on these sketches—as he must depend on the list of procedures—for he does not yet know enough about cabinets to enable him to solve the problem readily . . . or not to assume that the discrepancy is a problem in the first place.

We get a sense of how powerful this kind of knowledge of the object is when we watch an experienced carpenter confront the challenges of structure and assembly. One carpenter I observed was installing a set of sliding French doors into a constrained wall space. He stood back, chin in hand, surveying the frame, his eyes moving over it, occasionally nodding his head and saying something under his breath. When I asked him what he was doing, he said he was "picturing the door in my mind." Essentially, he was imagining the pieces as he would assemble them, thinking, for example, how the threshold will have to angle down, so that the rain will run off it, or picturing the sliding panels moving across the stationary ones, and where problems might develop with that. As well, he is imagining the look of the casings that came with the door, and realizing that they're too big, given the other woodwork in the room, and trying to visualize alternative casings he could fashion.

I find this intellectually rich. The carpenter is relying on a significant knowledge base about doors, some of it generic, some specific to this uncommon structure. He is performing a number of mostly visual operations on this knowledge, operations documented in the research literature on mental imagery: he is examining and combining elements of the assembly, moving them, comparing, substituting, or transforming them. And there are not only structural and mechanical goals driving these operations but aesthetic ones as well—for example, the look of the casings. He is assembling the structure in his mind's eye and is also reflecting on it. Thus, in fact, the task before this carpenter and what he does with it is more complex than the tasks involved in typical studies of mental imagery. The acquisition of such knowledge and the ability to use it this way is another sign of expertise. (This sense of the object has long been recognized as central to the expert's ability; I found crisp expression of it by a nineteenth-century shipbuilder: "[T]he most important part of the builder's craft [is] the carrying about the shape in his head as well as in the mould.") Felipe is at the beginning stages of developing a sense of cabinet structure. But watching him and his crew build their second wall cabinet, you see it developing.

There are some expected advances, of course. There is no confusion the second time around about the length of the top and the bottom panels; that earlier episode taught Felipe a lot. And I saw other evidence of an emerging cabinet sense. Unlike the previous cabinet, this cabinet requires a plastic laminate over its surface. Felipe is laying the cabinet's face frame over a long sheet of plastic and tracing the outline of the frame onto it. This will give him the covering for the frame but leave two fairly large door-sized squares of the plastic. Felipe stops, takes a step back, looks the cabinet over, and then reaches for his list of measurements and a tape measure. I ask him what he's doing. We're short on laminate, he explains, and here you'll have these two excess pieces of it cut away from the frame. We'll need to use them. But, he realizes, they won't cover the doors themselves, because the doors will be larger than the opening; they'll attach onto and over the face frame. So, he's trying to think ahead and picture where the as-yet-uncut surplus might go. What other, smaller pieces of the cabinet could be covered. That's what he's about to check. When I describe this event to Jerry Devries he smiles and says, "That's how a cabinetmaker thinks."

❑

Several times during the construction of the first wall cabinet—the one with the puzzling sixty-seven-inch top—Felipe would comment on the mathematics involved in cabinet assembly. And I asked him about it myself. His comments were a bit contradictory, and the contradiction resonated with something that was vexing me as well. At times he would note that the math is "simple," "just numbers," "only fractions." At other times, though, even within the same few sentences, his face registering perplexity, he would observe that "a lot of math is involved" and that "it's difficult."

Felipe has taken algebra and is currently enrolled in college math; he knows what more advanced mathematics looks like. On the face of it, the math involved in cabinet assembly is pretty simple: reading a ruler; adding and subtracting (and, less frequently, multiplying and dividing) whole numbers, mixed numbers, and fractions; working with the basic properties of squares and rectangles.

Yet, he says, "there's so many pieces you need to take into consideration, otherwise, you'll mess up somewhere."

Felipe's puzzlement, I think, is located in the intersection of traditional mathematics, learned most often in school, and the mathematics developed in the carpenter's shop. Traditional mathematics is in evidence throughout Mr. Devries's workshop: from the calculations students do to determine cost per board foot to measurements scribbled on scraps of paper spread across the room. Considered from the perspective of school math—that is, if lifted from context and presented as problems in a textbook—the operations here would be, as Felipe observes, fairly rudimentary, grade-school arithmetic. But as these measures and calculations play out in assembly—particularly an assembly that is unfamiliar—things get more complex, and thus Felipe and his crew move slowly and with some uncertainty. With an incomplete sense of a cabinet's structure, Felipe must keep a number of variables in mind, arrayed in three-dimensional space, with each variable having consequences for the other. The top of the cabinet will be shorter in length by the sum of the two rabbit cuts in the side panels—but what about the width of the top? Will it rest in a cut in the back panel, and if so, what are the implications for the measurements of the back panel? Will the top extend into or onto the face frame? What does that mean for the face frame? And so on. In neurologist Frank Wilson's phrasing, this young carpenter is developing the ability to "spatialize" mathematics—and as Felipe notes, that means taking "so many pieces . . . into consideration." Jerry Devries tells me that he has students taking calculus who have a hard time with such tasks.

There is a small but growing research literature on mathematics in the workplace—from the tailor's shop to the design studio—and a few of these studies focus on carpentry. Listening to Felipe puzzle over the nature of the mathematics of assembly led me to look more closely at the math in Jerry Devries's shop, and what I saw matched earlier studies, some of which were conducted in other cultures, such as South Africa, suggesting some cognitive commonality to the way carpenters do the work they do.

One of the findings of this research is that a wide range of mathematical concepts and operations is embodied in carpentry's artifacts and routines of practice, and in ways suited to the properties of materials and the demands of production. The carpenter's math is tangible and efficient. Take, for example, measurement. The ruler and framing square provide measurements, but so do objects created in the shop, like the layout stick, and one piece of wood, precisely cut, then functions as the measure for another. Tools are also used as measuring devices. A sixteen-inch claw hammer laid sideways on a wall provides a quick measure for the location of studs in a wall frame. And carpenters use their hands and fingers to measure and compare. ("I use my forefinger and thumb for calipers," reports master woodworker Sam Maloof.) They develop an eye for length and dimension, but also, my experts tell me, for relations and correspondences. Disciplined perception.

Working in the shop, the young carpenter learns a range of other mathematical concepts: symmetry, proportion, congruence, the properties of angles. Planing straight the edge of a board, cutting angles on the miter box, laying out the pieces of a cabinet's face frame to check for an even fit—through these activities, Mr. Devries's students see mathematical ideas manifested, and feel them, too, gaining a sense of trueness and error. Fractions were never more real to Felipe than during the episode with that cabinet top. We can return here to Richard Gregory's observation that tools embody solutions to past problems, and also note that tools—and other artifacts in the shop—contribute to a material understanding of mathematical abstractions. In fact, the abstractions can become, in a sense, tools themselves. I was watching a student installing a window frame into an unevenly cut opening; there was barely any wood along one side to take his nail. What to do? His teacher, who was watching, showed him how to "angle the nail in to find wood." With that, *angle* became another device in the student's repertoire. You can do things with an angle.

Abstraction is the essence of mathematics; the source of its power is its independence from the material world. What is worth considering, though, is the way this fact has been converted in our intellectual history into a series of judgments about the worth and status of kinds of mathematics—for example, that the more applied and materialized the mathematics is, the less intellectually substantial it is. (As schools of engineering were developing in the American research university, they were beset by such judgment.) Without disputing the conceptual power of abstraction, my time with Felipe left me wondering about this commonplace distinction between pure and applied, or abstract and concrete—and the problems with the distinction would intensify as I studied other kinds of work. When that carpenter visualizes the French doors and performs a number of cognitive operations on his mental image of them, his activity is directed by a general understanding of the basic geometry and physics of such structures. As routines of assembly, knowledge of structures, the ability to visualize, and material mathematics interact and develop in Felipe's practice, it would be difficult to mark exactly what is "concrete" and what is "abstract." Such distinction blurs in real-world problem-solving tasks. A proper vocabulary of work would need to include some means, some hybrid term perhaps, to render this complexity. "Tools are instruments," notes the early-twentieth-century educational tract cited earlier, "by which the hands give material expression to thought." Felipe's cabinet is thought materialized, and as such embodies a record of the interplay of general principles, specific artifacts, and human need.

◻

Felipe and I are standing in the small utility room attached to the school's main office. There are old filing cabinets, a refrigerator, a sink and small service area, a microwave, a coffeemaker, stacks of paper cups. Standard fare. Above the sink is Felipe's cabinet. He and his crew installed it several weeks ago—without any help from Mr. Devries. Its shelves are becoming crowded: paper plates, baskets, a few pots, condiments, the secretaries' coffee cups. Mrs. Gutierrez is with us. She is the office supervisor who commissioned the cabinet. She just loves it, she says. We've needed something like this for a long time. Felipe and company used a natural stain on the pine, and the cabinet shines in fluorescence. I open the other door, smooth on its hinges.

A call comes in for Mrs. Gutierrez. Back she goes to the front office. Silence. Then Felipe softly begins, "I didn't see it after we installed it, but, now, damn . . . I didn't know I could do that. Pretty nice. It looks nice." I close the door I opened. An easy click. I compliment Felipe, recalling Mrs. Gutierrez's praise, her words a measure of his achievement. "I feel good when people talk like that," he says. "The cabinet's not just there, and that's it. They're using it!"

There is a lovely poem of Marge Piercy's, "To Be of Use," in which she celebrates those who immerse themselves in "[t]he work of the world." I think of it here: "the thing worth doing well done/ has a shape that satisfies, clean and evident." The use of the cabinet offers Felipe, in this moment, a confirmation of the value of his effort—but in a way that goes beyond acknowledgment of his manual skill alone. The time he took, the uncertainties and revisions, the focus of his mind on the task—all of this now gains meaning from and locates Felipe in the sphere of social exchange. It is a heady thing to feel you can be of use.

REFLECTIVE TECHNIQUE

Electrical Wiring and Construction

For a very long time in the West, there has been a tendency among intellectual elites to distinguish between physical work and technical skill—labor, the mechanical arts, crafts and trades—and deliberative and philosophical activity, which emerges from leisure, or, at least, from a degree of distance from the world of work and commerce. This distinction is related to another: between pursuits that are ends in themselves and pursuits that are means to other ends, "pure" activity and knowledge versus the instrumental, applied, and practical, which possess less merit. These distinctions find early articulation in Classical Greece where they were part of a comprehensive philosophical system that celebrated the capacity of the human mind but that developed in a society reliant on slavery and servile labor. One consequence was that entire social and occupational groups were narrowly, and harshly, defined. In *The Republic*, Plato mocks the craftsman who would pursue philosophy, for his soul is "warped and maimed" by his work; such men are "incapable of culture." And Aristotle in *Politics* notes that "there is no element of virtue in any of the occupations in which the multitude of artisans and market-people and the wage-earning class take part." Because such occupations are "ignoble and inimical to goodness," Aristotle further proposes that their practitioners be denied citizenship. To be sure, the craftsperson—from cobbler to shipwright to potter—was essential to Greek civilization, and his skill was praised, but, wrote Plutarch, "It does not necessarily follow that if a work is delightful because of its gracefulness, the man who made it is worthy of our serious regard." Work of body and hand, then, has limiting, even harmful, consequences for civic status and engagement, for the ability to deliberate and interpret, for virtue.

I am reading again what the Greeks and others in the Classical tradition had to say about physical work as I visit these classrooms and job sites where young people are learning a trade. The distinctions between pure and applied, theoretical and practical are deeply familiar to me, resonant from undergraduate courses in philosophy and literature, from graduate study in education and psychology, and from years of professional life in a research university, where a range of institutional decisions and certifications—from course credit to disciplinary definition—are made on the pivot of the pure-applied differential. A lot of our schooling reinforces this way of thinking about human activity. Though there certainly are dissenting voices in Western intellectual history, from Saint Augustine to William Morris, it is striking how pervasive this perspective on human behavior is. It underlies many canonical treatises on art and on education. So when Felipe expresses pleasure over the utility of his cabinet, he would raise, for some, a set of judgments that lessens the merit of the object of his craft and the virtue of his activity.

Yet, when you get in close to that activity, watch it unfold over time and get a sense of the thought and motive that directs it, you gain continual evidence of many of the qualities that the classical philosophical distinctions tend to diminish. The work itself when seriously engaged—the traditions and values one acquires and the complex knowledge and skills developed—gives rise to a virtue of practice, an ethics and aesthetics, and a reflectiveness intermixed with technique. Furthermore, as we've been seeing, all this becomes part of the construction of one's sense of self.

There are many reasons why physical work is perceived as it is in our time, reasons stemming from our economic and social structure. But an element of our perception—particularly in some intellectual communities and institutions—is related to these long-standing distinctions, absorbed into new historical contexts. I want to consider the way these distinctions restrict, even categorically rule out, the possibility of the full expression of mind for whole groups of people, contributing to a stereotypic opinion of blue-collar workers. To help us arrive at a more philosophically generous view of mind and work, let me bring together a series of further vignettes, some from settings we've visited—Jon Guthier's plumbers and Jerry Devries's woodshop—but most from other sites, particularly two involving electrical wiring and construction.

One early event that got me to thinking about these issues occurred at a Habitat for Humanity construction site. As we were traveling to the site, I listened to a boy named Skip hold forth. Teen-magazine good looks, cocky, a mouth full of trouble, he was needling another boy about his acne and declaring that he was going to take care of someone else "for talking some shit about me." By the end of the ride, I found myself imagining the hell Skip creates for some of his teachers and surely for his vulnerable classmates. He was quickly becoming my least favorite kid.

Then we pulled into the job site. A cluster of house frames, stacks of lumber, young folks and old securing joists, nailing plywood to rafters, installing windows. The teacher, a skilled carpenter named Scott Butler, picked Skip and two other boys to spend the day with him and learn how to install windows. I went with them. And witnessed a remarkable transformation in Skip, almost from the moment he put on his tool belt.

His agitated arrogance and the nasty streak disappeared. Instead, Skip was focused on the work, thoughtful about it and considerate of those working with him—his language inflected now with "yes sir" and "excuse me." He attended to Mr. Butler as the teacher guided the young crew through a range of activities: from tricks for working in tight quarters, to modifying routines in order to solve emerging problems, to thinking about the consequences of a particular repair for subsequent construction. Skip's one moment of disgruntlement—an emotional peep when compared to the braying on the bus—came in response to a poorly cut window frame left by a previous crew. "Oh man," he said, shaking his head, "measuring is one of the first things we learn how to do."

Skip's transformation and the connection to craft he displays call to mind a passage in *Pedal to the Metal*, Lawrence Ouellet's sociological study of long-haul truck drivers. Himself a veteran trucker, Ouellet reflects on his and his buddies' high school disrespectful rebelliousness versus the ethic and "sense of honor" he encountered as he entered the truck-driver's community, the way the work of the road, while allowing a countercultural bearing, brought with it certain codes of conduct and standards of performance. To be sure, the codes of physical work can incorporate cultural biases about race and gender, and about poverty itself. And there can be a certain rigidity to some craft values, a one-right-way absolutism that can blend with social intolerance. We, of course, don't know how Skip will turn out. But, for now, getting the windows right makes its demands on his mind and manner. Something in the techniques he's learning and the traditions they embody, or the occasion to display competence, or the relation the work affords with Mr. Butler—who knows exactly what—creates for this boy at this juncture in his development the opportunity to act with deliberation and civility, experiment with alternative ways of being in the world.

⌁

I was writing this book during a time of anguished national conversation about young people—about their popular culture, their
goals and values, and, with the shock of schoolyard murders, their
internal torments and disconnection from the social fabric. Against
this backdrop, I was reading about virtue, right action, and finding
illustration of it in unexpected places, unexpected given our intellectual traditions and common biases. Now, I certainly witnessed
peer insult, distorted masculinity, virtual and real violence. We just
got a dose of it all from Skip. But young people's lives have many
dimensions to them, and, thus, I also witnessed behaviors that are
dearly sought in our national assays of adolescent experience. It is
as if our collective anxiety is leading us to look in the wrong places,
to seek pathology, and, as a result, to miss whole categories of activities that are principled and contribute to the social good.

During my visits I heard continual expression of—and saw material evidence to support—a desire to do a job correctly, not to
rush it, to make something work well. Take, as illustration, Nancy,
who, with another student in her automotive technology class, is
replacing the brake pads on her sister's car. She works through the
class period and into lunch. As she is finishing up, tightening
wheel nuts with a pneumatic wrench, she talks about the importance of good brakes, how she is "really picky about brakes," how
they can make the crucial difference in protecting both life and
property.

Or watch Peter repairing the sinks in a women's shelter. He
works with Joe, a retired plumber volunteering his time. Peter
works hard and fast, says he enjoys getting this experience with a
seasoned plumber, and is curious about the function of things.
He'll ask Joe to repeat a task or manipulate a device so he can see
how something works. At this moment, they're replacing the fau-

cets on a bathroom sink, and are about to fit the sink back into its cabinet. Peter takes a quick look at the drainpipe and p-trap, running his finger inside the trap. "Oh, look at this!" he says to Joe. The trap is corroded, and if you squat down, you can see the buildup of rust and debris. "We've gotta change this," he says, "we can't put it back together like this." The schedule for the day specifies faucets only, so Peter goes in search of his instructor, wanting to get approval for a new p-trap that he will then have to find in the crew's supplies. Peter's curiosity and his desire to do good work combine here toward action that both satisfies his sense of workmanship and yields benefit to others.

Nancy and Peter are meticulous about the work they do, aware of its consequences, exhibiting both pride in and commitment to doing a good job. There are social and ethical ramifications here. And as we've been seeing throughout this book, these craft values emerge from and contribute to a sense of who one is, principled action and identity intertwined, which, it seems to me, provides a good foundation for virtue. Consider Rudolfo and Charles.

Rudolfo is sanding a bookcase, showing me a small flaw along the base. Under a strip of oak that both decorates and reinforces the base—in a place that no one will be able to see once the bookcase is upright—Rudolfo points to a tiny gap in the otherwise flawless seam where strip and base join together. The gap is between one-sixteenth and one thirty-second of an inch wide. Wood inevitably warps, and, as Rudolfo explains, he placed his finishing nails "too high on the strip," thus not correcting for a small irregularity in the oak. Next time, he notes, he'll place the nails lower, checking the seam more carefully. Now, though, he's going to fill the gap with putty and sand it. "No one can see it," he explains, "but I want it to be right."

Charles is volunteering at a Habitat for Humanity site and is assembling the frames for the walls of one of the bedrooms.

These frames consist of two long, horizontal two-by-four boards with six shorter two-by-fours, called studs, nailed vertically in place sixteen inches apart. Charles begins by measuring and marking the sixteen-inch increments on the horizontal boards, and then lays out the vertical studs accordingly. He measures again. Then he begins nailing the studs in place, driving one nail, then another, stopping occasionally to check with his eye or a framing square the trueness of the frame. I ask Charles about this precision. He says that when the frame is finished, "I know it's going to be straight and well done." He pauses and adds: "That's the way I am." Charles's values motivate and guide his action: measuring twice, positioning his body, eyeballing the frame. The emerging frame, in turn, embodies those values, manifests them back to Charles, confirming his sense of himself.

□

"Hey, Justin, that's pretty!" Jim Padilla yells to the boy on the ladder, under the eaves, affixing the last fastening strap around a long stretch of electrical conduit. Mr. Padilla pulls two other boys over, pointing up. The sun is behind us, warm and bright on the stucco of the new house. "Look," Mr. Padilla says in his earnest, rolling voice, "you can barely see the conduit. Nice, huh? You always want to preserve the beauty of the home."

Jim Padilla, a stocky man with thick black hair and a full mustache, is the teacher of this crew of fledgling electricians, fifteen or so boys, high school juniors and seniors out of the classroom on their first job site, a modest tract house in need of outdoor lights and receptacles. Mr. Padilla moves on, his arms angling out from his chest as he walks, and stops at another ladder to talk to another boy fastening conduit under the eaves. "Hey, Mundo," he hollers up, "come down here a minute, *por favor*. I wanna show you something." Mundo makes his way down, rung after rung, setting foot alongside Mr. Padilla. The teacher points up to one of the straps on the underside of the roof. It is off-center. "Look, Mundo," says Mr. Padilla, "see, all the other straps are in the middle. That's good. Fix this one, OK? If the strap's in the middle it's stronger, and it looks better." Mundo nods and starts back up the ladder. Mr. Padilla places his hand on the boy's shoulder. He's not done yet. "We try hard not to show our straps, Mundo. We want to show as little evidence of the electrician's being here as possible."

The snug attachment of a conduit, the neat bend in it as it connects to a receptacle, the exact placement of a fastening strap where few will see—there is functional purpose to all this, but an aesthetic motive, too. ("What looks well works well," says one of the carpenters in Tracy Kidder's *House*.) To Jim Padilla's eye, such work is pleasant to behold, is "pretty," and he tries to train the eye of his students to see it as pretty, too. Being on a job site with Jim Padilla is like being in an artisan's studio, surrounded with evaluative craft-talk. Over time, the students acquire it, and the acquisition re-creates tradition in this time and place. A boy next to me stands back from his work, looks at it quietly, then turns to me and says, "That's nice, isn't it?" The look of the work becomes a mark of one's identity as an electrician. Showing a group of students the wiring in the electrical panel alongside the house, Mr. Padilla tells them: "Here's the thing, guys. Make it as neat as possible. Your signature is on this."

But it is an unusual signature, and an unusual aesthetic, given the aesthetic of display that so permeates both our popular and highbrow culture. Part of the appeal here is the care put into embedding one's work in the context of the house, out of view, even hidden. An experienced electrician I visited had removed a section of drywall and was commenting on a cluster of wires running along the frame. The braid was perfect, he said approvingly. That makes it easier, he explained, to single out a particular wire—the functional value—but also, it just looks good. The previous electrician's signature is woven into the braid, but anonymously so, and completely out of sight, seen, if at all, by another electrician, carpenter, or plumber over the life of the house.

If there is an aspect of Western intellectual history that diminishes the thought and virtue in physical work, there is, as well, a tendency to limit the meaning and occasion of aesthetic response. I am reminded of something one of Jerry Devries's students said in an English class. The teacher was introducing a list of vocabulary words, drawn from an essay they were reading. *Aesthetic* was one of them. After a few minutes of discussion, this boy, one of Jerry's more able students, raised his hand and respectfully suggested to his teacher that the word "doesn't have anything to do with us." His comment reveals the power of some traditional, and widespread, approaches to aesthetics, that it is a particular kind of response to "high art." Such definition is unfortunate here, for it compromises the student's understanding of his own activity.

Of course, there is a range of opinion in Western aesthetics about the nature and function of art, but what strikes me as I read in that literature is the immense intellectual effort put into differentiating that which is marked as art from other forms of human artifice. Tolstoy put it nicely: "[A] certain class of works which for some reason please a certain class of people is accepted as being art, and a definition of art is then devised to cover all these productions." And these definitions are often wrought comparatively: *art* is contrasted with other activity (for example, *craft*) and judged to be of a different, and superior, order. I am not suggesting that Felipe's cabinet or Justin's neat conduit is the cognitive or imaginative equivalent of *The Starry Night* or "Mood Indigo." What is worth considering, though, is the way the process of defining art tends to diminish other realms of artful behavior.

◻

Marcus lays a small spirit level on the top of one of the receptacle boxes, examines it, then tightens the fasteners affixing conduit to receptacle. He takes three or four steps back, folds his arms, and looks at the assembly, a long look, quiet. He takes a pair of pliers out of his back pocket, walks forward, taps another receptacle box, lightly, then again. He moves back, takes the scene in, focused amid the chatter of other students working on other assemblies. He returns to the box, taps it once more, puts the level over it. Perfect. He recedes again, leans against an adjoining wall, reflective.

Marcus is completing a mock-up of an assembly of outdoor lights and receptacles, not unlike the configuration Jim Padilla's crew is working on, but a bit more complicated, for he is further along in development, taking courses in a trade-technical college program in electrical construction and maintenance. Marcus is in his mid-forties, and wants to become an electrician after having worked in the airline industry for a number of years. The mock-up before him is one of twenty-five such assignments he and his peers must complete this term; it has taken days to think through and build.

In his brief essay on painting, "Making Pictures," D. H. Lawrence writes of the experience of "disappear[ing] into that canvas." There are times in this electrician's workshop when you sense that kind of absorption. It's a relatively quiet place. The students talk some while they're working, check in on each other, consult, hang out—but not a lot. Concentration. You occasionally hear an exclamation of frustration, *shit* or *goddamnit,* but it tends to be linked to a blunder or mishap—a porcelain fixture that cracks with the final turn of a screw or a finger whacked or pinched—rather than to a circuit that didn't test out. You could describe the students as patient, but, though not inaccurate, *patience* doesn't quite capture the feel of the room; there's a sense of engagement, a sense that these problems are worth solving. You give yourself over to the task; it takes what it takes. To pitch a fit at every failed test would be bad form.

What I am trying to describe here—this mode of engagement— is nicely rendered in studies of intelligence in other cultures, where "smart behavior" can include what Western psychologists would distinguish as qualities of emotion and personality. Among the Canadian Inuit, for example, competence at solving a puzzle, or fixing a snowmobile, or teaching a baby to walk is manifested through a blend of experience, skill, knowledge, and a calm perseverance. One's orientation to the task, one's way of being with it, is crucial. This ability is not considered to be innate; one learns it, is socialized into it.

I got to watch something akin to this process of socialization closer to home—with Jim Padilla and his students working under those eaves.

Hector, in a quarter-twist of his torso, arms over his head, is trying to fasten a conduit strap into tight quarters. "Mr. Padilla," he moans, "the screw won't go in. Dang, I can't get leverage!" Jim Padilla rests his foot on the bottom rung of the ladder, one hand on the rail, watching Hector, offering suggestions calmly, methodically. "Try a smaller screwdriver, Hector." Then, "Turn the hammer sideways." Then, "No? Well, start the hole with a nail." Mr. Padilla intersperses these suggestions with homilies and exhortations: "Hector, there's more than one way to get milk from a cow, *verdad?*" And, "I'm not gonna let you give up." And, eventually, Hector does get the vexing strap affixed—starting the hole with a nail does the trick, once he holds the hammer sideways—and he comes down the ladder, seemingly pleased with himself.

Imagine a developmental history of such experiences, surrounded by a discourse of persistence. I'm struck by something as

I go back through my notes. I find not a single instance where Jon Guthier, or Jerry Devries, or Jim Padilla is talking to his students, or to me, in a way that suggests that some kids have got it and some don't. There is no talk of innate talents or of deficits versus giftedness. They will note when a student is skillful, a good craftsperson, careful, promising. But these evaluations seem focused on what the youngsters accomplish, rather than on some pervasive quality of their cognitive and biomechanical endowment.

So here's Mr. Padilla with Hector, talking him through alternative solutions, encouraging persistence but with flexibility—that is, not a dogged grunting at the problem but an adaptive sequence of attempts. There's lots of ways to get milk from that cow, lots of variations, tricks of the trade. In fact, one could define tricks of the trade as embodiments of wiliness, ways that other workers have developed to overcome limits, tight spots, blunders. With such a delivered history of alternatives, and with it a frame of mind that encourages thinking alternatively, one, perhaps, has less need for a language of endowments and deficiencies.

Persistence, sticking with a problem and assuming there's a way to solve it, becomes a powerful motivator to continue, and a hedge against frustration—and against one's own sense of ineptitude. The young people working with Mr. Padilla get frustrated, to be sure, but their teacher guides them toward a different way of conceiving of the difficult moment. With the right frame of mind—and the right techniques—the problem just might be solvable, if you give it the time.

❑

Marcus and his fellow students at the technical college talk a lot about time. They talk about the time it takes to do something right, or about making an error because they were going too fast. You'll also see students redoing a task that was completed satisfactorily, but not up to their own standards ("I'll not settle for this," one says) and willingly giving up the time to do it again. Mastery is foregrounded; the clock recedes. Yet there is a clear tension between this task-oriented sense of time and the pressure of workplace production. (Some historians have noted similar tensions with the advent of industrialization.) These students have all held jobs; they're aware of the demands of the clock. They know they will have to become faster; as Marcus puts it, the job will be no place to train. So there is the hope that time given to mastery now will lead to surer, faster skills in the future. This is the economic context of their absorption. But it would be a mistake, I think, to attribute all motivation here to economic concerns and miss the other dimensions of their engagement.

I am intrigued by the feel and rhythm of this engagement, the oscillation between action and reflection that we saw with Marcus as he worked on the receptacle boxes. There's a reflective cast to the technical work these students do, a concentrated involvement, a disappearing into the task. "That's his world," the wife of an expert plumber tells me, "and he goes deep into it." That's what I sense here. A room, at times, lost in thought.

What, in this context, makes such engagement possible? What leads up to Marcus pondering his assembly? I spent several months observing him and his classmates, trying to catalog the different kinds of knowledge they acquire.

Marcus and his classmates learn a vocabulary and symbol system for electrical work. They read, interpret, and discuss electrical codes and perform a number of calculations related to them. They think and talk their way through multiple "scenarios"—various combinations of lights, appliances, switches, receptacles—using graphical displays developed from the electrical symbols. Several kinds of literacy and numeracy come into play: the mastery of new vocabulary and symbol systems; translating from one symbol system to another and using the symbols to solve problems with multiple variables; interpreting the codes and calculating from them. These codes, especially, raise an interesting set of social and educational issues. "You gotta be a lawyer" to read them, says Marcus. "The code is not written as an instructional manual," adds one of his classmates, "but is there to protect the industry, so that's tough, correlating the instructional aspect with the legal." As Marcus and company spend more time with experienced electricians, they'll further develop their knowledge of the code through talk and illustration, but now they work hard at deciphering it, learning to read the code for their own ends.

The conceptual work they do, then, is of some substance—and it is purposeful, must move outside the classroom to be realized and tested in assembly. Marcus observes that the time in class "gives you what you need to analyze" the tasks in the shop. The symbolic graphics help him "think ahead" as he builds an assembly, and the challenge is to "apply the concepts" he is learning to "new situations, new assemblies." It is in application that Marcus's knowledge gains its power, and this effective use becomes a test of the depth of his understanding.

Watching Marcus, you see the various cognitive and behavioral means he and his classmates have acquired to work the interface between classroom learning and assembly. He pins the symbolic representation of the assignment on the board alongside his emerging assembly and consults it as he works; sometimes he redraws parts of it on separate paper, using the sequence of symbols to assist him in thinking through the steps of assembly. He stands back from the assembly and with his index finger traces one of the multiple circuits through the conduits and switches, isolating a variable with the aid of a gesture. He reports visualizing the assembly, or a part of it, and, in fact, explains the need to imagine the assemblies when in class, to convert the symbolic representations into material networks of conduits and receptacles. He can then "take that image in my head right back out to the shop."

What Marcus and company reveal—and this resonates with the kind of thing we saw with Jerry Devries's carpenters—is the use of multiple representations of concepts and procedures, and a shuttling back and forth among them. In other words, these new electricians are making thought physical and, equally, converting the physical into images and symbols that they can manipulate.

Such work encourages a cognitive suppleness and contributes to a problem-solving cast of mind—evident with Jon Guthier's novice plumbers, but here in a different domain, and further along in development. Watch, for example, as Marcus and the others troubleshoot some problems in assembly. As they shift back and forth from graphics to assemblies and manually trace circuits, they speculate as to the cause of the problem. If you ask them, they'll talk in an experimentalist vocabulary of theories and hypotheses, and the steps they need to take to "test my theory." They are trained to proceed systematically. As one said, "You make sure each thing is doing what it should be doing, so you check them one at a time." Given the number of variables—and the increase in them as the assignments proceed—this focused, isolating orientation is crucial. And it is not mindless procedure. You hear the students articulate causal links, logical connections, as they take you through the elements of an assembly, then flick a switch, saying "and, indeed, the connection is made." Or they note that "in light of the wires coming from the panel" one can expect a particular outcome. This aspect of the work, at least for some, yields a motivating cognitive pleasure; the students describe it as a "brainteaser" or a "mechanical puzzle," expressing the intellectual kick found in the need to "problem-solve mechanically."

Finally, let me note again the role of workmanship and aesthetics, evident throughout as part of the developing electrician's knowledge base and value system. As mentioned earlier, there is often a relation between appearance and function: the graceful bend in a line of conduit looks good but also contributes to a secure assembly. It is not uncommon, though, that a student's efforts are more aesthetic than functional; something just doesn't look right to the disciplined eye. So one student trims off a fraction of the end of a conduit that will be hidden in a receptacle box, or another reconfigures a series of wires because, simply, "it was all fucking ugly." Your signature is in the braid of that wire.

These are some of the factors I can isolate that precede and inform Marcus standing before the assembly. He is eyeballing for symmetry, which has aesthetic and functional benefit. He is thinking about the circuitry, a final run-through. He feels a sense of accomplishment and a sense of things coming together, a sense of the whole. Marcus's experience, and the experiences of others like him, do not meet the Classical criteria for philosophical reflection or contemplation: that the object of contemplation is necessary and immutable, and that the contemplative act is purely intellectual, complete in itself, and free of personal gain. But isn't it worth pondering the degree to which such criteria limit the contemplative possibilities of human experience? To assume that contemplation cannot emerge from work of the hand, observes Christian philosopher Douglas Steere, is "to exclude all those . . . who are not favored by a large leisure." For that fact, the Classical definition also denies something we've witnessed: the interplay between action and reflection. We learn powerful things about the world not only by reflecting on it but also by acting on it—and what we learn through action can well move us to the contemplative. Marcus's configuration of objects and the channeling of electrical power it yields is his creation, one involving basic physical forces as well as human drives and needs. It is worthy of a long look, leaning against the side wall.

TWO LIVES

A Welder and a Foreman

Shift with me, now, from the development of skill in the task itself to the long stretch of tasks that, engaged over time, comprise a working life. Lisa Legohn, a tall African American woman who just turned forty, sits across from me in a small office that opens out onto the welding workshop at Los Angeles Trade Technical Community College. The office is all metal and concrete, industrial and spare, flatly bright under fluorescent lights. An applied metallurgy textbook sits on Lisa's desk, along with a copy of the Los Angeles welding code, several photocopied quizzes ("explain the following nondestructive-test symbols"), a stapler, and a tape dispenser. Across the wall behind the desk, and on the gray side panel of the old filing cabinet adjacent to it, there are prints and photographs of flower displays: bursts of roses, carnations, gladiolas. "I think of a flower," she is saying, "the same as I do a weld. There's a certain beauty . . . an art to it. It's not just metal joining metal."

Lisa entered the welding trade at nineteen. She began her training while still in high school—through a regional occupational program at the Watts Skills Center—and then went on to Trade Tech, to this program, in this school. "It started out as just a whim, as a practical joke. Welding . . . well, *this* oughta get my parents! But I ended up liking it. I was captivated by the instructor's presentation. He said that welding is the art of fusion. That got me, . . . the . . . art . . . of . . . fusion. By the time I finished the Skills Center program, I said, 'I'm going to be a welder.' I loved it. And there it was."

During the summer after her first year at Trade Tech, Lisa secured entry-level employment as a welder. "I was working at a hamburger stand, and the welding job was three times the pay. That was motivating! Plus I would be doing what I was learning about, the opportunity to do hands-on work. I was just fascinated. Oh, OK, now all of this is coming together. I mean, like learning about aluminum and how it was cut, instead of just reading about it, actually seeing it, actually putting it together." Lisa speaks fast here. "I was fabricating these truck ramps and these dock boards that trucks are going to use, and they're going to unload things, and I'm like, wow, I did that, *I* put this together."

There are themes in the particulars of this account of discovering a trade that we've heard in previous chapters: the importance of opportunities for training; the intellectual possibilities of manual work; the aesthetic dimension as well; the appreciation of utility; the sense of getting ahead and shaping a life. In Lisa Legohn's case, these themes emerge in a transformational juncture in the history of American labor. It was a point where the postwar industrial boom, changes in family structure, and the civil rights and women's movements intersected to disrupt traditional occupational patterns and increase the participation of women and racial minorities in a broader range of the workforce. And Lisa has that story to tell. Coworkers who tried to dump menial and repetitive tasks on her. The racial slurs and sexual banter in the surround, raised a decibel or two in her presence. Men verbally challenging her—"What are you doing here? Why aren't you at home?"—or threatening her physically. Lisa Legohn is a formidable presence—exuberant and determined—so part of this story is her response, from wit to confrontation to formal complaint, and the inner resources she drew on to mask the terrible hurt and stay the course.

One cannot appreciate, then, the full meaning of the themes of opportunity and engagement without keeping in mind this environment of insult, acknowledging Lisa's courage and the resilience of her defenses, and understanding, more generally, what *opportunity* comes to mean in this historical context, the individual and collective struggle to create it.

Part of the injury of occupational exclusion, along with its immediate economic effects, is the way it reinforces cultural biases that certain kinds of knowledge are the natural possession of some groups but not of others—women, for example, do not have technical minds. And such beliefs—coupled with actual hiring discrimination—profoundly limit the development of trade skill. But with affirmative action legislation and other social forces generating the occupational conditions for fuller participation, Lisa Legohn found and forged ways to become competent in the art of fusion. Building on her education at Trade Tech, she mastered multiple gas and electric welding methods—oxyacetylene, shielded metal-arc, gas-tungsten arc, plasma arc—each of which has advantages for different metals, structures, and conditions. (She, for example, got very good at stainless-steel pipe welding at a time when that skill was in high demand.) She enhanced her knowledge of metals and materials, and the various flaws they can contain. She developed an eye for welding defects—porosity, slag inclusion, cracks and their causes—and how to remedy them. She became a good troubleshooter. She acquired tricks of the trade, a sign that she was participating in an occupational tradition—as she puts it, "You're in awe because there's just not a text you can open up to find them." Terms and symbols became increasingly familiar, second nature, and she gained fluency in reading blueprints. Her account of reading blueprints—this from early in her career—gives a sense of the growth in skill she was experiencing: "When I started out, I could read them, sort of, but not really *see* them. I'd be on the job and have the print before me, and all these parts. So, I'd ask the foreman, or one of the lead welders, 'Should this go here? Or here?' And he'd say, 'OK, Lisa, take a look right here, see? This sketch represents *this* piece, right here—we put it right *here*.' And the more I did it . . . just like, one day, it was as if something was revealed. I got it! Oh, it fits." It's interesting to think about how many such moments of intellectual discovery in the workplace affirmative action made possible.

There is more to tell about Lisa Legohn's career as a welder and her transition to teaching the trade, but I want to pause here and introduce the second person whose working life I'll profile in this chapter, Joseph Meraglio, my one surviving uncle, who spent his early years in the Pennsylvania Railroad and, during the auto boom of the 1950s, moved to Ohio to become a career employee at General Motors. They are quite different lives in many ways, but I want to describe them in a manner that leads to a shared outcome: to illuminate the considerable role mind can play in a labor biography. So, for example, in addition to—or better, in concert with—Lisa Legohn's affirmative action narrative or her story of economic mobility, there is also in her working life the account of a vibrant mind engaging a trade. To be sure, these two people are atypical in the trajectories of their careers—Lisa became a teacher, and Joe would move off the assembly line and up through the supervisory ranks. These unusual turns, however, throw into relief, allow us to consider from another angle, the nuances of physical work, identity, and mental life.

◻

The light from the images on the screen—a welder's sparking fluorescence, a huge, glowing side rod, the white blast of a furnace— flickers across my uncle's face, and I can see that he's moved by the images and by the narrator's sonorous voice: "a reminder of a people and a city at work." We're lined up along the first row of this little theater in the new Railroader's Museum in Altoona, Pennsylvania: me, my uncle Joe, his wife, his middle daughter and son-in-law, and his two grandchildren. Altoona was created in the early 1850s as a company town for the Pennsylvania Railroad, and throughout the first half of the twentieth century was the site of the largest group of railroad shops in the world: more than two hundred acres of foundries, machine shops, paint and assembly facilities. All but one of my uncles worked at some point in the PRR; my uncle Frank, machinist and welder, would retire there. We are in Altoona a few days before our family reunion, and Joe wants to make a day of it, showing his grandsons where he was born, the traces of Little Italy, his grammar school and church, my uncle Herk's old pool hall, the streets he ran, and the memorials to the PRR, like this three-story museum, a much snazzier place than the one I visited many years before with my uncle Frank.

The film incorporates a number of old photographs that have a severe beauty to them. They are sharp black and white, the sun streaming through high windows onto the shop floor: massive presses, boiler shells, trip-hammers taller than a man. A geometry of light and shadow that doesn't reveal what Frank and Joe knew: the numbing cold or exhausting heat, the dirt and noise, the myriad injuries. Though this is a commissioned film—and thus is fairly sanitized—the harsh reality of the work is revealed in momentary clips. "The whole place shook," says a retired worker. "It was a dangerous operation," says another. Unforgiving production. It is hard to imagine the output of the Altoona yards. In 1942 alone, they repaired 1,600 steam locomotives; they built 7,000 freight cars, nearly 20 a day; they employed 17,000 people, a stunning percentage of the city's workforce. Joe watches, his hands resting on his lap, one over the other.

Joe's father, my grandfather, lost his leg in these shops in 1921, the year Joe was born. All the Meraglio kids started working very young. Joe sold papers, shined shoes, ran numbers. Soon after completing the eighth grade, he dropped out of school for, he figured (this he tells me in his gravelly voice after the film), "I'll be in the railroad, so how's school gonna help me there?" He followed his father, as did so many children of immigrants, into the yards, starting, as his father did, as a "laborer," sweeping the debris from the machines, picking up scrap, lugging materials. "The goal at that time," he explains, "was to move from *laborer* to *helper*," for "being a helper was like an apprenticeship." Over the next few years, he would work as a helper in the construction and masonry department, in the foundry, and in the locomotive shop, learning, by watching and doing, the fundamentals of carpentry and bricklaying, of metalwork, machining, and machine repair. He dwells on the locomotive shop.

"It was very, very dirty and a lot of noise. I was on what they called 'the ash pan gang,' replacing the ash pans under the engines—they would rust from the heat, the water, the salt. . . ." (I recall that it was an ash pan falling from an overhead lift that crushed my grandfather's leg.) The mechanic Joe worked for, "a German fella," liked Joe's work, so when that mechanic was transferred to the crew building a new engine—what was to be the grandest of the PRR's steam locomotives, the sleek, futuristic T-1— he asked Joe to join him, and Joe jumped at the chance. My uncle liked the work and was "getting pretty good at it," learning, for example, how to read a blueprint (his description of the process closely matches Lisa Legohn's), and with that reading, a sense of the sequencing of complex assembly—a skill, he adds, that would be a great asset when he later joined General Motors.

Then the war. Rather than be drafted, Joe joined the navy as a radioman in order to learn something about that technology. He saw intense action on the USS *Arkansas*, participated in three invasions—the Philippines, Iwo Jima, and Okinawa—returning in 1945, quiet about the war, inwardly shaken. He rejoined the T-1 crew, but, as the narrator of the film put it with vague finality, "beyond Altoona, there were forces of change [leading to] the end of the steam era." As diesel replaced steam, the Altoona shops, which were a center of steam engine manufacture, began a decline that would dramatically alter the city's economy, its demographics and opportunity structure, and its image of itself. My parents' restaurant failed, and they moved west. Several years later Joe, joined by Frank, would follow them to Los Angeles in search of work, a brief interlude, hired by a division of the Union Pacific Railroad to repair refrigerator cars. Then he returned to Altoona, finding sporadic employment with the faltering PRR and some freelance painting and plastering, using the skills he learned in the railroad. In 1954, a call came from his brother Herk who had gone ahead to Cleveland to work for Fisher Body, a division of General Motors, the largest corporation in the world. "The industry was booming. I got hired the very next day. And when I found out what you done for the amount of money they paid, 'Well,' I thought, 'that's pretty damned good.' "

Joe was hired as a wet sander. Once a car body was primed, the rough finish would be smoothed out by hand with water and sandpaper. It was "wet, cold, and nasty" work, but it was steady—a big thing for Joe after all the postwar fluctuation in Altoona—and held the promise of advancement, "if you had the right attitude and work ethic." From the sand pit, Joe Meraglio would launch a thirty-three-year career with General Motors, rising to superintendent of the paint and body departments at the Lordstown plant outside of Youngstown, Ohio. It is the kind of career trajectory that was of its time—wet sanding is a thing of the past—and is no longer possible for someone with an eighth-grade education.

We'll continue to follow that career momentarily, but this mention of education and its relation to economic opportunity provides entry back to Lisa Legohn, who has tightly blended work and education in her own career.

◻

"Learn to Earn" the bright script reads, writ large right beneath LOS ANGELES TRADE TECHNICAL COMMUNITY COLLEGE. Since its inception in 1925, the college has provided local vocational training, expanding its academic curriculum after World War II, moving into this cluster of buildings in the late 1950s. The college is due south of downtown Los Angeles, surrounded by car dealerships, small industry, and assorted commerce. The nearby housing, down side streets, off the main drag, is modest, some apartments and single-family homes. It's a working-class neighborhood, mostly African American and Latino, and many of the Latinos are recent immigrants. Learn to Earn. Lisa Legohn got her associate-of-arts degree here in 1981. On the first of my visits to interview her, there was a street fair bustling at the main entrance, under the college logo, food wagons, T-shirts, stuffed animals, balloons rising in curved arrays over students streaming in and out of the campus.

Lisa had been welding for several years when a friend encouraged her to continue her education, maybe with an eye to teaching the trade that had captivated her. She began a night program at Long Beach State University to get a teaching credential and work toward a bachelor's degree in vocational education. Lisa quickly secured a part-time position at Compton Community College, southeast of downtown L.A.; she was a pipe welder during the day, a student for two nights a week, and a teacher on the other two. Over time, Lisa would teach as well on other campuses and in industry. In 1997, a full-time position opened at Trade Tech. Lisa interviewed and was hired, an instructor of gas and electric welding in the Department of Construction Technology, coming back home.

Lisa still works as a welder occasionally; in fact, on the day of my final visit, she had just finished a job for the community college district. "It's something I like to do." She nods, shrugs. "It grabs you. It's part of you." Another nod, a smile. "I don't think I'd want to teach anything else."

So we talk about her teaching. She says that she enjoys "coming back here and being able to share how welding can open so many avenues. It's about equipping people and giving them opportunity." As she is talking about opportunity, she turns to thoughts of technical education.

"There's this idea that academics and the trades don't go together, but they do. A vocation combines theory and practical application. The more theoretics you have, the better welder it makes you." So, for example, Lisa teaches her students how and why their welding instruments work—the basic principles—which aids them in troubleshooting, in being systematic in "rectifying a problem in the weld: 'OK, I've checked this, I've checked this, I've checked this . . . so the problem has to be in the metal itself. So let's test the steel.' " Equipping people, then, involves reasoning "about cause and effect," and Lisa values, takes pedagogical pleasure in, engaging her students in this interface of the conceptual and the technical. I think here of a nice phrase from the mathematician Alfred North Whitehead—that technical education involves "the art of utilizing knowledge."

What's the hardest thing about teaching, I ask, your biggest challenge?

Lisa shifts in her chair, pauses. Across the shop, a fellow is hammering on a bar he's just welded, "peening" it to reduce stresses in the weld. Two others, one a Mexican boxer called "The Canary," have just ignited their torches—the *pop* of flame—and are adjusting the mix of oxygen and acetylene. Welders a century ago would have sought the same balance. "The hardest thing," says Lisa, "is conveying that there is no instant gratification—but doing it without breaking one's spirit. 'How can I motivate this individual,' I ask myself. 'How can I bring out the best in this person?' That's my biggest challenge. These programs take two years. Two years of sacrifice. It's hard to imagine, hard to see the reward. But I say to them, 'I sat where you sat. I felt the same feelings.' "

A student comes over to show her a weld. It looks irregular, bumpy. She tells him to hold his elbow up, that the angle of his electrode is too acute, and that's causing the irregularity. He leaves, and Lisa talks for a while about the craft, the artistry of welding. "It's like calligraphy . . . or signatures. You can have thirty beautiful signatures, and they all look different—and that's how it is with welding. I can show you how to do it, but then you develop a style of your own." She takes me across the shop to one of the benches. There are strips of metal on it, layered with samples of students' welds. "The keys to welding," she explains, "are travel—how fast you're moving—and heat, and angle." She calls my attention to two welds. One looks good, "but notice the little lack of fusion in here. When you analyze it, you see that the ripples could be a little more consistent." Then we look at the other. "Run your finger over it," she tells me. "Look at how tight the ripples are, little half crescents, close to each other, a lot of definition, but very smooth." We walk slowly back to her desk, talking further about her work here at Trade Tech.

"You have to remember the makeup of this community college. We have a lot of poor people here. They may not have a home or a car. They're working five or six days a week. And there's other problems surrounding their lives—you can't imagine the horrific stories they have to tell. The fact that some of our students get here daily is a success. This gets to how I define matriculation. They may need remedial English. They may need tutors. But they also need a chance."

Teaching and learning, for Lisa, gain significance in an economic context. The acquisition of metallurgical knowledge and related welding skill is in the service of decent wages and security—with the possibility of some advancement as one learns more. Thus learning to earn, given the right work environments, begets further learning—think of Lisa refining her ability to read blueprints. One's cognitive-manual repertoire develops through monetary incentives; to "equip people" has both pedagogical and economic meaning.

As Lisa articulates it, there is a strong human development aspect to this view, combined with an ethic of service. To enroll in college and pursue a course of study involves various kinds of support, assistance, guidance. I think here of the times I saw her pull aside a student who had missed class for a long talk out of earshot, or give one a ride home after school, good for catching up and checking in. "I sat where you sat. I felt the same feelings." This ethic of service extends beyond the personal level, needs to be institutional as well: remedial courses, tutorial centers, a college's sense of mission. Therefore—and this is a further, related, dimension of Lisa's philosophy—instruction has to be sensitive to its setting, emerging from and responsive to the community in which Trade Tech is located.

There is a traditional language used to define educational goals and courses of study that would label the above approach as "instrumental" or "vocational." And, clearly, it is. The purpose of the welding program is to train for work, though, as practiced by Lisa, the economic purpose is inflected with craft and aesthetic values and a strong sense of care. Within this language, the vocational orientation is often contrasted with the liberal course of study, and the contrast yields the kind of binary oppositions mentioned in the last chapter: narrow versus well-rounded, practical versus intellectual, commercial and materialistic versus humanistic. What strikes me as I listen again to the tapes of Lisa's interview—with these binaries drifting in and out of my mind—is how unbinary her account is, how many elements compose it, *compose* it, constitute it in orchestral interplay, the cadence of her voice, the multiple registers and topics: childhood memories, early work stories, social-political observations, moral evaluations and testaments of will, technical detail, colloquialisms and specialized terminology, aesthetic judgments, a theory of learning, metaphor, troubleshooting and hypothetico-deductive reasoning, religious invocation, a driving intellectual curiosity, sequences of procedures, and more. They are all of a piece, lived in full complex expression.

This richness reminds us again of the limitations of so much of the language we use to characterize not only working life but also the education of working people. Consider Lisa Legohn's life, then, as an educational text.

The gaining of skill and the attendant acquisition of knowledge, even if delivered in reductive ways, has the potential to spark the play of mind and contribute to broader views. Welding, as we've seen, provides for Lisa a medium of aesthetic expression and judgment. It also necessitates the development of a technical literacy, which begets further learning. And it provides the arena to develop and live out craft values and related social responsibility. "A bridge is only as strong as its weakest weld," she tells her students. "You're like a surgeon, but you're working on metal. You're taking two separate entities and making them one. So take it to heart."

And something I've heard again and again, heard, for that fact, from several of Lisa's students, is the sense of agency that the acquisition of technical knowledge and skill provides. It's significant that Lisa uses words like *equip* and *empower*. Yes, for those students of Lisa's whom I met, the empowerment occurs within a life world terribly affected by poverty and race. Neither Lisa nor her students are naive about that; they know better than anyone. Furthermore, the work they're taking on, as Lisa puts it, "is hot and dirty," and depending on their place of employment, they may encounter personal and organizational restrictions on their further development. But to see only constraint, to not simultaneously understand possibility, is to miss the full sweep of what Lisa knows.

It is to miss what it means to someone to gain through tangible, demonstrable skill the ability to exercise some control, to give some direction to things, to feel security within reach—something people born into economic security cannot fully appreciate. This sense of agency, this imagining of a future not turbulent, spawns longer views, elaborates purpose. The relation of skill to hope.

❑

For Joe Meraglio, the shop floor provided what school did not, was, for him, "like schooling," a place where "you're constantly learning." The intellectual benefits of my uncle's work experience derive from his career path, the variety of jobs he held and their expanding challenge and responsibility. The path was an unusual one in the auto industry—the limited mobility from the assembly line to supervisory roles is well documented—so I would not want to generalize about the economic and educational opportunities at places like General Motors. Rather, I'd like to consider the way thought plays out in a particular working life, and some of the lessons this life might offer.

As we saw, Joe's career at GM began in that area of the paint department where car bodies, after they had been primed, were sanded to a smooth finish. It was hard, low-tech labor—basically a piece of sandpaper and a water hose—and, like all assembly line work, called for an economy of movement, working smart to hold exhaustion at bay. Though it was classified as unskilled, there was definitely a technique to wet sanding. In a sociological study of the auto assembly line conducted close to the time when my uncle was entering GM—thus giving us a close look at the work he did—one wet sander lists methodically the number of strokes he delivers to each section of the body: eight around the drip rail, six on the left corner panel. Another stresses the importance of applying the right pressure to the sandpaper—not too much or too little—and of responding to the characteristics of the body before you: "the paint varies and you have to go the way that goes." Wet sanding took a certain touch, and, as was the case with the men in the study, Joe developed a feel and an eye for the work.

From wet sander, Joe bid on and got another job on the line, that of paint repairman, a little more pay and a little less nasty. An inspector would examine the car bodies and mark with chalk any defects in the paint, mostly from dirt, in the air, off workers' clothes. It was Joe's job to sand down the defect, repaint that area of the body, forward it to an oven, then polish the repainted area to blend it with the overall coat. There was a little variety to the work, a different set of routines, and a different phase of the paint process. And a few more cents an hour. I visited a GM plant with my uncle later in his career. Working on the line is noisy, repetitive, and taxing, and the pace—a perennial source of labor-management dispute—is grueling. But to do the work competently and survive requires some of the skills we've seen in earlier chapters: finding the most efficient way to use one's body and developing a set of routines to work quickly and preserve energy. As Joe says, "There's really no such thing as unskilled work."

But once jobs like these are mastered, there is little variety and little new learning; the work, for many, quickly becomes monotonous, justified only by the pay and benefits. As Joe characterizes it: "You put four screws in this thing, put four screws in this thing, you know. You do it one hundred times in an hour, eight hundred times in a day, four screws in this thing—and it would get to the point where a guy figures that if the screw went in, good, and if it didn't, the hell with it." And, though assembly line wages in the auto industry are relatively high, the wage rates between types of jobs are compressed. So transferring to different jobs on the line can, for a time, stave off boredom, but not significantly raise your income. Joe was married, and he and his wife wanted to start a family, so when he was offered a chance to try out for a foreman's position, he took it. Back to wet sanding to supervise the thirty-two men who were doing what he had done a few years before.

Unlike line workers, whose labor is stationary and predictable, a foreman is on the move, feeling the pressure from his bosses, dealing with the people and machines in his section, confronting a range of problems, trivial to profound, technological and human surprise. In that midcentury study of the assembly line I mentioned earlier, the researchers tracked the activities of a representative foreman, and the pattern of his activity resonates with my uncle's account of his day. In one eight-hour period, the foreman walked over four miles and took part in nearly four hundred different incidents, about one per minute. A significant number of those incidents involved his own workers or, to a lesser degree, the foreman on either side of his section, and they generally had to do with the maintenance of timely and quality work: supervision and direction, but a good deal of pitching in, supplying tools and materials, and responding to emergencies. (Later in the century, collective bargaining agreements would restrict some of these activities.) The foreman observed, tested, talked, demonstrated, handled tools, instruments, or parts and—this is crucial—did it all quickly, on the fly, his talk interrupted continually as another, and yet another, thing arose. As with the waitresses we saw at rush hour, the effective foreman must quickly judge the demands made on him or her, parcel out physical and mental resources, keep a number of ongoing events in mind, return to that which had been interrupted, and maintain a cool head under pressure. And though the immediacy and barrage of the demands on his attention made it hard to think beyond the moment, it's interesting to consider the kinds of things my uncle learned in the midst of it all.

Joe Meraglio learned more about the basics of paint chemistry and of plating and baking. He gained a practical understanding of a wider range of machines and of human-machine interaction. He got a better sense of production processes—you can't figure out the cause of a problem in assembly unless you know what happens up the line from your section. Some of this he learned during the in-house training the company provided, but a lot of it was acquired on the shop floor, through the flow of activity. One of his educational resources was a young paint chemist with whom he formed a friendship; the chemist wanted to observe production, and Joe was eager to learn about research and development. My uncle also learned, or further clarified, an approach to supervision. As we'll see, there were things about Joe's background that contributed significantly to his management style, but he also encountered, via the company's seminars, current psychological theory on human relations, motivation, and job satisfaction. And Joe was afforded continual opportunity to troubleshoot and solve problems, testing his ability to think on his feet, gaining confidence. One of the frequently discussed restrictions of work on the assembly line is its narrow focus. The foreman's position facilitated for my uncle a broader view of production, a bigger picture.

After four years as foreman of wet sanding, Joe was promoted to general foreman of the whole paint department. This was 1960. His field of supervision expanded considerably—seven foremen and about one hundred personnel—as did the sweep of production he would have to come to know. There was a significant instructional dimension to this work—at least as Joe defined it—from

showing new workers how to perform a job efficiently to developing and advancing people along and off the line. The general foreman is also responsible for the department's budget, so Joe would
learn some basic finance and accounting, adding an economic
perspective to his understanding of production.

The automotive industry in our time has been notoriously sensitive to fluctuations in the economy and to international competition. My uncle's career had developed in Cleveland's Fisher Body
plant, but in 1968 GM announced that, to cut costs, it was moving
the factory's bodywork to Detroit. Such conversions and closings
have become a wrenching part of life in the auto industry, making
transfers and layoffs commonplace. The superintendent above Joe
was being transferred to Lordstown, the new plant twenty or so
miles outside of Youngstown, and asked Joe to join him, retaining
his position as general foreman of the paint department. With
three kids under ten, and fresh memories of the failing railroad,
Joe said yes. Lordstown was touted as GM's state-of-the-art facility,
and several years after Joe's arrival it would be cranked up to inhumane levels of production. The result was a bitter strike in 1972—
well rendered in the opening chapter of Stanley Aronowitz's study
of working-class life, *False Promises*—and, for some time afterward,
the strike left an atmosphere of contention and distrust. As Joe explained, twenty years after the fact, there were still bad feelings between some managers and workers.

Joe would remain a general foreman at Lordstown until 1978
when he was promoted to shift superintendent, and from there to
superintendent over the entire paint and body shop, the position
from which he retired in 1987. These positions involved Joe in
long-range planning and in a larger sweep of economic and industrial issues, including union negotiations, which he saw as "the
hardest part of the job." Joe had been a member of the United Auto
Workers—still was, actually, though inactive because of his super-

visory status—and believed that "people who work on the line need a union behind them to protect their rights." But he was also middle management, feeling the intense pressure of production quotas. Though my uncle has a thick skin, and has developed through his life a quiet resolve, this last decade and a half would exact a price. He had open-heart surgery in 1979. But this period also brought with it the opportunity to engage technical, organizational, and personnel problems of a sort rarely available to people like Joe Meraglio, coming off the line, with limited formal education and social capital. The shop floor as curriculum.

This survey of Joe Meraglio's working life reminds us that even in industrialized work settings where so much is automated and bureaucratized, where so much of the intimate knowledge of craft and machine is designed out of production apparatus and human interaction is channeled by work rules and protocol—that even in such tightly regulated sociotechnical systems, someone like my uncle could think his way through the day, taking on complex industrial and human problems. This is not to deny the many barriers and frustrations Joe faced within such a system, particularly as it was manifest at General Motors during the 1950s and '60s, before, as Joe put it, "the Japanese, Ralph Nader, and the oil embargo changed the auto industry." Joe and others in the paint department saw flaws in the priming and painting processes, at the least, saw the poor quality resulting from the breakneck speed, and "we'd bring this up in meetings, so they'd appoint a committee. But nothing would change. It was as always, you know, put on a whole lotta chrome. Make it shiny." Still, Joe engaged the work, and found ways to insert himself into it. Here are several examples.

In one of the operations in the paint shop, a worker sprayed a six-inch strip on a quarter panel. The spray gun delivered a twelve-inch spray, so the panel had to be masked off, and the overspray—some of which flew back onto the operator—was significant. Joe wondered why the gun couldn't be outfitted to deliver a narrower spray, and spoke to the supplier, who, in fact, was able to fashion an adjustable air cap for the spray gun. This device eliminated the need for masking, which cut cost, and also made the job cleaner; the painter "didn't have to eat all that overspray." Another example involved the ovens that bake the car body once it had been primed or painted. The ovens were divided into zones, each with its own temperature regulation. Joe speculated that you could lower the temperature in one of the middle zones—thus cutting energy costs— and still maintain adequate overall heat. The supervisor over Joe was doubtful, but Joe knew what the finished product should look like, and when he saw the results of his experiment, he knew he was right.

There are several things to note about these examples. They reveal a penchant for problem solving, but more so bear resemblance to what one pair of psychologists call *problem finding*. Joe worked under a general directive to cut costs, but he sought out the ways to do it, defining particular practices as problems to be solved based on his direct experience with assembly line technology. This mention of experience leads to a further point: the value of direct, immediate knowledge of how a machine works, the on-the-ground look and feel of the spray gun and the oven. In *Engineering and the Mind's Eye*, engineer and historian Eugene Ferguson laments the loss of such knowledge in the training of engineers, the increased reliance on mathematical abstraction devoid of the empirical encounter with mechanical structures and processes. Joe had limited formal knowledge of how the mechanisms under his supervision worked, but he was savvy about them, knew how to experiment with them—and his supervisory position allowed him to bring that kind of knowledge to bear on production.

Another realm in which Joe's yen for problem finding and problem solving emerged was in personnel and management. It was

Joe's responsibility—from foreman to superintendent, in Cleveland and at Lordstown—to keep GM's furious production schedule going, to monitor the quality of that production, and to cut costs wherever possible. He is straightforward about that during the interviews. Call it the pressure from above—and it clearly pits boss against worker. No wonder that accounts of factory life—from Harvey Swados's *On the Line* to Ben Hamper's *Rivethead*—depict the foreman as a brute or a troublesome fool. But, finally, it is the people on the line who meet or fall behind or sabotage a schedule. And everyone I've talked to who has worked assembly notes the difference in one's working life a decent foreman can make. Joe had a bedrock belief in the capability of his workforce; as he says several times, "People build a job." Make no mistake, my uncle knew the informal codes of the shop floor. "You're not gonna like what I'm about to tell you," I can hear him say, or, with his characteristic bluntness, "Let's cut the bullshit." But his no-nonsense demeanor was modulated by a hard-bitten empathy. The supervisor who hasn't worked on the line, Joe says, tapping his index finger hard on the chair, "has no idea of the mental exhaustion or the physical exhaustion that goes with the work." Call this understanding a force from below. It was from this in-between space that Joe addressed a range of employee problems, finding the right job for an assembler who couldn't keep up, talking to someone who was chronically late or absent and jointly trying to work things out. "Most of the foremen would scream and raise hell. Well, my theory was to talk to the man first and find out why he wasn't there. What's his reason? Sometimes there'd be a serious problem."

This hybrid perspective on the needs of workers and the demands of management led Joe to think of ways to improve efficiency on the line while relieving some of the stress on the assemblers—again, Joe's penchant for problem finding, here manifested in the human domain. He, for example, had each person in a unit learn the other members' jobs, thus they could rotate across stations, relieving some of the monotony of the task. He also arranged things so that, through this rotation, assemblers could get longer and more frequent breaks. Such an experiment required Joe to argue his case on a number of fronts, the stuff of a rhetorical education. He had to persuade the people on the line, an easy sell; the union, who had to approve any modification in job duties; and the managers above him, who were wary of the change. The experiment worked and was scaled up, yielding both worker satisfaction and improved quality, and the resulting efficiency trimmed costs, which benefited Joe as well.

There is an interesting parallel, I think, between the source of Joe's management style and the kind of knowledge he relied on to solve technical problems: both are experiential and empirical. General Motors did provide supervisors with a steady stream of management training—on personnel issues, benefits, work rules, group dynamics—but Joe credits his ability with people to three sources: his coming of age in Altoona and all it enabled him to understand about work and hardship; his service in the navy, learning how so many guys from different backgrounds lived and saw the world; and his time on the assembly line. Humble beginnings and hard work are by no means a guarantee of decency and broader views; poverty and labor can make one fearful and mean. But Joe Meraglio's background, from all I can tell, did contribute to both a theory and an ethic about supervision. Take, for example, his observations about the significant population of marginally educated workers at Lordstown, many of whom were from the economically depressed coalfields of West Virginia and neighboring Pennsylvania cities like Uniontown. "People looked down on them, but, you know, I was born on the wrong side of the tracks, too. I thought to myself, 'These guys are just like me.' Coming out of the mines like they did, they knew nothing but hard work. Hell, wet sanding was easy next to mining coal." Joe talks a lot about the importance of putting yourself "in the other guy's shoes." What makes this expression meaningful is that he had the kind of personal history that enabled him to find a common ground.

◻

It is the end of the day, and Lisa Legohn is looking across the workshop, hands on hips, a slow gaze. The shop is nearly empty. Enrollment has dropped over the years, nowhere near as many people as when Lisa was developing her skill at those stations, the exuberant young woman, getting her movements right, the materials, the torch. Over the last few decades, a good deal of factory welding has been automated; I recall a computerized welding device at Lordstown that would simultaneously hit forty spots on a frame. Still, Lisa says, there is decent work to be had, in construction, in some industries, in small shops. "If you're a good stainless-steel tube welder right now," she explains, "you can write your own ticket."

I see the boxer at the far end of the shop and motion toward him, the Canary. He is putting his mask away and taking off his leather apron. Lisa tells me to hold on for a minute, walks to her desk, comes back and hands me an article from L.A.'s Spanish-language newspaper, *La Opinion*. It is about "El Canario." I will later have one of my students translate it for me. It's the kind of piece written about a promising young fighter, the excitement of the ring, his string of victories, the power of his punch, his tenacity. But it is also an immigrant's tale, and refers, two or three times, to his education at Trade Tech. "A canary is longing to sing . . . anxious to begin a new kind of life, in the ring, and at school." "Boxing," the young man tells the reporter, "isn't something you can do your whole life, so formal schooling will help me survive in the future."

In *Outliving the Self*, psychologist John Kotre writes of "technical generativity," the passing on of a skill, and the values associated with it, to a new generation. "I see students graduate," Lisa says, "they come back, five, ten years later, and they say, 'This is my family. This is my son. You helped me get my first job.' That's a joy I can't explain—not that I would do it for free." She laughs. "But I love what I do. It's a blessing from God." Kotre would call it her legacy.

Lisa closes up her office. On our way out, we run into another of her students, a woman in her mid-to-late thirties. As we're walking to the parking lot, up on the roof of one of the buildings, Lisa is called aside by a colleague for some quick school politics. The student and I continue talking. She tells me that she is about to graduate. She is soft-spoken but open, and is, it becomes clear, quietly, deeply pleased with her accomplishment. She came back to school after what sounds like very hard times, and schooling itself—as Lisa observed earlier about many of her students—has not been easy, a long, tough haul for her. But here she is, a welder, a job lined up, a modicum of order, a second chance.

◻

When Joe Meraglio turned eighty, his oldest daughter, a graphic designer, put together a collection of snapshots of her father's life, from faded first communion photos to family portraits taken a few years back. I am looking at photographs from the mid-1950s, just after Joe's migration from Altoona to Cleveland.

In one photo, he is sitting sideways on a chair at the dining room table, a cup of coffee before him. A window shade is half open; it is dark outside. He is in his midthirties and looks tired, his chin resting on the palm of his hand. A note under the photo reads "first furnished apartment." Other photos follow. The kitchen. The living room. Another has his brothers, Herk and Russ, talking, smoking; another is of my aunt, pregnant, by the door. There are shots of Joe holding his infant daughters, of Joe and his wife outside their first house, purchased just before he made general foreman, his foot up on the bumper of a car in the driveway. These are snapshots of beginnings—first apartment, first house, children being born. They give a visual sense of the life Joe Meraglio was creating out of his labor in the sand pit and from the flurry of demands that fell on his shoulders as foreman.

I have many notes written over the last few decades—notes from earlier attempts to capture our family history—that shed further light on this period of Joe's life. He spoke about growing up in Altoona, acutely aware of living on the wrong side of the tracks, the multiple faces of poverty, hustling to sell enough newspapers to buy a loaf of yesterday's bread. He remembered walking his father to work in the winter, steadying him, his cumbersome artificial leg precarious on the ice. And he remembered the children of businessmen, of supervisors arriving at church, in cars, in new clothes. An ongoing debate in social analyses of the working class in the United States concerns their degree of "class consciousness," and the ways that such consciousness is veiled and mystified, the ways that workers are duped by the social order. Though there may well be things they don't know and though they may say seemingly naive things for public consumption, I haven't known many working people who were privately stupid about their situation. As Joe put it simply, "I felt we were cheated out of life." He came to realize that "there was no future for me in Altoona." So, he'd have to get out, "work a little harder, get down to it and grind."

The interview, the notes, the snapshots half a century old give a sense of the longing that drove Joe Meraglio to Cleveland, the gleam of the future, the possible world, difficult as hell, extending before him. For all its pain—the pressure, the long hours, the toll on his health—work in the auto industry provided my uncle with a field of competence and development, a fulfillment of his sense of what it means to be a man, and a powerful feeling of achievement, his legacy in his children and the opportunity he could provide for them.

RETHINKING HAND AND BRAIN

The labor biographies of Lisa Legohn and Joe Meraglio have threaded through them the stock occupational terminology that, as we've seen, define work in America: skilled versus unskilled labor, for example, or experiential knowledge versus formal (or school) knowledge, or mental versus manual activity. The master category that plays across all these—one that reflects the Western, Cartesian divide between body and mind—is the opposition of hand to brain.

In this chapter, I'd like to push further on the issue of the hand-brain binary. I'll begin with a portrait of a late-nineteenth-century laborer, for our current representations of work are, I think, shaped by certain historical simplifications of the work that precedes our own. From there, we'll move to a comparative discussion of three types of higher status work that involve a blending of body and mind: surgery, physical therapy, and teaching. Using this comparison, I want to raise, from other locations in the occupational status hierarchy, questions about the terminological assurances—such as the distinction between the conceptual and the manual—that underpin the way we classify work. Finally, we'll consider the process of occupational classification itself, along with some of its historical and methodological complications. Each section is a brief treatment, only touching upon the full sweep and scope of the underlying topics. But collectively they will serve, I hope, as a further invitation to reimagine and unsettle our prevailing vocabulary of work.

⌷

As my uncle Joe and his family were filing out of that theater in the Railroader's Museum, he caught my arm. "You know," he said, "what they left out of that story was the fact that a lot of those men couldn't speak English." We drift over by a street scene of old Altoona. "They were like your grandfather, off the farm, didn't know those tools, hell, never saw a steam engine in their lives. But they learned what to do, and they coordinated what they did."

This is not the typical depiction of those workers, or, for that fact, of the American worker in general, immigrant or native-born. Take, as a classic example, one drafted a decade or so before my grandfather entered the stockyard, Frederick Winslow Taylor's portrayal of a laborer named Schmidt in *The Principles of Scientific Management*—one of the most reproduced portraits of a laborer in Western occupational literature. It captures American industry's traditional separation of managerial intelligence from worker production.

Taylor was a fierce systematizer and a tireless promoter of time study and industrial efficiency. He uses Schmidt to illustrate how even the most basic of tasks—in this case, the loading of pig iron—could be analytically broken down by the scientific manager into a series of maximally effective movements, with a resulting bonus in wages and a boom in productivity. Schmidt, Taylor claimed, jumped his rate from twelve and a half tons of pig iron per day—each "pig" an oblong casting of iron weighing close to one hundred pounds—to an astonishing tonnage of forty-seven.

Before he introduces Schmidt, Taylor sets the scene with a dispassionate analysis of the loading of pig iron at Bethlehem Steel, Schmidt's place of employment. Enter Schmidt, "a little Pennsylvania Dutchman," seemingly inexhaustible (he "trots" to and from

work), frugal, in the process of building "a little house for himself."
Then comes this interaction between Taylor and Schmidt:

> "Schmidt, are you a high-priced man?"
>
> "Vell, I don't know vat you mean."
>
> "Oh, yes, you do. What I want to know is whether you are a high-priced man or not."
>
> "Vell, I don't know vat you mean."
>
> "Oh, come now, you answer my questions. What I want to find out is whether you are a high-priced man or one of these cheap fellows here. What I want to find out is whether you want to earn $1.85 a day or whether you are satisfied with $1.15, just the same as all those cheap fellows are getting."
>
> "Did I vant $1.85 a day? Vas dot a high-priced man? Vell, yes, I vas a high-priced man."
>
> "Oh, you're aggravating me. Of course you want $1.85 a day—every one wants it! ... For goodness' sake answer my questions, and don't waste any more of my time. Now come over here. You see that pile of pig iron?" ...

Taylor badgers Schmidt for a little while longer—one wonders what Schmidt thinks of all this—and then introduces him to the supervisor who will direct his scientifically calibrated labor:

> "Well, if you are a high-priced man, you will do exactly as this man tells you tomorrow, from morning till night. When he tells you to pick up a pig and walk, you pick it up and you walk, and when he tells you to sit down and rest, you sit down. You do that right straight through the day. And what's more, no back talk. Now a high-priced man does just what he's told to do, and no back talk. Do you understand that? When this man tells you to walk, you walk; when he tells you to sit down, you sit down, and you don't talk back at him."

"This seems to be rather rough talk," Taylor admits, but "[w]ith a man of the mentally sluggish type of Schmidt it is appropriate and not unkind." Later, Taylor observes that Schmidt "happened to be a man of the type of an ox . . . a man so stupid that he was unfitted to do most kinds of laboring work, even."

There's much to say about this depiction, and a number of critics, beginning with Upton Sinclair, have collectively said it: the insidious mix of scientific pretension, class and ethnic bias, and paternalism; the antagonistic management stance, the kind of authoritarian control that would lead to industrial inflexibility; the absolute gulf between managerial brains and worker brawn; the ruthlessness of full-blown industrial capitalism. All true. In addition, though, I keep thinking of Schmidt himself, rereading Taylor's rendering, trying to imagine him . . . and with him, my grandfather, Tony.

Anthony Meraglio, too, was a small man, judging from the one photo I have of him, wisps of hair hanging over a broad forehead, large, sad eyes, narrow shoulders, maybe 5'3" or 5'4", but, like his son, my uncle Frank, he had those big, thick hands, one hand halfway in his pocket, the other raising a glass, a pose, looking into the camera. Not that long after Schmidt encountered Taylor's stopwatch, Tony would be hauling and hoisting scrap metal and ash in the Altoona yards of the Pennsylvania Railroad. Like Schmidt, he was part of a huge increase of manual laborers in the American workforce, a 300 percent increase from 1870 to 1910, 1,200 percent in Schmidt's iron and steel industry, over 600 percent in the booming railroads. "The key to industrial growth in the middle and late nineteenth century," writes labor historian David Montgomery, "was more people devoting more of their lives to working harder than ever before." ("The hard work of America," an Irish immigrant wrote concisely in a letter home, "is no joke.") By one estimate, there were nearly ten million such men toiling in the

United States, making the nation's domination of steel and rail possible. Schmidt was one such worker, Anthony Meraglio another.

We know so little about these men; even less about their interior lives. A small number left letters or diaries; in a handful of cases, they or their children wrote memoirs or fiction, like Thomas Bell's *Out of This Furnace*, a multigenerational account of a Slovakian family in the steel town of Braddock, Pennsylvania. During Schmidt's and Tony Meraglio's time, few unions admitted common laborers, so their voices are absent from that record. And although sociologists and social reformers visited mill towns and urban tenements, their focus was more on family life and childrearing practices than on the work the men did, how they did it, what they made of it. We do get a glimpse into the experience of such work from a few adventurous academics and journalists who sought employment on pick and shovel gangs, in machine shops, and in steel mills—and they give testament to the danger and drudgery of the work itself, albeit through a middle-class lens.

It is a piecemeal record, at best. What is typically offered in its place, even down to our time, is the sense that this vast, widely diverse population of laborers was, yes, hardworking, even courageous, but intellectually substandard, their deficiency rooted in their cultural and linguistic difference, or their rural origins, or their lack of formal education, or the very work they did—hazardous, dirty, defiled.

So let us, as one labor journalist puts it, give workers back their heads; let us reimagine Schmidt beyond the borders of Taylor's page, follow him through the plant, out into his world, down the road home. Though Taylor claims that a man like Schmidt "is so stupid that the word 'percentage' has no meaning to him," Taylor also tells us that Schmidt is building a house from his meager earnings. So, Schmidt had to calculate and budget, and even if he could not do formal arithmetic—we don't know if he could or couldn't—he would have to be competent in the carpenter's material mathematics. And for him to plan and execute even a simple structure, use hand tools effectively, solicit and coordinate aid— well, we get a sense of all that is required from our time in Jerry Devries's workshop.

Taylor does not tell us if Schmidt is literate, but does note that many of the laborers "were foreigners and unable to read and write." If Schmidt were illiterate, did he, like Tony Meraglio, develop informal literate networks to take care of personal and civic needs? We know that ethnic communities were rich in fraternal organizations—for Tony it was the nearby Sons of Italy—that served as places of entertainment, but also as sites of political discussion and the exchange of news about the old country. Literate members would write letters, read newspapers aloud, both in their native language and in English, and act as linguistic and culture brokers with mainstream institutions. The parish church or synagogue was another source of exposure to literate practices and social exchange, and, for some, a place of reflection. Though Bethlehem Steel and the Pennsylvania Railroad machine shops were not yet sites of significant union activity, labor unrest had already erupted in some sectors of steel and rail, and concerns about safety, work conditions, and the length of the workday were in the air. Though Schmidt and Tony were not union members, they might well have heard the early rumblings about these issues and would have been interested in them, might have talked about them to others in the yard, the saloon, the neighborhood. The point is that one cannot assume—as so many have—that the men looking back at us impassively from those photographs of the open ditch or the pouring of fiery steel, faded, blurring to silver, had no mental life, were sluggish, dull, like oxen.

This assumption is not only historically suspect, it also serves us poorly now. It contributes to the longstanding belief articulated by John Hoerr in the introduction that the wage worker lacks intellectual competence, and that belief, in turn, has contributed to the stratified work culture that has so bedeviled American industry over the last few decades. Even as some industries have seen a significant restructuring of the workplace—and with it a redefinition of the worker's capability—we continue to classify entire categories of work, and workers, as having less mental virtue, or as remnants of an outdated era. "Smart people," said one senior executive interviewed by the MIT Commission on Industrial Productivity, may just not be needed in manufacturing. And as we move to other kinds of contemporary work, consider how these beliefs—inflected with biases about immigration, class, the grime or cleanliness of a task—play out in the way, say, busboys or gardeners, cannery workers or domestics are perceived. As one of the maids in *Nickel and Dimed* succinctly puts it, "They think we're stupid."

❑

In one of those early firsthand accounts of physical work written by reform-minded academics, a sociologist named Amy Tanner concluded that her supervisor at the apartment house where she waitressed "sinned chiefly in [her] inability to imagine" what the waitress's work entailed. The portraits in this book provide the opportunity to engage in such an act of imagination. The tools of imagination have involved close observation of work and how it gets done, accounts of the work by people who do it, and a blending of disciplinary perspectives on it—how it came to be, the psychology, biomechanics, and aesthetics of its execution, the social context in which it unfolds.

Yet another device for seeing differently would be to consider higher-status kinds of work with the insights gained through blue-collar study. What might happen if we turn the epistemological tables, look not at the waitress or plumber through the lens of white-collar achievement, but, rather, look at work at the other end of the occupational scale with a waitress's or plumber's knowledge in mind? It was this idea that led me to spend a summer studying the education of general surgeons—work that involves manual skill but is high in status—while I was also observing young carpenters learning their craft. I wanted to understand, as best as I could, surgeons' practice on their own terms, but wanted to look, as well, for what cognitive scientist Rogers Hall calls "points of contact" between quite different kinds of activity. I am not suggesting—and I want to be clear about this—that surgery is parallel to carpentry or plumbing or styling hair. In addition to their typical risks and consequences, they are different on many levels: the knowledge base, the number and complexity of the variables involved, the amount of training required, both the material compensation and the symbolism that surround them. It would be simplistic and reductive to equate them. But if we give the kinds of physical work we've been observing the credit they're due and bring their lessons to bear on other work of different occupational status, we might catch instructive glimpses of similitude, resonances at the level of hand, eye, and brain.

Why is it important to catch these resonances and reflect on them? For reasons not unrelated to our reimagining of Schmidt: a further attempt to correct a deficit-oriented perception of entire occupational categories and, hand in glove, to appreciate the degree to which powerful techniques and strategies of mind and body are manifest in a wide sweep of work. We as a society have developed a popular occupational vocabulary that leads us to make easy but substantial distinctions between work of body and brain, of white collar and blue—these days expressed as the new knowledge work versus old-style industry and service. Neck up and neck down. While these distinctions surely have meaning in terms of status and income, they may be less definitive than we think and may blind us to commonalities in the way different kinds of work actually get done at the level of immediate, day-to-day practice. We gain, I believe, a richer appreciation of competent performance, a broader sense of it, by observing, for example, the sequencing and pacing of tasks in a range of occupational contexts, or the strategic combining of the senses in service of both the tradesperson's and the surgeon's diagnosis. So, it is the fledgling carpenters and electricians, my uncles Frank and Joe, Rose Meraglio Rose who breed the conviction that leads me to the stool alongside Ronald Tompkins, MD, the two of us watching on his computer screen a laparoscopic gallbladder surgery.

◻

"See, he's pulling away the fat and connective tissue that obscures the cystic artery and the cystic duct." I lean in, watching the instrument gently tug at and lay back the tissue; Tompkins's finger guides my sight to the artery and duct, exposed now. I see them. That morning, he had me test the instruments myself on a display, and, try as I might, I went wildly far and wide over the mark. I ask him about the touch this work takes, the developed manual finesse. He laughs. "I remember telling the guy who taught me that it's like trying to eat spaghetti with chopsticks—and doing it by looking in a mirror over your head!" The week before I had viewed the same surgery with a first-year resident. "It's very difficult," he explained, "because your arc of movement is exaggerated, a slight movement of your hand will result in a pretty significant movement of the instrument." Watching the sure moves on the screen, I'm struck by the retraining of hand and eye these extensions of hand and eye require.

Ron Tompkins has been a surgeon for thirty-nine years, was chief of General Surgery here at UCLA. He has been my guide through this medical world, introducing me to residents and other

senior surgeons and arranging entry to instructional and assessment settings. We sit before the screen close to the end of my time
in the medical center, trying to pull together some of what I've
learned.

The surgeon's instrument is moving onto some small vascular
structures. "See these little vessels right here," Tompkins continues. "They're coming out of the liver directly into the gallbladder."
Again his finger guides me. "They're tiny, but they bleed like hell if
you don't cauterize them. That's what he's doing now." And a tiny
puff of smoke comes off the vessel.

I ask Tompkins about the anatomy here. That first-year resident
could recognize basic structures, but was still learning about detail
and variation. He spoke as well about the difference between learning the anatomy from a textbook or even from a cadaver—which is
inert, bloodless, without pulsation—and elaborating and refining
one's knowledge through the living human body. "Ducts in the
biliary system," Tompkins agrees, "have a wide variation. And,
yes, a textbook may have a chart of twenty variations, but then
you'll go in and find a misplaced artery." He continues, explaining
the importance of hands-on experience, guided by more senior
surgeons—"no, don't feel down there, feel up here"—integrating
textbook and laboratory knowledge with this knowledge of how
things actually feel and look.

Tompkins pauses the CD and talks a bit about the importance of
visualizing the anatomy, speaking almost geographically about the
interior of the body, in terms of landmarks and signposts and
planes of tissue. (One of Tompkins's colleagues speculated with
me that surgeons "think graphically ... have a lot of images
stored.") Vision is also crucial in assessing pathology. One of the
residents I interviewed described his first encounter with abdomi-
nal surgery, where the supervising surgeon said, "Oh, this looks
great," but to the resident "it looks like this nasty, open wound."

Over time, however, the resident noted, "you develop an eye for what looks good and what doesn't. . . . You get to the point where you feel comfortable looking at something and evaluating it." As happens with immersion in other kinds of work, the young surgeon's perception is becoming more disciplined.

This visual and topographical orientation interacts with touch, and, turning attention back to the gallbladder procedure progressing now on the screen, Tompkins notes the physical limitations in current laparoscopic technique. "You lose that tactile sense that a lot of us have grown up with. You might be looking at something on the anterior surface, but you need to know what's behind it, so you get your fingers behind there and you feel: does it feel like a tumor, or a lymph node, or does it feel like a blood vessel—you know, you can feel the pulsation." I'm reminded here of the expert plumber "seeing" with his fingers as he feels structures that are hidden from sight. If the surgeon who speculated about a storehouse of images is right, I suspect that there is, in a surgeon's knowledge, a storehouse of the feel of things as well. In a sense, the geographical language Tompkins and company use is not metaphorical. The surgeon's knowledge of anatomy has to be physical. He or she will be working in tissue, moving it, tugging on it, cutting into it. Knowing is visual, tactile, practical. But, and this recalls my attempt in the chapter on the young carpenters to complicate easy distinctions between abstract and concrete knowledge, what is seen and felt is freighted with meaning, and abstractions about physiology or pathology are useless unless embodied. This bears resemblance to—but is not the same as—a distinction made by some psychologists between procedural knowledge (knowing how to do something) and declarative knowledge (knowing about something), but here, I believe, there is an intermingling rather than a distinguishing between the two. One thinks one's way through an operation by feel and image as much as by proposition.

I want to dwell a bit longer on this blending of the ideational and the tactile, for, in educational and occupational discourse, the conceptual is so often separated from the physical—and given more status. About a year before my time in the medical center, I observed the training of physical therapists, a different field of health care that also requires manual skill, but in a way that integrates, no, *fuses* touch and concept. Take, for example, the key notion of resistance.

Put simply, *resistance* refers to the stiffness of a musculoskeletal structure—the degree of flexibility or fluidity of movement of a knee or vertebrae—and a physical therapist tests resistance by manipulating the structure by hand through its potential range of motion. Resistance is a concept of key diagnostic importance, for it provides a way to understand and convey how severely a patient's mobility is restricted and provides information, tactile data, that contributes to diagnosis and treatment. Physical therapy students first learn about resistance in coursework and textbooks, but then must blend book knowledge with clinical experience for resistance to become more than an inert concept, to be truly known and to be of use. The effective assessment of resistance requires that the physical therapist's manual technique—the positioning and motion of hands and body—be skillful and adroit; otherwise the inefficiencies in the therapist's own movements will contaminate the information sought about the patient's range of motion. The therapist's body, then, not only provides the means of treatment but also becomes the instrument that receives information from the patient's body. The therapist's hands are both tool and gauge.

As therapists train, their tactile sense of resistance becomes more discriminating. And one of the things that makes the development of this discrimination difficult is the number of musculoskeletal structures involved, each with its own range of motion—from the limited movement of spiral vertebrae to the wide swing of the shoulder. A therapist must also gain a sense of the range of normal variation, person by person. As one experienced therapist explained it: "You need to get a feel for all the feels. Then you'll form an idea. . . . You need to get a sense in your hand." Resistance, truly known, is an average of feels, a tactile abstraction, a kinesthetic concept. It's quite hard, here—as it has been in a number of the occupations we've observed so far—to separate hand from idea.

Let us now return to Dr. Tompkins's narration. At various stages of the gallbladder surgery, Tompkins has been talking about the importance of technique—in laparoscopic or open procedure— and the interplay of technique and the body. The importance of "being gentle on the tissue . . . knowing what tissue will take and what it won't take." And though direct touch is critical, surgeons, with experience, develop the ability to feel through their instruments. As we saw with the developing tradespersons, the skillful use of the tool provides feedback to the hand. It is not surprising, given their stage of development, that the first-year residents I interviewed spoke at length about matters of technique. They talked about the many instruments, learning their names and their histories, learning how best to hold and manipulate them, the different opinions one gets from supervising physicians, how you weigh these opinions and integrate them to get at *your* skill. The scalpel held lightly but firmly, the appropriate pressure on tissue. There is the use of the needle, how you drive it, the motion you make. And the tension on the suture, the tying of a knot, how much of the tail of the knot to cut, how that length varies by material. They described one surgeon who will take hold of your hand, show you how to position it, where exactly to put your finger on an instrument, the proper rotation of your wrist. And they talked about tricks of the trade, their value, the good feeling of learning the effective, handy technique that makes their lives easier and signals membership in a surgical tradition. Mastering all this, the residents told me, is anxious, frustrating, at times humiliating, work. But when you begin to get it, begin to *feel* it—then there's the thrill of adroit, purposeful action, the fluent use of tools, a skill encoded in your body. I think of carpenter Jeff Taylor's observation quoted a few chapters back: "At a certain point, upon a day, you almost become the work, a moving and cognitive part of the tool in your own hand."

Beyond technique, or, more precisely, developing from it, is a competence we've seen before: the ability to manage the steps in a process. Not only getting each technical move right, but arranging the moves properly and fluidly. I had the opportunity to observe more experienced, fourth-year residents operating on a series of plastic models—removing an embolism, resecting a colon—and, to a person, each commented on the challenge, at their stage, of knowing what to do next, and next—each necessary step anticipated and followed in order—and what decisions to make when there is no supervising surgeon present to guide them. ("Assisted performance," said one senior surgeon, "can hide incompetence.") This is a key developmental juncture in a surgeon's professional life. The evaluation form for these simulated operations included categories for the economy of movement and the flow of the operation—for rhythm, timing, sequencing. This fluidity, in part, results from simple material adjustments and those tricks of the trade—holding an instrument one way rather than another, positioning a clamp just so—but also emerges from the quality of the on-the-spot decisions the surgeon makes. Though surgical procedures involve predictable sequences of steps, one must continually respond to variations in the patient's anatomy, the residue of trauma or prior surgeries, the surgeon's own mistakes—a nick, a clumsy move— and the unexpected responses of the patient's body. As with the other kinds of work we've seen, effective decision making requires not only a repertoire of skillful routines but also a developed sense of how to modify routines in order to gain a desired effect, a technical suppleness.

The surgeon on the screen is bringing things to a close. I ask Dr. Tompkins what might have happened if, say, the gallbladder had been in an odd position or if the surgeon had run into scar tissue from a previous surgery. "You've got to be prepared for these things," he says, "and you've got to be able to judge when it's not safe to continue this laparoscopic procedure and convert to open surgery. That can be a psychological problem for some surgeons—younger ones particularly—because they feel that if they can't complete it that somehow their skill level is low, and people will talk about them. But it's not a failure to convert to an open procedure. It's just good judgment."

Ron Tompkins continues to talk about judgment. Tompkins is a low-key kind of guy, carries with him his small-town-in-Ohio origins, but the topic of judgment catches him, and he turns it over and over as we talk. It is a topic that other senior surgeons I met focus on as well—perhaps the most pressing issue as they attempt to train young surgeons.

Good surgical judgment, they tell me, involves the information one has about the patient. And it involves what one knows about the procedure in question—what's been published about it, what techniques detailed, what probabilities of good outcome. This book knowledge, as we've been seeing, is augmented, revised, made incarnate through experience—yours or another's. Are you in a position to consult, is a colleague close by, or available by phone? "I get calls all the time," Tompkins notes, "from surgeons who are in the middle of an operation. They'll say, you know, 'I've never run into this before, what would you do?' And sometimes I'm able to say, 'Well, I've seen it a couple of times, and this is what I did, and it worked out all right.' " This business of consulting brings up several key issues having to do with one's psychology and character.

Do you know your limitations? If surgery involves, as one writer puts it, "a practical-minded obsession," doing and doing and doing a task, and replaying one's doing of it, until mastering it, then it also involves being clear-eyed about what one cannot do. In his study of the training of surgical residents, *Forgive and Remember*, Charles L. Bosk suggests that it is not surgical error per se that marks someone as a poor surgeon—anyone can err—but rather how the person handles error, accepts responsibility for it, evaluates it, sets out to correct it. A surgeon, observes Dr. Tompkins, has to be supremely confident to do the work—and part of that confidence is a protection against the emotional weight of disease—but also has to be aware of his or her limitations . . . a phrase Tompkins uses repeatedly.

Surgical judgment emerges from a physical knowledge of anatomy, from technical finesse, from procedural skill. And, as with so many of the kinds of work we've been observing, important craft values are woven through this competence: persistence, self-monitoring, knowing limits. "You know," Tompkins reflects, leaning back from the computer and turning directly to me, "you can talk about judgment and describe it more than you can define it. You can describe situations where it comes into play, and by describing those situations, then you can, kind of, put flesh on the thing." Drawing on a blend of knowledge, skill, and character, surgical judgment is, if I understand it, contextual and in the moment. And though it involves abstractions (for example, probabilities of outcomes or generalizations about disease processes), it is also profoundly immediate and physical. There is a tendency in twentieth-century intellectual life to create mathematical or logical models to represent reasoning and decision making. I think it would be pretty difficult to model surgical judgment. Surgical judgment provides yet another example of the way dichotomies such as concrete versus abstract and technique versus reflection break down in practice. The surgeon's judgment is simultaneously technical and deliberative, and that mix is the source of its power.

☐

Reimagining the mental life of the laborer Schmidt and considering general surgery—or physical therapy—as examples of knowledge embodied and materialized help us complicate generalizations, both historical and contemporary, about categories of work, the people who do the work, and what the work requires. Another type of work comes to mind, quite different from surgery or physical therapy, work I know intimately: teaching. In discussions of the new information society, teaching is categorized as "high knowledge" work, and, in many ways, it clearly is, requiring disciplinary knowledge acquired through formal schooling. But consider how much of the work, particularly in the elementary and secondary grades, calls for a wide array of physical and social skills, particularly when it is done well.

There is a range of teaching styles, of course, and grade level, subject matter, and local cultural norms—not to mention the specifics of one's personal history and training—and all affect the way one does the work. Regardless of these differences, however, teaching is inherently performative. So the way one locates oneself in a room and moves about it is important, as are pacing, tempo, gesture, and the use of one's voice. For many teachers, materials are also critical—from illustrated books, to watercolors and acrylics, to a pulley and an incline—and the manner of their use matters, the tricks of the trade. And how does one use space, organize desks, chairs and tables, displays? Then there is the social choreography, the ways one encourages or constrains student interaction. Consider the woodshop teacher Jerry Devries, for example, pairing a less skilled student with one more skilled, or directing one student's question to another, or sending a kid across the room to work on a peer's project.

Reading the student audience is critical, and, in the best of cases, involves social skills and cultural understandings gained to a degree, perhaps, through formal schooling, but developed more often via lived experience, formal and informal apprenticeships, mentoring. How do you engage the room? When and how do you ask questions? How long do you stay with a student or move on? When and how do you assert authority? The whole issue of authority is exceedingly complex and emerges only in part from the formal knowledge one pursues; it emerges more profoundly from an ethic of care, from moral bearing, from values made manifest in action.

There is more to list, but I'll stop here to make a broader point. Though traditional teacher education programs would separate out some of the above from knowledge of subject matter and teach it as classroom management or methods, such a separation says more about the vagaries of ed school development and disciplinary specialization than it does about the way competent teaching gets done. Pacing, organizing space, and so on are not, in practice, ancillary to subject matter knowledge; in the work of the effective teacher they blend inextricably with subject matter, become what educational psychologist Lee Shulman calls the "wisdom of practice," in a sense *are* the subject matter.

Of course, the teacher is schooled in child development and reading theory or in disciplines like literature or mathematics. But teachers do things with this knowledge. Knowledge gains its pedagogical meaning in use; it is organized, selected, augmented for a social purpose. The analogies or metaphors one selects, the illustrations, what one decides to play up or play down, one's familiarity with the typical misunderstandings of key concepts or errors of execution—all this emerges in contact with others. Subject matter becomes the means to engage the world of the student, the terms of a particular kind of cognitively oriented social interaction. It's not just that the effective teacher is alert socially—good at reading cues, anticipating responses, and the like—it's also that the social purpose of the work transforms the meaning of one's knowledge and, I believe, the way it becomes organized and understood by the teacher over time. (Perhaps this is analogous to the surgeon's and the physical therapist's knowledge of anatomy; it transforms from a memorization of textbook fact to a mode of action.) The richness of a teacher's knowledge enhances the repertoire of engagement with students, and, conversely, this relation adds a layer of meaning, a human dynamism, to disciplinary knowledge. Teaching, then, can be fruitfully understood as a particular kind of knowledge work that manifests significant elements of craft and service work, knowledge understood in a broader way, embodied, enacted, relational.

◻

Examining the surgeon's—or physical therapist's or teacher's—activity through the perspective gained from studying manual and service work has provided a conceptual reach that privilege obscures. Mind vibrant across a range of occupations. What we see, though, is qualified quickly, sadly by the sheer, cold economic distinctions between occupations. Material reality reasserts itself. I would watch the young carpenters in the morning and then in the afternoon drive across town, northeast to west, across class divides to the surgical residents and their teachers. Each kind of work was powerful on its own terms—the majesty of fashioning the environment, the science and mystery of strategically opening the body—but also resonant through the shared dynamic of hand and brain.

Yet the future of these two groups extends thus: on average, the surgeon will earn at least five times the income of the carpenter. Their lives will vary significantly by physical demand—as carpenter Jeff Taylor observes, there are no old house framers—vary by job stability, by benefits, by access to resources and respect, by social standing.

The way work gets defined, then, has huge material consequences—and social and civic consequences, as well. To be sure, these definitions are based on some significant differences in the work itself, and in our society, and in many others, a price follows these distinctions. This is not the place to attempt a detailed analysis of the occupational categories that codify the distinctions; such an analysis would involve multiple disciplines and topics. But I do want to raise two issues about the categories that are relevant to our line of inquiry.

First, as a number of historians and sociologists have documented, occupational distinctions and categories are influenced by interest groups and the economic and political forces of the time. Consider the classification of manual work as skilled, semiskilled, or unskilled. This labeling is commonplace and consequential, yet, as labor historian David Montgomery observes, such distinction is "itself a cultural boundary that shift[s] in response to workplace struggles." It was partly out of craft traditions, for example, and partly as an attempt to protect their own status and job control in the face of mechanization that many late-nineteenth-century machinists' unions excluded entire categories of workers as unskilled. One machinists' lodge resisted the admission of boilermakers because, as they put it, such admission "would not be advancing in that social and intellectual scale that is desirable." Another example comes from welding. In an attempt to settle early-twentieth-century disputes among various railroad craft unions, the American Federation of Labor and, later, the U.S. secretary of labor declared that welding is "a tool rather than a trade." In effect, this judgment stripped from welders any claim of special skill and prevented them from organizing as a separate trade. According to one historian of the field, the judgment "has probably done more damage to the welding industry than any other single event." Clearly there are distinctions among kinds of manual work— distinctions emerging from requisite training, dexterity, modes of problem solving, and so on—but how those distinctions are encoded and what they mean is influenced by a wide arc of social and political forces.

The second point to make about occupational categories is this: given their modern origins in industrial psychology and related fields, they tend to be developed from analyses of work by outside observers or from the examination of documents like job descriptions. Such analyses can yield detailed categories—and the recent revision of the Department of Labor's Standard Occupational Classification System is remarkable in its level of refinement. But these analyses can also diminish or miss entirely characteristics of the work in question, not immediately evident to the outside observer, but known to the practitioner, in the flow of work. The Department of Labor's discussion of surgeons, for example, lists the importance of shifting between different sources of information, but does not give a sense of the integration required of the tactile, visual, and conceptual. The discussion of waiters and waitresses correctly identifies *memorization* and *manual dexterity* as important abilities, but rates *coordination* (adjusting actions in relation to others' actions) as a skill fairly low in importance, and *negotiation* (bringing others together and trying to reconcile differences) as not important at all, a zero on a scale of one to one hundred.

Now, within the terms and context of this classification system, the Department of Labor analysts are making a legitimate point about waiters and waitresses. They are more or less independent agents, and their work requires neither a formal coordination of effort nor a mediating of disparate views. Waitresses are not office managers. But when you gain access to the insider's view, the degree of informal coordination and negotiation—especially in a busy restaurant—can be significant, emerging quickly, unpredictably, in a system that, as we saw in the first chapter, is rich in potential conflict. My point is not to deny the very real differences between restaurant work and office management, but rather to illustrate the way occupational categories can limit our understanding of those qualities of work that are less formal, not codified, or lie beneath the level of observation.

I find myself thinking of Joe Meraglio's dictum that there's no such thing as unskilled work. Sure, building a flight of stairs involves more variables, techniques, and training than does digging a ditch or hoisting freight. But even the most basic labor requires thought and technique if it's to be done effectively and without injury—as anyone knows, quips longshoreman Reg Theriault, who has just got through moving his first refrigerator. In fact, Theriault's account of physical work, *How to Tell When You're Tired*, could be read as an insider's catalog of how to push, lift, and stack wisely. It's interesting to note, recalling Schmidt, Tony Meraglio, and F. W. Taylor's clipboard, that these physical techniques typically do not come from time-and-motion experts but are developed by the people themselves who do the work and are passed on from more seasoned workers to newcomers. The wisdom of heavy lifting.

You can't deny the importance of perspective here. Where you grow up, in what circumstances, what you can see up close, what you come to know. Growing up, I saw a lot of people doing things that took know-how, finesse, a touch, some thought: a guy standing before a load of crates, still, thinking the move through before starting, or a waitress handling the quick demands of the counter, orchestrating satisfaction. I saw poor work, too, or should I say, learned to see it through the evaluations of those around me, judgments of ineptitude or carelessness. People commented on how hard someone worked, or the look of a job when done, or the quality of a repair, saying that it was skillful or half-assed or "Mickey Mouse." "Your uncle Joe busts his ass," people would say, or "Your mother's a damned good waitress." The sad thing, I see now, was that these judgments could also be skewed by the speaker's own biases—about race, about gender—by his or her own desire to exclude.

Mixed with talk about the quality of work were testaments to wiliness, to outsmarting the boss, to beating or sabotaging the production schedule. But, by and large, the tone of all this was different, not so much one of admiration as of indictment, an assertion of will. The work these people did took its toll, was exhausting and dangerous. Interwoven with assessment of endurance and competence there were tales of damage: a finger, an eye, a burn seared across the calf, the forearm, the cheek. And the work, often, was unsteady, layoffs, plant closings, fluctuations that pulled the rug right out from under you. And, then, there were the injuries of class; the shit you had to take. No wonder that through all this talk ran a refrain about one's kids doing easier work, steadier, the desire for a generational shift to white collar. "Boys, the family luck has run out," a steelworker from Bethlehem—where Schmidt had toiled generations before—tells his sons. "You better get an education because there's not going to be a job like I had or your grandfather had."

Joe Meraglio is proud that he was able to send his kids to college. Like so many Americans of his generation, he embraces, even in the face of economic fluctuation, the credo of social mobility— work hard and you will do better—and believes in using the benefits of mobility to improve the prospects of your children. And, like so many, he sees education as the current springboard for opportunity. It's a belief that for some time has led the nation to support public education: education as engine of mobility. In sending his kids to college, though, Joe Meraglio locates himself in a tension familiar to many Americans: on the one hand, a belief in advancement through education and a pride in making it possible, but, on the other, worry that more advanced education will change things, make kids grow distant, put on airs, at the worst, regard the lives of their parents with disdain. This tension is real, though it is at times overplayed or simplified in literary accounts of working-class kids going away to college. In reality, region, ethnicity, gender, the particulars of one's family history make the relations between generations complex, thick with compromise and negotiation. Still, the tension exists.

This tension—familiar, close, human—is coupled with another in American social history, one extending back to the early Republic: the tension between practical life, experience, and common sense versus schooling, book learning, and intellectual pursuits. This opposition overlaps with many of the dichotomies we've been discussing, though the American experience has tended, in some eras and in some domains, to value the practical and experiential over the schooled and theoretical. Richard Hofstadter's classic *Anti-Intellectualism in American Life* is a chronicle of this antagonism, and of the gradual ascendance of school-based expertise in the nation's culture. This tension has its intimate expression, too, poignantly rendered by a friend who writes to me of his father, a skilled tradesperson who "did it all, plumbing, electrical, masonry, carpentry, even cars, the whole bit. But what arrogance went with that, what despising of my book smarts. He made me see myself for years as a cretin." Bookish folk fought back, of course. Look at the long line of withering portraits in our literature of the practical man, Sinclair Lewis's Babbitt foremost among them. And, for that fact, on quite a different front, you could read F. W. Taylor's treatise on scientific management, with which I opened this chapter, as an argument for the superiority of a learned, detached, academic approach to practical matters, a defense of the knowledge of "scientific laws"—which, unfortunately, grinds up the laborer Schmidt in its rhetorical mill. The over-the-top quality of some of Taylor's language is, perhaps, evidence of the hard sell he felt he had to make.

People in Joe Meraglio's shoes, then, live amid the push and pull of these historical antagonisms. Joe believes deeply in the value of his work and in what it yields for him and his family. He is proud, as well, of all he's learned: the school of hard knocks, maybe, but a school open to a guy like him. In line with another American dynamic, however, he wants his kids to be freed from this work—via a mechanism, though, that sparks its own suspicions. Talking about a new generation of foremen straight out of college, Joe says, "they have no idea what it feels like to work on that line." Joe expresses a working-class resentment, perhaps, but he's defending what he knows and how he came to know it; yet he voices his complaint in the same stretch of the interview in which he expresses pleasure in sending his kids to college.

It is this kind of nuance that tends to get leveled out in the binary oppositions that have been my concern:

brain—hand
abstract—concrete
intellectual—practical
academic—vocational
pure—applied
reflective—technical
new knowledge work—old industrial work
neck up—neck down

These each have their own lineage, but play off of one another. They are commonplace in educational and occupational discourse, in policy talk, in opinion pieces and editorials. They can be useful as shorthand, quick conceptualizations that enable us to follow a line of thought, make distinctions, wrap our minds around things. But they can also compartmentalize thought. For it is interaction, interweaving, ambiguity, fuzzy borders, that more characterizes human activity—and surely where mind and work are concerned. The binaries make us think we understand multifaceted historical, social, and psychological phenomena better than we do, and—my concern here—they limit our ability to see, and to honor, the considerable play of mind in physical work. Admittedly, it's hard to avoid the terms, so strongly do they inflect our language. I use them throughout *The Mind at Work*, though, I hope, in a way that complicates them.

One of the most influential of the dichotomies above, particularly in the lives of young people, has been the distinction between the academic and the vocational. This distinction characterized the high school curriculum for much of the past century and has defined, therefore, entire courses of study. So much follows: the kind of instruction one receives, the crowd one associates with, the status one feels in the yards and corridors. Though it has been the focus of significant reform over the past two decades, vocational education—and, more generally, the divide between the academic and the vocational curriculum—has been one of the most long-standing and visible institutional manifestations of our culture's beliefs about hand and brain, mind and work. Thus, I think, it has a great deal to teach us about the contradictions and consequences of those beliefs.

HAND AND BRAIN IN SCHOOL

The Paradox of Vocational Education

When I went to high school, students were placed, upon entrance, into one of three or four curricular "tracks." Most readers beyond their thirties will remember them. There were, typically, an academic or college preparatory track (and, in some schools, honors or advanced placement courses); one or two variations of a general education track; and a vocational track. Like many children of the working class, I began my high school career in the vocational track. What makes my story unusual, particularly for the time, was that I was moved out of it and into college prep. I got to see both worlds. Though I had little sense at sixteen as to what this move would mean for my future, I could certainly tell that the courses were different and that, well, it somehow felt different to be in school.

Tracking developed as the comprehensive high school—the large high school most of us know—was taking shape in the early decades of the twentieth century. Before that, the high school was modeled on the college curriculum, what we would recognize as academic or liberal studies: branches of mathematics, Classical and foreign languages, life and physical sciences, history, English, and rhetoric. So students in a given high school took more or less the same subjects. There was some social-class mixing among these students, within a restricted range—the children of skilled tradespersons, merchants, and lawyers comingling—but few from the poor or the wealthy. It is important to note, though, that by 1890, only 6.7 percent of American fourteen- to seventeen-year-olds were enrolled in high school. These numbers would change dramatically during the first decades of the twentieth century, and these changes would form the demographic backdrop for curriculum tracking. Tracking was the school's response to huge numbers of students who differed in preparation, interest, and aspiration—an attempt to match students with a course of study that fit their varied achievements and prospects. As educational researchers Norton Grubb and Marvin Lazerson point out, this differentiating of the curriculum helped make American schooling more accessible— there's a place for everyone—but in the process made the quality of participation highly unequal.

Here is how tracking worked. Through some criterion, or mix of criteria—tests of achievement or ability (in my high school, I believe it was an IQ test), prior record and teacher recommendation, and sometimes parental or student choice—students were placed into different curricular tracks. Depending on the school, it might have been possible for students to take some courses together, across tracks, though in my school, we remained in separate groups, even for PE. All high school students are required to take a certain number of academic courses—English, math, social studies—and these courses were among the most tracked; the content and mode of instruction of, say, an English course taken by vocational students would typically be quite different from that offered to those preparing for college. (In my case, I moved from a curriculum heavy with grammar worksheets and occasional short writing assignments to a Homer-through-Hemingway reading list and critical essays on literary and philosophical themes.) And, for those students in vocationally oriented courses, there was not much likelihood that kids from the academic track would be working alongside them. Since placement in these tracks correlated with social class, the result was distinct educational experiences that varied by parental income.

The practice of tracking has been the focus of significant reform over the past two or three decades, and, more recently, vocational education has also come under reform scrutiny. Though the grouping of students—by previous record, or by a measure of ability, or both—continues, most high schools no longer structure curriculum as single, contained tracks. Students can, at least in theory, choose among a wider array of courses. Typically, then, there is no longer a vocational track, though there are vocational courses—from clerical to carpentry to cosmetology. Enrollments in some vocational courses have been declining, however, and there is an ongoing debate as to whether or not VocEd provides useful preparation for today's economy. As a result, a number of traditional VocEd programs have been scaling back, shifting toward new technology, or creating course sequences that combine academic with vocational material. One indicator of these changes has been an alteration in name. In some policy and professional circles, vocational education is now called career and technical education. For purposes of clarity, I will use the older, more familiar name throughout. And I will say more about the VocEd reforms shortly.

Although the official policy of placing students into an exclusively vocational track has been largely abandoned, there remain patterns of inequality in the courses students take. I certainly see these patterns in the schools I visit. Vocational courses still tend to be the domain of working-class students and students of color, and some of the courses exhibit the same limiting characteristics that led to the need for reform in the first place.

There is a dimension to this inequality that is central to the concerns of this book. It is summed up by the authors of a recent historical analysis from the National Center for Research in Vocational Education: "[V]ocational teachers emphasized job-specific skills to the almost complete exclusion of theoretical content. One result was that the intellectual development of vocational students tended to be limited at a relatively early age." This, I think, is a remarkable statement. We charge the school with cognitive development, yet in the very curriculum that places work at its core, we find a restriction of intellectual growth. The report captures the fundamental paradox of vocational education as it has been practiced in the United States: its diminishment of the intellectual dimension of common work and of the people who do it. This state of affairs provides an extended illustration of the degree to which the hand-brain division runs deep and wide in our social and institutional life. To understand the paradox, we need to know more about the history of VocEd.

❑

Tasks and lessons drawn from the world of physical work have been incorporated into the curriculum since the nineteenth century. One motive for these lessons was middle-class alarm over the rise of the factory and the mechanization of work—and the social conditions wrought by these changes. To include material drawn from work—primarily from the trades and agriculture—would, it was hoped, preserve respect for the value of labor and for traditional notions of the work ethic, a moral outcome.

A different, though not entirely unrelated, set of motives had to do with the content of curriculum, and with pedagogy itself. Influenced by both European and American educational theorists, and reflecting larger cultural tensions between "practical" and "bookish" pursuits, some reformers sought a curriculum that engaged a wider range of the child's physical and mental capacities. The reformers also saw standard classroom practice as repetitive and sterile. "Throw in the fire," wrote one advocate, "those modern instruments of torture, the spelling and defining books." Some level of manual activity would engage hand as well as brain, make the curriculum more meaningful, and better prepare young people for modern industrial life.

Physical work was also a part of the curriculum in some utopian communities and schools for the ministry. It was an element in the remedial and redemptive program in reform schools for urban youth. And it was central to the restrictive curriculum given to Native Americans and African Americans in segregated institutions. But for some advocates of "manual training," lessons involving physical tasks were seen as part of every child's curriculum. Students were not to be separated into a "manual" or an "academic" course of study; everyone could benefit from learning about mechanical principles, the properties of materials, and the use of tools.

The moral and educational goals behind such pursuits continue to affect discussion of these matters down to our time. Consider these remarks from a recent essay written by a *Los Angeles Times* journalist. Celebrating the "honor and satisfaction in creating things with one's hands," the author asks, "Shouldn't we make room in our schools to expand students' experience . . . to reconnect their hands to their minds . . . ?" And, "What our schools teach—and increasingly what we demand in the way of test scores—is growing regrettably narrower and more conformist." There is resonance here with certain of those nineteenth-century reformers: concern about a limited curriculum and a desire for a wider range of human engagement.

The history that follows the early reforms—stretching from the late 1890s to World War I—is consequential, and will lead to a fully developed vocational education program. Essentially what happens is this: the attempt to transform the general curriculum through manual tasks fades and a movement begins to create an "industrial education" that is separate from the standard academic course of study. The history is fascinating—if, at times, disturbing—and demonstrates the truth of an observation made by those who study curriculum reform: that any major change in curriculum represents the intersection of multiple social forces and, therefore, reflects concerns and debates going on in the culture at large.

Let's tease out some of these forces and concerns. First, there are the numbers: a growing urban—significantly immigrant—population combines with child labor and compulsory education laws to send many more children to the classroom for longer periods of time. This increase in numbers coincides with the era's changing notions of adolescence, family life, and schooling; with fears about immigrants and concerns about how to educate and socialize them; and with continuing anxiety about the social effects of mass industrialization—particularly labor unrest and the concentration of the urban poor.

There is also significant lobbying from business—via leadership and interest groups like the National Association of Manufacturers—to closely align school with work, emphasizing job training over liberal education. Though there were diverse voices in the business community, many connected vocational education with the promise of national economic development and with a conservative vision of the social order. Some powerful educational leaders—the president of Harvard among them—agreed, arguing that we need to "sort [pupils] by their evident or probable destinies" and prepare them to be "effective economic units." Organized labor was, at first, wary of such exclusionary vocational training, for they feared it would deprive working-class children of a full education and, as well, would generate a cadre of low-paid workers. (The American Federation of Labor had already labeled trade schools as "scab hatcheries.") Under the politically wily AF of L president Samuel Gompers, however, organized labor would eventually join and influence the shape and structure of the emerging vocational education enterprise—mandating, for example, that vocational training would not begin before a child's basic education had been secured and that labor would be represented on VocEd governing boards.

There were other elements in the development of vocational education. Proponents of child-study psychology and Progressive education, like some earlier critics, wanted to rethink the old-fashioned high school curriculum, finding it too tied to a dated Classical tradition and the collegiate course of study. But of particular interest here were those reformers who, following the mood of the times, were calling for more scientific and efficient administration of the schools (the educational equivalent of F. W. Taylor's "scientific management"). These calls for efficiency would intersect with the emerging discipline of mental measurement—the IQ test—leading to a systematic classifying of students through assessment of their abilities and life prospects. There was a good deal of educational talk about the limited mental capacity of various immigrant groups and working-class populations as well as judgments about some students being intellectually suited for abstract thought and others being "manually minded." Curricula would be developed suitable for each, leading to an effective, stratified society.

The vocational education movement would gain its national legitimization in 1917 via legislation sponsored by two Georgia congressmen: the Smith-Hughes Act. The legislation would significantly increase the professional ranks of vocational teachers and administrators, encourage the growth of VocEd teacher-training programs, and foster agricultural education and home economics. And, though local control was the norm, the new legislation— partially out of a desire to protect the burgeoning vocational programs from the traditional academic elite—would, in essence, mandate separate governing boards, funding streams, and instructional programs. This would institutionalize the academic-vocational divide at the administrative as well as the classroom level. Two years after its passage, all forty-eight states had, in some way, initiated vocationally oriented courses in line with Smith-Hughes guidelines. The VocEd program that I, that so many, would encounter was shaped here.

The basic stated goal of vocational education was to enable a broader range of young people to stay in school and secure a place in work and society. This goal emerged over time from a dynamic mix of cultural anxieties and social forces, demographic shifts, industrial transformation, and the interests of political, business, and educational elites. What is telling is that within the mix are assumptions about learning and instruction, mind and work, about the cognitive capacities of particular groups within the social order, and about the structure of the social order itself.

With this brief history in mind, let me return to the paradox of VocEd.

Though vocational education has been robust through much of the twentieth century—it has a commonsense quality to it as well as a powerful lobby—it has encountered opposition and critique on several fronts. John Dewey was among the first of many to raise concerns about its narrow focus on job training and its separation of young people essentially by social class. "Social predestination," he called it. And, ironically, by midcentury, several national studies were revealing that VocEd was not doing a very good job of preparing students for industry. One of the principal reasons was an unimaginative and restricted curriculum. As well, there was a mismatch between the curriculum and the workplace—and the changing nature of the workplace itself. The possibility that traditional vocational education was not transferring well to employment settings was vexing indeed, given VocEd's foundational claims of preparing young people for the world of work. Such concerns have been at the heart of more recent calls from government and industry to reform vocational education.

A further issue involved gender stereotyping and racial segregation. Girls were channeled into clerical courses (which, however, were successful in leading to employment) and into courses like home economics, which did little to prepare them for work outside of the domestic sphere—or domestic labor. Few women were placed in industrial training courses (though special training was made available in some states during World War II to meet emergency production needs). Black Americans, especially in the South, but not only there, were virtually excluded from many forms of mechanical and technical training. One Depression-era survey of eighteen states, for example, found only a single Black student (of 838 surveyed) enrolled in a welding program. Critics wondered if vocational education was creating employment opportunity or was reinforcing the prevailing social order and opportunity structure. Although vocational legislation in the 1960s and '70s—in the spirit of the times—addressed such discrimination, this concern remains today.

And there is another, not unrelated, matter of inequality. A long line of sociological studies—from A. B. Hollingshead's *Elmstown's Youth* to Jeannie Oakes's *Keeping Track*—demonstrates systematic bias at play in the way students get placed in various curricular tracks. (And in a posttracking environment, these biases continue to affect course placement and selection.) For all the administrative rationality and meritocratic logic of the differentiated curriculum, academic counseling can be irregular and inconsistent, can be affected by, among other things, parental power and teachers' and counselors' beliefs about race and about social class. There is troubling evidence, for example, that working-class and racial minority kids with records of achievement comparable to their mainstream peers will more frequently end up in general education or vocational courses. A further problem is that a course of study heavy in vocational classes yields not only different status within the school but also dramatically different educational resources and outcomes—an obvious one is that a traditional vocational curriculum will not provide the courses required to enter college. One of the early reservations about establishing a separate vocational curriculum was that it would institutionalize a dual system of education, segregating young people essentially by social class, creating a school system more European than American. This, pretty clearly, is what happened.

Finally, there are the intellectual limitations of vocational education—an issue underscored by the authors of the national report cited a few pages back. Criticism of the cognitive content of the VocEd curriculum—and there has been a lot of it over the century—has frequently come from those schooled in the humanities or the life and physical sciences. While their critique has merit, it also has an unfortunate quality to it. It is typically framed in the very terms that the VocEd community rejects, and that early legislation tried to protect against: a comparison with the college-prep course of study. Such critique privileges the academic over the vocational and plays into long-standing turf battles—and, one could argue, reinscribes class biases about manual and service work. These objections are, at the least, worth considering. What intrigues me, though, is that *within* the vocational education enterprise—on its own terms, not comparatively—there has been scant attention paid to the intellectual dimension of common work, to the cognitive possibility of the salon, the welding shop, the construction site.

Now, this is not to deny that many a vocational instructor has taught well and has made a difference in young people's lives. My stepfather, a very handy guy, locates the origins of his skill some sixty years ago with a Mr. Foster, his high school woodshop teacher, and one of the hair salon owners in chapter 2 got her start in a high school program. I also want to underscore the fact that some vocational teachers—such as the talented people we met earlier in this book—have concerned themselves with the full development of the students in their charge, have provided good counsel, and have structured students' experiences to foster both trade skill and a problem-solving cast of mind. When you get in close to good vocational instruction—just as when you get close to work done well—the intellectual content of the practice is clear, though it may not be expressed in typical academic terms.

Rather, my concern is with the core themes of the vocational education profession itself, the dominant discussions in its journals and conferences, its public face. At various points in its history—particularly when it has had to define itself and clarify its goals—vocational education has directly addressed the cognitive dimension of its course of study. But overall the treatment tends to be brief and intermittent. I surveyed a thirty-year span of the field's main journals, and though many topics were covered—from teacher training and development to current hot topics like high technology and school-to-work initiatives—overall there was limited attention paid to the kinds of intellectual activity detailed in the previous chapters. For example, I found only a handful of articles on the way students develop knowledge of a field, or on hypothesis testing and problem solving, or on the interplay of thought and action. The issues covered, for the most part, weren't framed in a way that gave one a sense of the cognitive base of the subjects students were taking. When topics were covered that had strong intellectual content—such as mathematics or communication— they tended to have a remedial focus, or they were a response to policy directives from outside the profession, like a Department of Labor report on the general cognitive demands of the new workplace. Individual teachers may acknowledge the thought that it takes to do work well, but if, in an educational context, the cognitive features of an entire field of study are muted, there will be intellectual and social consequences for the students involved.

In our historical overview of vocational education we saw some of the reasons that, I believe, underlie this culling out of intellectual concerns from VocEd. There was considerable effort that went into developing VocEd as a distinct educational program, separate from, even defined in opposition to, the academic curriculum. This separation was justified by the belief, a reasonable one at the time, that the fledging vocational education project would be overwhelmed and poached upon by the more powerful academic course of study if it did not have separate curricula, teacher career paths, professional organizations and venues, and funding mechanisms. But, as I noted, the separation was also justified by theories of intelligence that defined entire social groups as "hand-minded" and others as "abstract-minded." Combined with these theories were beliefs about the purpose of schooling: that the task of the efficient school system is to guide people into their likely place in the social order. So hand-minded—primarily immigrant and working class—children would be trained for manual work. These beliefs were woven through the organizational development of vocational education.

While the institutional separation of VocEd had its political and bureaucratic rationale, it also cemented in the deep biases of the culture about physical versus mental activity. Furthermore, there were no bridging mechanisms built in between the vocational and academic realms to enable creative interaction, to foster cross-disciplinary discussion that could expand and enlighten, for example, the use of tools or the development of literacy. I think here of something I saw at a Habitat for Humanity site that crystallized this issue for me. I was watching Scott Butler—the teacher we met in chapter 5—as he was guiding two of his students inserting windows into a house frame.

They have just placed an assembled window into its space in the frame. They are looking it over, eyeballing the edges, checking it with a spirit level. They're following procedure, and everything seems OK. They're ready to fasten the window in place. Mr. Butler takes a few easy steps toward them and asks them to come here a moment, to walk with him around to the other side of the window, inside the house. "Take a look from here," he says. The boys inspect the edge of the frame—and see the problem. The plywood that forms the frame on this side of the window assembly has been cut unevenly, and at several places there is not enough wood to receive the nails that the boys were about to drive from the other side. They are visibly struck by this, say they wouldn't have thought of this. But, geez, now that they see it. . . .

In many ways, this is a small thing. A further routine step in the procedure of window installation—though Mr. Butler sets it up nicely. But it also could be thought of as a metaphor for the vocational-academic divide. Though a routine move, and though utterly functional—you've got to see if your window assembly will be secure—this strategic shifting of physical location represented for me the shifting in perspective that is such a key element of intellectual development. It contributes to the solving of problems in many domains, to a more complex understanding of human behavior, to adopting a point of view in literature and the arts. A lot could emerge from this moment. The day-to-day at the Habitat job site was full of such episodes, and their cross-disciplinary potential was, for the most part, lost to the English teacher or the psychology teacher, sealed off by the physical and conceptual barriers in the curriculum.

The result is separate professional spheres, each narrowly defined. And it is the academic curriculum, not the vocational, that has gotten identified as the place where intelligence is manifest. Such separation can't help but play out on the ground. Play out in the way school people talk, in the formal and informal terms and categories they use. Thus a language of abstraction, smarts, big ideas surrounds the academic course of study, which is symbolically, structurally, and often geographically on the other side of the campus from the domain of the manual, the concrete, the practical, the gritty.

◻

As I noted earlier, the last two decades have seen a broad range of reforms aimed at the high school, and the issue of curricular tracking in general, and the vocational-academic divide in particular, has been integral to a number of them. Dissatisfaction with VocEd, has, for example, led to the most significant vocational legislation since Smith-Hughes in 1917, the Carl D. Perkins Vocational Education and Applied Technology Act of 1990. This act was followed by the less-sweeping but complementary School-to-Work Opportunities Act of 1994. (The school-to-work legislation expired in 2001 while the Perkins Act is facing contentious reauthorization as this book goes into print.) What makes this combined legislation particularly relevant to the discussion so far is its stress on amending existing programs or creating new ones to better integrate academic and vocational education, thus providing a richer range of options for careers or for further training or education. So, for example, preceding the Perkins Act, but spurred by it, are career academies (typically, small schools within schools) that, at their best, offer coordinated sequences of academic and vocational courses organized around an occupational theme. Thus, the chemistry course in a graphic arts academy that I visited a while back had students engaging concepts and problems related to ink, paper, and printing processes which carried over to their work in the graphic arts lab, where they were producing small books of essays they had written in their humanities course.

The new vocational legislation also provided incentives for school districts to establish effective pathways from secondary to postsecondary education; young people would be better prepared for and institutionally guided toward more advanced study or occupational training. Some of the courses in that graphic arts academy, for example, were structured so that they integrated trade skills with material that fulfilled college admissions requirements. Students could also elect courses at a nearby community college during their senior year, further directing them beyond their high school course of study.

Finally the legislation encouraged districts to develop systems to better integrate school and work. School-to-work programs have existed for a long time. At their least imaginative, they simply place kids in business settings where they perform low-level tasks with little educational content. But the new legislation encouraged the schoolhouse and workplace to become more porous, enhancing the curriculum with industry tasks and standards and providing at the job site apprentice-like supervision and instruction, and a fuller sense of an occupation's scope and sweep.

This legislation, especially the Perkins Act, was unusual in its emphasis on *both* academic and occupational competency—and for a broad range of American high schoolers. Its expansive and integrative impulse ran contrary to much earlier VocEd policy, and thus it and the reforms it encouraged are collectively of some educational importance. Yet, any reform movement produces widely varied results. As economist and educational researcher Norton Grubb concludes after a comprehensive review of this "new vocationalism" in the schools, many efforts are little more than minor adjustments to the status quo—adding a few written exams to an introduction to technology or slapping onto a course in fashion design a prepackaged basic math program. But some efforts are ambitious, involving a cross section of a school's faculty over many months in developing a curriculum that integrates academic and vocational material. And in a few cases, a visionary faculty uses VocEd reform as the occasion to reimagine the very structure of high school itself and with it the academic-vocational divide. Drawing both on John Dewey and on recent cognitive psychology, they develop curricula that merge rather than reinforce disciplines, that find in the occupational world rich educational content, that blend learning and doing through projects, public presentations, and portfolios of creative and scholarly work.

Unfortunately, such innovation is rare. Intellectual enrichment, when it occurs, is typically achieved by beefing up the vocational side of things with traditional academic content and courses. As a practical matter, this makes sense; if a primary goal of the reforms is to make more students eligible for college, then they need to have the prerequisite academic courses. But conceptually such practice doesn't move us much beyond the definitions of knowledge codified in early VocEd legislation and played out in its history. A related concern is that the culture's biases about mind and work—which have so influenced schooling—are infrequently raised in these reform deliberations. Thus, as education scholar Theodore Lewis puts it, vocational knowledge is not perceived as valid school knowledge. The intelligence we've seen in service work, in the trades, on the factory floor is not typically a part of the conversation, and this absence limits a creative rethinking of the academic-vocational divide.

□

We began this chapter with the paradox of American vocational education: the role it has played in restricting the intellectual possibilities of work. Yet those VocEd pioneers were clearly right about some things. Though they would undercut it in practice, they voiced a legitimate call to honor the educational importance of the hand as well as the brain. Also, they—like John Dewey, who would come to disagree with them on so much else—saw the limitations of a curriculum built on the memorization and recitation of texts, an approach to learning that easily became static and insular. And, finally, they were on target about the fact that many, many kids— kids like my uncle Joe Meraglio—found little in the traditional classroom to engage them, and they hoped that a vocational course of study would keep such young people in school. These issues are still with us.

They are captured in something I witnessed in a high school electronics class. In the middle of his workshop, the teacher had built the frame of a very small house. The frame was bare except for wires running across and through the beams, wires and recep- tacles, some wall switches, various light fixtures, and a power panel, door open. Students test their skills on this simulated resi- dence, sections of the classroom's tiled floor taped off and marked *washer, garbage disposal, T.V.* On this day, Tyler and Mariana are hooking up the lights and running the wires to the power panel. They are just about done, Mariana giving the circuit breakers in the panel one last look.

There is a group of younger students present, new boys and girls just entering the program. I stand amid them. We are all back a little ways from the house. Tyler and Mariana say they're ready, so the teacher walks over to the classroom's central power source and flips a switch. It works! The whole house lights up, ceiling lights, wall lights, floods. "Wow," exclaims a boy by me, under his breath. "Man," he says, "that's crazy!"

Young people who find little of interest in the traditional cur- riculum can be intrigued by the world of work. I would find out that this fellow was such a student; he had already come to believe that school wasn't for him. Though the reasons for dropping out can involve much more than curriculum, this program might catch him. This might help keep him in school and aid him in fashioning an occupation for himself, an opening through the intersection of technology and desire. The big question is, what would await him? A restricted pathway that defines him and the electrician's trade in the narrowest of intellectual, as well as economic, terms? Or a curriculum that assumes curiosity and the ability to learn, and that, while situated in the illuminated house frame, seeks connection to writing, to mathematics, to the economics of the trade, to the meaning of shelter and light across time?

Debates about vocational education, though politically weighty, tend to take place at the margins of school reform efforts. But as I've conducted the research for this book, I've come to believe that the vocational-academic divide could become the site of a broadly significant conversation, one that would not only affect VocEd but extend far beyond it. Some of those early VocEd topics were never adequately addressed, and they remain, I believe, among the key occupational and educational issues facing us today.

There is the issue of intelligence itself: its definition, the limits of our standard measures of it, and our lack of appreciation of its manifestation in the everyday. There is the set of cultural assumptions that attribute low intelligence to entire categories of work and to the people who do the work, often poor people, people of color, and immigrants. There is our impoverished sense of what work, any kind of work, requires and an arrogant denial of the intricate human dimension of technology. For all our talk about the new workplace and the need for smart workers, many believe, as does this manager of a Motorola plant overseas, that "we really need to get the human element out of the process." What else but human consciousness makes the process work?

There is the issue of differences in aptitude and interest, in the things we like to do with our minds. Though our schools have put some effort into dealing with this kind of heterogeneity, they end up responding to difference in pretty simplistic ways. We develop limited categories for courses and for placement, which are administratively efficient but cognitively reductive—and we quickly rank-order them. Given, for example, the distinctions we make between the academic and the vocational, difference quickly devolves to deficiency. As one policy expert said to me in exasperation, ideas for vocational programs tend to "get implemented in the lowest, least imaginative form possible." My sense is that, with a few exceptions, most policy and curricular deliberations about vocational education have embedded in them assumptions of cognitive limitation—and these assumptions shrink our curricular imagination.

To vitalize that imagination, we need to rethink our notions about mind and work, but also need to reassess long-standing and seemingly self-evident distinctions among levels and kinds of knowledge. Certainly, distinctions can be made; expressions of mind are wide and varied. But there is a tendency, in the school as in the culture at large, to view all knowledge and skill associated with physical work as rudimentary, even primitive, "neck down" activity. It is instructive, therefore, to look back at the work done by the young plumbers, carpenters, and electricians we visited and consider how often there was evidence of the kinds of cognitive operations—making fine discriminations, for example, or separating out variables, or weighing alternatives—that are central to higher-status academic and professional endeavors. A related issue, as we've been seeing, is that the traditional, and weighty, separations between "pure" and "applied" knowledge, between "skill" and "concept," between "theoretical" and "practical" tend to neatly segment a more elaborate reality. The more time I spend amid different intellectual disciplines and amid different spheres of work, the less sure I find these distinctions to be. They harden in debates over the purpose of education or in disciplinary and professional power plays, but they blur and morph in actual practice, both blue-collar and white.

And then there is the issue, much in public talk these days, of the purpose of work, which gives rise to a cluster of further issues: meaning and identity, tradition and ethics, values, human connection. The school has not done a very good job of addressing them; when they do appear in conventional vocational courses, the treatment is frequently abstract or trivial . . . and the students could care less. Yet there are so many moments in the practice of challenging work where values, ethical questions, connections of self to tradition emerge naturally, and with consequence, ripe for thoughtful consideration. Surrounding such issues, influencing them at every level of working life, are the profound effects of social location, economics, politics. The early architects of VocEd wiped these concerns from the curriculum, and vocational education has been pretty anemic on such topics since. (Historically, unions have served as the schoolhouse on these issues for many American workers.) The tragedy here is that young people are at the stage where they're realizing how important work will be in their lives, how it will frame who they are and what they can do in the world. They are desperate to be somebody, to possess agency and competence, to have a grasp on the forces that affect them. This is not easy to get to—kids are so self-protecting and adults often so inept—but the desire quivers within adolescent life.

All of the above, it seems to me, plays in and out of the basic question, the Jeffersonian question, about the purpose of schooling in a democracy. Throughout the early history of vocational education, both advocates and opponents relied on democratic rhetoric to make their cases: It is democratic to provide all students with a similar course of study—at that time, the academic curriculum. Or, no, it is democratic to respond to the individual needs of quite different students. As I've considered it, I don't think this is the most fruitful way to frame the debate. The vocational-academic divide leads us to consider the Jeffersonian question in more nuanced ways.

For some critics, schooling should be freed of economic motive and vocational content. Though unrealistic, and, to a degree, elitist—if you're poor, how can you bleach school of the hope of advancement—there is merit in this position when one considers how crassly practical some have tried to make schooling. (One influential early-twentieth-century superintendent wanted to evaluate subjects in the curriculum based on each subject's "unit cost" per pupil recitation.) But economic motives have long driven mass education in the United States. In addition to his claims of the intellectual, civic, and moral benefits of the common school, Horace Mann devoted an entire report to its economic benefit. And one could certainly argue that the strictly academic curriculum has long served as a vocational course of study for the middle and upper classes. It seems that the key issue here is how narrowly or richly "vocation" is conceived and whether the child is defined solely as an economic being.

I know a telling, and awful, illustration of this issue, relayed to me by a teacher who was part of a VocEd reform team. The team was trying to incorporate more explicit literacy instruction into the curriculum, and was meeting strong resistance from a veteran auto mechanics teacher. He said that his students didn't need reading instruction from him, that he showed them what they needed to know, or they learned it from watching others or viewing instructional videos. To be sure, a good deal of trade skill is learned not from texts but from observation and practice, and it is also conceivable that what we have here is petulant resistance to incursion from the "academic" side of things—a reminder of the perennial suspicion and turf skirmishes along the academic-vocational divide.

But, Lord, what a terribly restricted notion of vocation this teacher expresses—that his students' working lives will not need to extend toward reading and writing—and what a pinched definition of cognitive and civic development he seems to hold.

It is accounts like this, combined with the earlier-cited record of inequality, that have led in the last two decades not only to VocEd reform but also to impassioned calls to dramatically alter or even dismantle vocational education itself. There have been the many attempts to "detrack" schools, to move beyond the vocational-general-academic scheme and develop courses and teaching methods that can accommodate a wider mix of students—a common educational experience that could well include vocational options. There is, as well, a related effort to create in middle and high schools a "college culture," that is, to foster change in a school's organization—from curriculum to counseling to parental involvement—so that, to quote one research team, "college is a reasonable expectation for all students." And, finally, in a few cases, there have been recommendations to structure curricular equality by having all students enter high school in a college preparatory curriculum, from which they could then choose to exit for a different course of study. This approach, one floated in my own state of California, would counter the shameful record of counseling so many poor and minority young people into noncollege curricula.

Though there is a legitimate debate in policy circles as to the wisdom—economic or developmental—of trying to send everyone to college, I am sympathetic to these college-for-all reforms and have written things consonant with them. While it is true that there are currently well-paying technologically oriented jobs that do not require a baccalaureate degree, on average a college degree still has a significant economic impact over the course of one's working life. Furthermore, when you become familiar with the history of discrimination surrounding curricular tracking and with the systematic restriction of educational opportunity for entire groups of Americans to the lowest-level training ... well, there's little doubt about the democratic redress underlying these initiatives.

These attempts to broaden access to postsecondary education, however, require a carefully executed course of study, since many students need help with demanding academic material. As well, there needs to be a robust counseling program (not an easy task, given how overextended most high school counselors are) to assist students—especially first-generation college-goers—in making wise curricular choices. Furthermore, there are delicate social issues here. How do you encourage young people to consider college, take the right courses, perhaps leave their peers behind, look to work other than the work their parents do—how do you do that in a way that doesn't diminish who their parents are or how they make a living? Parents want economic mobility for their children, but enabling this mobility through schooling can be a tricky matter. As one policy analyst I spoke with aptly put it: "How do you honor a student's construction worker father while creating the conditions for his child to not be a construction worker?"

There is a related issue, one that can emerge in a school's institutional dynamics: a belittling of the work and the intellectual potential represented in vocational education programs. It is desirable to expand educational opportunity by enriching curriculum and providing more options for matriculation. But this must be done in a way that honors the diverse richness of cognition, that grounds itself in a capacious philosophy of mind. I'm not sure it is often the case. Some reform efforts leave unchanged the narrow definitions of disciplines and mental activity and, thereby, contribute to the sense many working-class kids have of scholastic alienation, of disconnection, of the sense that this intellectual—or aesthetic, or contemplative—business is not for them.

The core problem, it seems to me, is not that the school offers

multiple curricula; in theory, varied courses of study could be enriching. The problem is that even after tracking there are biases at
play in who gets what curriculum. Furthermore, the curricular options are built on terribly diminished, and self-fulfilling, assumptions about the cognitive capacity of large numbers of students.
After a while, young people figure this out. They develop a sense
of whose mind is certified by the school—a pertinent phrase from
Richard Sennett and Jonathan Cobb's *The Hidden Injuries of Class*—
who is intellectually competent, invested with hope, marked with
an aura of futurity.

Now, the kids who end up on the vocational side of things, as is
the case with any social group, are a resourceful lot. They respond
in a variety of ways to their situation, from making the most of it,
to assuming a protective disengagement, to creating a storm of
trouble. And some, like those young plumbers and carpenters,
find spaces of achievement, frequently in the workshop, lab, or job
site. But what is so disturbing on a societal level—taking the school
as a miniature society—is that young people at a key developmental juncture have to form their sense of self and their conception
of their intelligence within the tensions and restrictions of the
academic-vocational divide. They have to define themselves, either
in compliance or in rejection, within these institutional dynamics—
unless they drop out ... which creates its own stigmatized mess.
One of the results of all this is that some kids—no matter how
sharp they may be in other aspects of their lives—come to think of
themselves as intellectually inferior, not too bright, dummies. This
can even be the case—as I've witnessed innumerable times in my
life—when people dismiss book smarts, mock it, develop identities
in opposition to it. Even as they shun the academic domain, they
identify intelligence with it, trapping themselves within the very
terms they reject.

A number of vocationally oriented students have mediocre edu-

cations. Some are considerably unprepared, and their underpreparation is related to their social class background: poor schools, limited resources, hard times. They tend not to do well in their
academic courses, and their performance supports the school's belief that they cannot handle intellectually challenging material.
This belief is often reinforced by the students themselves, by their
many indications that they just don't like school—and don't trust
it, either. The teacher's challenge here—and this is where good
teaching comes in—is to be clearheaded in separating out a student's poor performance or detachment and defensiveness from
intellectual possibility. And when the conditions are right—the
right teacher, or approach, or moment in a young person's life—
when this clicks, wary students can be engaged, caught up, sometimes to their surprise. "Man, that's crazy!"

There is a further, related challenge. Not to assume—as many
curriculum developers seem to—that poor academic preparation
forgoes sustained and serious involvement with core disciplinary
topics and with material of intellectual consequence. By and large,
our schools have responded to underpreparation with reductive,
trivial curricula, "skills-and-drills," revealing once again assumptions about the cognitive capacity of those students on the VocEd
side of the vocational-academic divide.

It is hard work to teach creatively in the intersection of the academic and the vocational. It involves the delicate negotiation of
turf and subject-area status, which sparks teachers' suspicions and
self-protection—the touchy personnel dimension of the academic-
vocational split. Then there is the bureaucratic dimension: the
finessing of work rules, curriculum frameworks, and district guidelines. And there is the crossing of disciplinary boundaries and
culturally sanctioned domains of knowledge, something that the
typical undergraduate curriculum and teacher education program
does not prepare one to do. Thus even the most willing of teachers

is hampered by traditional vocabularies and definitions that make
it so hard, for example, to articulate—and then to teach—the cognitive and aesthetic dimensions of manual skill.

It *is* hard work. It means developing classroom activities that au-
thentically represent the intellectual demands of the workplace
and, conversely, bringing academic content to life through occupational tasks and simulations. It means that the house or the automobile or the computer could be the core of a rich, integrated
curriculum: one that includes social and technical history, science
and economics, and hands-on assembly and repair. It means learning about new subject areas and making unfamiliar connections:
the historian investigating the health care or travel industry, or the
machinist engaging the humanities. It means fostering not only
basic mathematical skill but also an appreciation of mathematics, a
mathematical sensibility, through the particulars of the print shop,
the restaurant, the hospital lab. It means seeking out the many literate possibilities running through young people's lives—on the
street, in church, in romance—and connecting them to the language of the stage, the poem, but the contract, too, and the list of
procedures, and the Bill of Rights. And, of course, such teaching
might well mean providing instruction in "basic skills," but in a
manner that puts the skill in context, considers its purpose, pushes
toward meaning beyond rote performance.

The teachers who do this work are trying to fashion a quality
education for a larger number than usual of American youngsters.
From what I've seen—and research supports this—they increase
the number of students who graduate thoughtful and articulate,
able to talk about what they're learning and of themselves as learn-
ers, able to act in and on the world. "It's the most powerful thing,"
says one teacher, "that I've ever done in education." While these
educational experiments can involve all children, I am impressed
by the special meaning they have for students who are not on the

educational fast track, the great mass of young humanity. This kind of teaching represents a significant change in established beliefs about the capacity of such students. The typical language in policy documents used to describe these young people is a language of practicality and preparation, inflected with a sense of their limitation. There is little sense of promise, of the excitement of cognitive and civic development. What I'm seeking is a deeper, richer, more involving orientation toward working people and their children, akin to a fundamental political commitment or article of educational faith.

It is the kind of belief in human potential that enables social movements, the extraordinary emergence of agency and strategy where little was thought possible. It is noteworthy, in this regard, that voter registration activist Bob Moses developed his program to teach algebra to children in poor communities from his political organizing experience. In the same way that the civil rights movement assumed that all people are capable of political deliberation and participation, the Algebra Project assumes that everyone—absent brain injury—is capable of understanding the conceptual fundamentals of algebra. "How can a culture be created," writes Moses and his colleagues, "in . . . which every child is expected to be as good as possible in his or her mathematical development?"

It is important to note that in the early days of debate over vocational education, there were compelling voices articulating this kind of belief in the capacity of the common person and in the necessity of connecting education to an egalitarian vision of human and cultural development. There was John Dewey and Jane Addams, but others as well, academics and state-level committee members. But that view of mass education was erased from final policy. It needs to be reclaimed, for it is so pertinent now.

Without such bedrock beliefs and commitments, we will never transform vocational education or bridge the academic-vocational divide. We will continue to take good ideas and squander them, dumb them down, trivialize them, for the beliefs about intelligence and the social order that underlie a curriculum are as important as the content of the curriculum itself. It is at this point that democratic principles and educational practice become one, an act of intellectual and civic realization. Thus it is that those teachers who do work diligently at the breach between the academic and the vocational are engaged in a kind of applied political philosophy. They challenge the culture's assumptions about hand and brain, and the rigid system of educational theory and method that emerged from them, making the schoolhouse more truly democratic by honoring the fundamental intelligence of a broad range of human activity.

CONCLUSION

Working Life

NO TRESPASSING, it says. *"This railroad, all sidings, yards, buildings, and lands connected therewith, are the private property of Consolidated Rail Corporation. . . ."* Conrail. The company that took over the failing offspring of the Pennsylvania Railroad. Someone has scrawled *Fuck you* across it. And someone, in neat, blue script, has written along the margin: *Gotta be prudent.* My mother and I used to stand on the landing of the fire escape behind my parents' restaurant, holding tight onto the iron grille, looking at the furious vast expanse of shop yards below: the engines crisscrossing in slow force, the screech of metal on metal, the fire in the smoke. "The scream of the engine is heard at all hours of the day and night . . . ," wrote Altoona's first historian. "The roar of the fires, the clang of machinery . . . never cease from the rising to the setting of the sun." Now I'm leaning into the fence and looking at suspension springs and running gear, rusted and covered with the delicate cream of Queen Anne's lace.

The occupational landscape of the country has changed dramatically since my mother moved west to her long series of waitressing jobs, since my uncles dug in for the railroad layoffs or followed the rust belt to the auto industry. Over the next three decades many would also move on or weather layoffs and plant closings in Lackawanna, New York, in Kenosha, Wisconsin, in the mill towns around Pittsburgh, Pennsylvania, in Flint, Michigan. The railroad would continue to decline. Steel, another of the great smokestack industries, would begin to come apart as well. The auto industry has been rocked to its core. Still other manufacturing industries have been transformed and dispersed to cheaper labor markets south of the border or overseas. Globalization. New industries, based on new technologies, are emerging, providing good jobs for some and many more that bear resemblance to old-style factory work, cleaner, safer, but with similar production characteristics, and, generally, with less compensation. The influence of unions, with a few exceptions, has declined. Wages and benefits, by most any measure, have declined as well. The protections of the welfare state are being systemically eroded. The jobs that are plentiful—particularly for people with limited education and modest resources—tend to be in lower-wage service industries, waitressing among the top five occupations projected for growth. When my mother said long ago that, hard as it was, she knew that she could always find work waiting tables, she was right.

So a new generation moves out onto this changed landscape, driven by the same motives that brought Frank and Joe into the PRR; that led Joe to travel to Cleveland, then to Youngstown; that brought my mother, anxious and uncertain, across country. This search for work, this particular kind of search for a job is a restless, unsettling business. You need work, need it to keep the roof over your and your family's heads. You need the wages, desperately, but you need the security, too, a place to go, structure for your day. For some, the job also brings social connection beyond home and neighborhood. And, for everyone, given the tremendous moral weight work carries in our country, the job brings a sense of virtue and validation. Thus when you can't find work, or it is torn away— I think of this looking through the fence at the rusted fields— you're not only in economic but also in existential free-fall. "The habit of work," write the authors of *Poor People's Movements*, "and the wages of work, underpin a way of life."

But when you do find work, the conditions in which you work—in the restaurant or salon, the factory or office, or with tools out in the field—the conditions may limit, at times profoundly, the various satisfactions the work can offer. Many have commented on the continued tendency toward de-skilling and surveillance. And although physical work is safer overall and more protected than in my grandfather's day, certain jobs remain very dangerous—witness the meatpacking industry—and all are driven by intense schedules. Hiring, firing, and advancement are, in some settings, less capricious than they were at midcentury, but blue-collar and service workers still live in uncertainty and live, as well, with the occupational and social assaults on dignity that Sennett and Cobb so aptly call the hidden injuries of class.

Yet, for all the limitation and insult, most working men and women try to find meaning in what they do—through the activity of the work itself or through what their wages make possible outside of the workplace. This effort is testament to a remarkable strength of mind. People work within constraint—sometimes the inhumane control of the assembly line or the "electronic sweatshop"—yet seek some expression of self, some agency, some small way of saying *I am here.*

There is an extensive philosophical and sociological literature on the meaning of work, and running through much of it is the notion that work provides human beings with a means of engaging the environment, putting their impress on the world. If we accept this notion—and it seems to resonate within a Western cultural context—then we have to acknowledge the everpresence of mind in the work people do, at the least, the monitoring and directing of one's behavior that enables even the simplest of tasks,

and the motives one brings to a task, the reasons for doing it—
from economic to social to aesthetic—that affect the execution
of it.

There is nothing particularly new about this claim; it seems self-
evident. But consider the ways our industrial history has violated it
and our social distinctions continue to diminish it. It is a way of
thinking about those who do physical work that I rarely hear expressed. So let us turn once more to the people in this book and
draw from their stories a different account of the mind at work, as
an expansive human resource, emerging in all the commonplace
spaces and events of our daily lives, from the rise of a staircase to
the preparation of a meal.

◻

We have witnessed a number of ways that the body is used tacti-
cally, purposefully, from the waitress balancing plates on the move,
to the plumber seeking leverage in close quarters, to the hairstylist
adroit with scissors and comb, to a welder coming in on a seam at
just the right angle. Though such activity becomes routine with experience, it was at some point learned through observation, trial
and error, and, often, physical or verbal assistance from another.
Such learning involves various cognitive processes, not the least of
which is the learner's self-observation and consequent modification of movement. How many times I observed novices talking to
themselves as they took on a new task, or shaking head or hand as
if to erase an attempt and try again. Furthermore, as we've heard
from experts, even mastered routines can involve a degree of self-
monitoring—at the minimum a peripheral awareness—to avoid
both injury and error. Also, some of what we saw and heard suggests that our traditional notions of routine performance could
keep us from appreciating the many instances within routine
where quick decisions and adjustments are made. I'm struck too

by the thinking-in-motion that some work requires, by all the mental activity that can be involved in simply getting from one place to another: the waitress rushing back to the kitchen or the foreman walking the line. As we've seen, they are attending to the environment, are vigilant, and must respond to tasks that emerge quickly, assess and prioritize them—and, then, be able to anticipate next moves. All this requires considerable knowledge of the work and of the specific workplace itself.

Much of the physical activity in this book involves tools and instruments, and they, in turn, require the studied refinement of stance, grip, balance, and fine motor skills. But manipulating a tool is intimately tied to knowledge of what a particular tool can do in a particular situation—and do better than other similar tools. One must also know the characteristics of the material one is engaging, how it reacts to various cutting or compressing devices, or degrees of heat, or lines of force. Some of this demands judgment, the weighing of options, the consideration of multiple variables, and, occasionally, the creative use of a tool in an unexpected way. (Watch the experienced carpenter or mechanic with an eye for this improvisation.) Little wonder, then, that psychologist Howard Gardner, after surveying a range of research to frame his argument for a "bodily-kinesthetic intelligence," notes "a close link between the use of the body and the deployment of other cognitive powers." Neurologist Frank Wilson puts it more vividly: "The brain does not live inside the head, even though that is its formal habitat. It reaches out to the body, and with the body it reaches out to the world. . . . [B]rain is hand and hand is brain."

In working with the material world, one's senses can become attuned to aspects of the environment, a training or disciplining of perception that both enhances one's knowledge and reciprocally informs perception. There is the carpenter's eye for length, line, and angle; the mechanic's troubleshooting ear; and, more broadly, the way the feel of things—shape, texture, motion—carries meaning in hairstyling or in plumbing. It is hard to separate sense data from concept here. Consider how diagnosis and judgment can be based on such disciplined perception, and how disparate perceptual information can be strategically compared or combined in solving a problem. A good example is the mechanic who relies on sound, vibration, even smell to understand what cannot be seen directly.

We saw continual evidence of the particular way that the mental processes long studied in the psychologist's laboratory are manifest in physical work. There is, for example, the role played by attention and memory in the busy restaurant. There is the grouping of tasks to maximize efficiency and the use of categories—this is an x kind of valve, this is a y hair problem—to direct action. Procedural knowledge is ever-present: the steps in a process, serial order, sequence—and the modification of procedure to achieve particular goals. For that fact, the way knowledge of one's field is represented and organized, the "architecture" of knowledge, is central to expert performance. I think here of woodshop teacher Jerry Devries's "cabinet sense" versus that of his student Felipe or of the functional mixture of theory, technique, and aesthetics displayed by the welder Lisa Legohn.

Planning and problem solving have been studied since the earliest days of modern cognitive psychology and are considered to be core elements in Western definitions of intelligence. We saw evidence of planning across the chapters, attempts to think through and direct upcoming activity. To work is to solve problems. Some problems, like a faulty circuit, can be fairly straightforward and solved by applying well-established procedures. Other problems are less clear, as when Jerry Devries's students try to determine the cause of flawed construction, not only testing out variables but determining what they are in the first place. Is the source of the problem in the power tools, in the materials, or in the assembly process itself? (And some problems, like those involving human relations—from the hair salon to the construction site—can be downright messy, requiring on-the-spot assessment, testing, and negotiation.) There are yet more workplace processes investigated in the laboratory—mental imagery, the timing and rhythm of behavior—but I think this accounting of cognition makes its point: that the world of everyday work provides a rich display of the kinds of mental activity long valued by those who study human thought. The big difference between the psychologist's laboratory and the workplace is that the processes and activities are not isolated but blend, embedded in the real-time flow of work, in all its rituals, routines, distractions, and social complexity.

The above discussion has been focused on the individual, but a good deal of physical work is social and interactive. Examples range from two movers determining how to get a stove down a flight of stairs to the kind of sharing and distributing of tasks we saw with Jon Guthier's plumbers or in Jerry Devries's woodshop. Such mutual effort requires some degree of coordination and negotiation, which might or might not involve speech. ("[W]e worked well together," writes longshoreman Reg Theriault, "anticipating each other's moves . . . lifting with me in an even, steady swing.") And this kind of coordinated effort can also include planning: an analysis of component parts, steps in a process, desired goals. Words and gestures—and sometimes the quick pencil sketch— run throughout, if for no other reason than to get the rhythm right. And it is common for workers to shift among ways of explaining or demonstrating, and, depending on the crew, shift among shared languages as well.

How important it is, then, to consider the social and communicative dimension of physical work, not only because that dimension yields its own human pleasures and irritants but also because it provides the medium for—some would say constitutes—so much of work's intelligence.

For all kinds of reasons, some less-than-admirable, workers are aware of each other, if just peripherally, and through this awareness can learn and monitor. Recall Jerry Devries hearing the problem with his students' use of power tools. Workers can guide action through nods of the head, gestures of the hand, even via a glance that directs a coworker's attention. Workers move in concert with each other, and in some settings the coordination of movement is critical. Someone should record and chart the interacting streams of movement in the busy restaurant, much of which occurs automatically, but contains quick instances of conscious adjustment. And, of course, talk flows through all this interaction.

It might seem odd, at first blush, to consider workplace language this way, given both the popular and high-brow ridicule heaped on blue-collar speech. Yet, as we have seen, the ongoing flow of talk at work provides the channel for organizing and distributing tasks, for troubleshooting and problem solving, for learning new information and revising old. For that fact, there's a significant amount of teaching that takes place at work, often informal and indirect. Joe Meraglio saw much of his supervisor's job as involving instruction, and, on quite a different front, the hairstylist Deborah had to leave a one-chair salon because she longed for the kind of stylist-to-stylist interaction that would teach her new things.

And talk does not need to be directed toward specific goals and actions to be cognitively rich. A recent example presented itself when I was visiting a friend in the hospital. Two nurses' aides—two young women—were working at the next bed, hidden behind a curtain, attending to a patient who was unconscious. As they changed the bed, they talked softly about what they did on their days off, their schedule for the week—that sort of thing. But as they talked, they also made observations and asked questions about the patient: one asking the other why the woman was wearing wrist restraints; both commenting on the trouble the staff was having getting her diet from her residential facility and the dangers of not knowing it; and both observing what I assume was unusual bruising and wondering if she was on Coumadin, a blood thinner—a question one of them would ask the nurse when she entered the room. The curiosity and reasoning of these aides are notable, but other aspects of the conversation are important as well. Their talk serves to reinforce what they know, to test and refine it, to build on the known to learn new things, and to experience their own competence, which is an enactment of identity. It is both display and inquiry, emerging from chitchat about leisure time and the workplace.

With waitressing and styling hair, we saw occupations where language and communication are central to the work itself, help constitute it. In fact, the interpretive aspect of talk is critical: recall the number of verbal techniques (interwoven with graphics and gestures) that the stylist uses to come to an understanding of the client's desire. Language, spoken or signed, is intimately tied to social interaction, is its enabling cultural tool, and social interaction requires thought as well as feeling. Whether you believe that there is a trait we can define as "social intelligence," or, simply, as one research team puts it, that "social behavior is intelligent," it's pretty clear that the social interaction in a good deal of service work presents its own cognitive demands: observing and interpreting behavior and expression, inferring mood and motive, taking on the perspective of others, responding appropriately to social cues, and knowing when you're understood.

Not only is social behavior intelligent, but intelligent social behavior can, itself, become the vehicle for enhancing what one knows about nonsocial domains as well. It's worth speculating as to how much of what Joe Meraglio and the welder Lisa Legohn learned about, say, reading blueprints came as a function of their socially adept interaction with more experienced workmates. And the hairstylist with limited social facility would probably be restricted in what she or he could learn about a client's history of hair treatments, about habits and routines that affect hair care, and about the particulars of a client's desire. The social and the cognitive, though traditionally separate areas of psychological investigation, intimately connect in the ongoing life of the workplace.

The study of values is also separate from the study of cognitive processing or technical skill, yet, as is evident throughout these pages, aesthetic and craft values direct behavior as powerfully as do plans and strategies, leading one to measure, trim, balance, adjust, redo. Recall here the novice electrician rewiring his perfectly functional fixture because he thought it looked ugly. These values focus attention and sustain involvement; they affect the choice of tool, material, and product and the choice of technique; and they stimulate and guide problem solving, for that fact contributes to problem finding in the flow of work activity. This intersection of value and action is central to the way one leads one's working life, and one's sense of who one is. "I love cutting this way," says the hairstylist Vanessa. "I go in and add my own touch, a signature."

Let me close this cognitive summary by considering the use of symbol systems: numbers, graphics, and written language. Verbal and numerical abilities lie at the heart of Western measures of intelligence, and many of the kinds of work we've been considering are typically thought to require relatively little of such proficiency. Compared to certain kinds of white-collar occupations, that's true. But let us get a little closer to this issue, for symbols flow throughout physical work.

Most workplaces are thick with numbers. On tools and gauges, as measurements, as indicators of pressure or concentration or temperature, as guides to sequence, on ingredient labels, on lists and spreadsheets, as markers of quantity and price. Certain jobs require workers to perform calculations, to check and verify, and, at times, to collect and interpret data. A fair amount of basic math can be involved, and some workers develop a good, if informal, sense of number and pattern. As well, there is material mathematics, mathematical functions embodied in materials and actions. The cognitive demands of such math—the number of interrelated variables, the planning, the estimations—can be, as we saw in Jerry Devries's woodshop, considerable, particularly when one is still developing competence. Another important thing to note is that a simple mathematical act can extend quickly beyond itself. Measuring, for example, can involve more than recording the dimensions of an object. I was watching a cabinetmaker measure a long strip of wood. He read a number off the tape out loud, looked back over his shoulder to the kitchen wall, turned back to his task and took another measurement, then paused for a moment in thought. He was trying to solve a problem with the molding, and the measurement became a key element in his deliberation about structure and appearance. Lower-order mathematics, as the authors of one recent report put it, becomes "a rich source of higher-order thinking."

The workplace is also rich in graphics. Directions, plans, and reference books contain numerous illustrations. Some are fairly representational of the object in question; others, like blueprints, are more specialized in depiction and purpose, and require training to understand. A whole array of esoteric symbols can be involved, "visual jargon" for switches and receptacles, or pipe fittings, or types of welds. Workers often generate illustrations themselves, quickly, in the unfolding events of the job, illustrations meant to aid communication and forward activity. How frequently I saw someone suddenly grab a pencil—shifting the medium of representation from speech and gesture to the graphical—to sketch something while talking on a scrap of paper or on a piece of material itself. (Many a panel of plywood nailed into place has such a sketch drawn on its reverse side.) Those sketches can illustrate dimension, function, relation, sequence, or more, and often contain words, numbers, and specialized notations intermixed with lines, angles, and curves. This strategic blending of symbols displays a flexible disciplinary and communicative competence—the worker has to recognize the need to mix or switch media—and signals membership in a skilled occupational community.

Though many kinds of physical work have not required high levels of literacy, more reading occurs in the average workplace than is generally thought: from manuals and catalogs, to work orders and invoices, to lists, labels, and forms. These texts are coupled with other activities, so, for example, people read to specify a production quota or to be guided in the use of an instrument or a product. (People who are marginally literate or who are not literate in English often develop a range of compensatory strategies to enable them to do such work.) These tasks require a familiarity with specialized vocabularies and with different kinds of texts, and they require a repertoire of reading strategies that vary by purpose: for example, the scanning of a list for a piece of information versus the interpretation of a customer's or coworker's written notes. Some manufacturing and service jobs involve a good deal of "paperwork" to document and trace, integrated throughout one's work routines. The use of such texts, once mastered, becomes familiar and repetitive, not requiring much interpretation, though they may well be incorporated into an interpretive act, part of assessing a situation or solving a problem. Other kinds of texts—codes and collective bargaining agreements, for example—define work, contribute to the standardization of parts and processes, and regulate social and economic relations. Such documents form a legal and organizational surround. They are typically not read in the immediate activity of work—the information in them is usually conveyed orally by peers and supervisors—but they can quickly move to the foreground of activity during labor negotiations, organizational restructuring, or the reassessment of a standard procedure.

Writing, of a limited sort, is also distributed throughout the workplace. It is used to label, to list, to record activity. It can be structured by a form or be sketchy, part of talking or thinking through a problem. It can initiate action, as in a restaurant order or a report of machine malfunction, or it can be private, as in the list or diagram hastily written as a memory aid. (Think of all those scraps of paper surrounding Jerry Devries's novice carpenters.) If the worker is in training—in the shop or in a classroom—he or she may take notes from demonstration or lecture, annotate written texts, and linguistically simplify or graphically render instructions in manuals or training materials. And in some cases, the worker—particularly in new or restructured industries—may need to draft reports and recommendations about production processes.

Traditional treatments of literacy tend to classify most of the above uses of reading and writing as basic, rudimentary: they are instrumental, repetitive, often involve limited amounts of text, infrequently call for interpretation or analysis of the text itself. There is a descriptive truth to such judgments: the uses of literacy in the common workplace do tend toward the abbreviated and routine. But I think there is also an implicit comparison here that sells workplace literacy short, a comparison with literary expression or with the uses of written language in the professions or the academy. While reading and writing in many professions are more routine and scripted than the comparison implies, it is surely true that, say, writing a legal brief requires significantly more literacy skill than filling out a form when a machine breaks down. Still, as someone who studies language and cognition, I've come to think we underestimate the significance of common workplace literacy.

As I've been arguing, our traditional categories and binaries can blinker our understanding: analytic moments can be embedded in routine, and seemingly basic reading and writing can be cognitively richer than they seem. The writing of just a single word, perhaps along with other notations, can represent much more than the word itself denotes. To the carpenter planning a roof or the paint shop foreman troubleshooting on the auto assembly line, the scribbled words *eaves* or *primer* can carry with them an understanding of a structure or a process, a history of experience, and a series of options for action. Also, I'm struck by the degree to which workers shift among different symbol systems—and frequently combine them—to make things happen. This shifting and combining is often done with others, is interactive and, at times, collaborative. Because all this occurs so frequently and in the flow of other activity—its very everydayness—I think we can miss the remarkable thing about it: the coordinated use of word, number, and line to initiate and direct action.

There would be much to learn by changing our line of sight and asking what all these forms of symbolic activity are on their own terms, in context—how they interact, what it takes to do them well, what they make happen in the world, how they might connect to other literate or mathematical behaviors, in and outside of the workplace. Such questions would yield a fuller, more nuanced understanding than we typically have of the many ways people live with words and numbers.

❑

It seems to me that both economic and social policy considerations follow from this summary of the mind at work.

I have attempted to demonstrate the robust and varied cognitive dimension of physical work. But, clearly, certain organizational structures, management philosophies, or modes of supervision can either foster or constrain the expression of intelligence. So one important economic and human development question is this: What opportunities does the workplace provide to actualize one's cognitive potential? I do not mean only through formal training and education programs—though it's important to note that such programs are surprisingly scarce, and, too often, are not well conceived or executed. ("Fewer than 10 percent of front-line American workers now receive training of any kind," notes a Department of Labor report.) Rather, I'm thinking about the very experience of work itself. Is work organized so that people have incentives to be smart, to learn more, to display competence? Just about every worker I interviewed commented in some way on such issues, making distinctions between kinds of work (being a plumber versus being an operative on an assembly line) or among particular employers: one hair salon or welding shop over another, even one factory rather than another.

In previous chapters, I raised concern about the ease with which the current distinction between an "old work order" and a "new work order" can rhetorically render twentieth-century industrial workers as cognitively substandard. Yet a legitimate element of the old work–new work discussion is that in some traditional jobs workers have to use their brains in spite of—or in resistance to—the way their work is structured and supervised. Currently, there are sectors in the new industrial order calling for a fuller intellectual engagement of their workforce. Let's consider this call, for, in theory, it could provide an occupational climate that opens up the cognitive possibilities of work and acknowledges the capacity of the people who do it.

Since the early 1980s, and with increasing frequency, business leaders, economists, and legislators have been claiming that a restructuring of the economy and transformations in the way work is organized are creating demand for a new kind of worker, skilled and adaptable. Within some industries changes in modes of production and delivery of service give the edge to workers with higher levels of literacy and numeracy who can learn new techniques and processes (particularly, but not only, those involving computer technology); who can collaborate with others; who can adopt a big-picture, systemic view of things; and who can solve problems and engage in front-line decision making. These qualities are frequently characterized as the postindustrial "workplace competencies" or "new basic skills," necessary to secure jobs with decent wages and some promise of advancement.

There is a genuine debate among economists as to how pervasively the American workplace is being restructured, and thus how much current work truly requires and fosters these new basics. (By one estimate, about 35 percent of firms with fifty or more employees are reorganizing in this way. Yet at the same time industry is seeking these new basic skills it has also been globally pursuing cheaper labor—which can be less skilled. Clearly, there are multiple and varied forces of transformation at work in American industry.) Also, some workplaces that have tried to reorganize themselves have, in fact, been unable to overcome old-style managerial structures and corporate culture. Still, given these caveats, it's clear that some workplaces—if, perhaps, a smaller percentage than is thought—are undergoing significant change, and it is hard to deny both the economic as well as the personal value of acquiring the "new basic skills." Though some studies demonstrate that there is not a clear relationship between skill level and wages—and the rhetoric of training and skills itself can obscure broader economic problems—a good basic education poises one for more options, both within and across occupations. And there are some well-documented cases of businesses that are striving to develop and utilize a fuller intellectual engagement from their workforce.

But consider studies like those carried out by literacy researcher Glynda Hull and her associates. They spent several years investigating the production of computer circuit boards in a reorganized, high-tech workplace in Silicon Valley. What they found was that although the front-line assemblers were expected to be literate and analytical, the managerial structure of the factory, assumptions by managers about the mental capacity of the (mostly immigrant) assemblers, and a reductive notion of reading (as simply decoding print without a need to know the context of its use) all contributed to a restricted development of literacy skill among these workers. There was little organizational incentive for workers, as Hull puts it, to imagine themselves as literate, to develop a literate identity. The conditions of work directly affect not only job satisfaction but also the expression of values and the display of intelligence. Hull's cautionary tale reminds us that even at a time of much talk about occupational change—and on the part of some, a real desire for it—there remain in effect powerful beliefs about mind and work that sabotage reform and constrain human potential. We saw these dynamics at play in the development of vocational education, and research like Hull's reveals them in business as well.

Economic and educational opportunity is typically defined in terms of slots, positions, openings, or, more generally, by the absence of structural barriers to advancement. Just so. Such definitions have been used by the courts to force opportunity where little existed. But there is another dimension to opportunity, not as obvious, less verifiable, but exceedingly important. As we just saw, it has to do with beliefs and assumptions: beliefs about mental capacity, about human difference, about the social order, and about the nature of work and what it can become.

This conception of opportunity gives us another way to think about failure in the workplace. Poor performance may well stem from personal limitations in skill or motivation but also can be grounded on, or at least complicated by, structures and assumptions in the workplace itself. Workers are acutely aware of this—the way they are treated as well as the way they are defined. (In this regard, one could read the history of union activity not only as a record of economic struggle but also as an assertion of ability in the face of managerial denial.) Along with assessments of individual performance, we can ask at the organizational level: What does the workplace invite and what does it limit or deny?

❑

We can ask a similar question of the society at large. In his classic study of the shifts in the kinds of intelligence expressed by the American people in the eighteenth and nineteenth centuries, historian Daniel Calhoun illustrates how the notion of intelligence is not a fixed entity, but is defined in time and place. He also helps us to understand how, through the process of defining, a society can validate some expressions of intelligence and award less merit to, even deny, others. As Calhoun summarizes this aspect of his study, intelligence is, among other things, a function "of the public ideas that surround, sustain, and even express [an individual's] mind." And, focusing on schooling as a place in the culture where intelligence is shaped, Calhoun continues, "intelligence is partly the result of what happens when the older generation communicates certain ideas about the intellectual behavior the young should display."

In writing this book, I have tried to get us to reflect on the public ideas that surround, sustain, and give expression to the thought in common work. My intention has not been to diminish the kinds of ability that have increasingly formed the core of our century's conception of intelligence—school-related verbal and quantitative facility—for they clearly enable extraordinary achievement. (And, of course, they are evident in some of the work we've been exploring.) Rather, I have tried to illustrate other spaces in the picture of human cognition and get us to consider why we so often view this picture partially—and the effect that partial perception has on the way we think about mind, work, school, and social class.

If the questions I've raised have merit, then, I think, they lead to a further question: What set of ideas about intelligence should we develop and promote, particularly in a democratic society? Whatever the basic neurochemical mechanisms of cognition are, most psychologists today would agree with Calhoun's assertion that the way intelligence is defined and manifested is culture-bound, affected by historical and social circumstances. So it becomes a legitimate act for a culture to ponder its ideas about intelligence: What do our ideas enable or restrict in education, in the economy, in social and political life? And how do our ideas map onto our foundational beliefs about the person?

As an ideal, democracy assumes the capacity of the common person to learn, to think independently, to decide thoughtfully. The emergence of this belief marks a key juncture in Western political philosophy, and such belief is central to the way we in the United States, during our best moments, define ourselves as citizens. Our major philosophical and educational thinkers—Jefferson, Horace Mann, John Dewey—have affirmed this potential among us, our intelligence as a people.

This belief correlates with support for popular democracy, for extended public education (the common school, land-grant colleges, community colleges), for the growth of libraries, for a range of compensatory and second-chance programs. The belief relates, as well, to many smaller-scale efforts developed by particular groups of citizens: from nineteenth-century mechanics' institutes and lyceums to a range of local mutual improvement and educational societies that continue to emerge through our own time. And the belief is intimately tied to a free press and to the wide dissemination—now via the Internet as well—of periodicals, newsletters, informational tracts, and more.

But central as it is, this belief in common intelligence is far from stable. As was noted a moment ago, the definition of "intelligence" shifts over time. A fluid definition of intelligence is, of itself, not necessarily a threat to a democratic conception of mind, but it does mean that it can be affected by repressive social conditions. A good example can be found in the early decades of the twentieth century when eugenicist theories of racial, ethnic, and class inferiority held particularly strong sway among a number of the early developers and interpreters of the IQ test in America.

Of broader concern is the presence of antiegalitarian beliefs throughout our nation's history and character. Various regional biases have led us to attribute different levels of intelligence to entire sections of the country and to the sound and structure of the language spoken in them. Theories of cognitive differences were used to withhold both education and the vote from women and African Americans, and assumptions about the inferior mental capacities of women and racial and ethnic minorities have shaped entire programs of study in the nineteenth- and twentieth-century social and biological sciences. The immigrants' foreign tongues and unfamiliarity with American customs translated, for many, into dullness, rigidity of thought, or childlike cognition. And there is an elaborate relation, part economic and part symbolic, between occupation and social class—a relation that carries with it assumptions about intelligence.

The belief in the capacity of our people, then, requires a continual reaffirmation, and a sensitivity to the ways it can be diminished. For though some of these biases about intelligence have been challenged and curtailed, they, altered, mutated, are still with us. They represent an antidemocratic tension in our social history, a set of beliefs that can emerge as a foul common sense, seemingly self-evident, ready for use. Witness the success of *The Bell Curve* a decade ago, a book built on an argument about the relation between IQ and economic and social advancement that included in it (methodologically and statistically flawed) analyses of African American inferiority. We are not at all free of the tendency to frame a measure of mind and separate ourselves by it.

My hope is that this book and the many sources represented in it—from research in the social and psychological sciences to the commentary of the participants themselves—can contribute to such a reaffirmation. These sources are testament to a dynamic, multidimensional model of intelligence and a conception of knowledge that doesn't separate hand from brain; that articulates the many kinds of knowing involved in work; that appreciates the interplay of the cognitive, the social, the aesthetic; that is more abundant and varied than a model built on hierarchies and binaries. In fact, as a number of firsthand accounts of intellectual and creative effort would certify, this is a more accurate model of *all* the mind's work: from the planning of a pitched roof, to the diagnosing of joint pain, to the crafting of a line of poetry.

The models and language we use have social consequences; that is Calhoun's point. And it is one worth pondering at this historical moment, as we undergo transformations in the workplace, as we struggle with ways to provide a quality education for all. Of course, matters of the economy and of education are affected by a number of forces, but the beliefs we carry about people figure into policy, both in its development and in the rhetoric of its implementation. "Given that there are ineradicable differences among human beings," writes philosopher Albert Borgmann, "in what respect are we equal? And to what does equality entitle each of us? The norm of self-realization [a central tenet of democratic theory] suggests that we are all equal in being capable of developing our common and various talents and that we have a right to the opportunities for such development." The specific talents that get recognized and valued and the nature and distribution of opportunity are both subject to a society's assumptions about ability and achievement.

If we believe common work to be mindless, that belief will affect the work we create in the future. If we don't appreciate, if we in some ways constrict, the full range of everyday cognition, then we will develop limited educational programs and fail to make fresh and meaningful instructional connections among disparate kinds of skill and knowledge. If we think that whole categories of people—identified by class, by occupation—are not that bright, then we reinforce social separations and cripple our ability to talk across our current cultural divides.

To affirm our capacity as a people is not to deny the obvious variability among us. Nor is it to retreat to some softhearted notion of mind. We mistake narrowness for rigor, but actually we are not rigorous enough. To acknowledge our collective capacity is to take the concept of variability seriously. Not as slots along a simplified cognitive continuum or as a neat high-low distribution, but as a bountiful and layered field, where many processes and domains of knowledge interact. Such a model demands more not less from those of us who teach, or who organize work, or who develop social policy. To affirm this conception of mind and work is to be vigilant for the intelligence not only in the boardroom but on the shop floor; in the laboratory and alongside the house frame; in the classroom, the garage, the busy restaurant, vibrant with desire and strategic movement. This is a model of mind that befits the democratic imagination.

AFTERWORD: ON METHOD

There are a number of involved and contentious discussions going on these days in psychology, anthropology, and the cognitive sciences about the nature of cognition and the legitimacy of various methods of studying it. A comprehensive treatment of these discussions is beyond the scope of a book like this, but let me give a brief overview of them.

Some researchers believe that the best way to study cognition is within the structured environment of the psychologist's laboratory where conditions can be experimentally controlled. Researchers with quite different beliefs contend that naturally occurring settings—like the workplaces described in this book—provide the most accurate perspectives on the way human beings use their minds; experimental control may be sacrificed, but authenticity is gained. My own preference in doing the research for *The Mind at Work* is toward the use of naturalistic methods, though I rely on other researchers' laboratory studies (for example, of memory or attention) when they are appropriate—as in the discussion of the waitress's memory for food orders.

These questions of method intersect with further questions about the nature of cognition itself. Some scholars hold, in a tradition that goes back at least to Descartes's single and distinct *cogito,* that cognition is best modeled and studied as an individual phenomenon. The standard metaphor compares the mind to an information-processing computer. Others hold that a better metaphor is that of an ecology or an orchestra. It misleads us, they claim, to focus on that individual computer, when cognition both develops and functions in dynamic interaction with the world beyond the individual brain. Thus these scholars tend to study cognition as a system: individuals in concert with each other and with tools, symbols, and conventions delivered by the culture.

A related debate concerns the role context—the lived environment—plays in thinking. Do our mental structures and processes exist and function in some generalized way, irrespective of the particular setting we're in, or is thinking intimately dependent on the specifics of the settings we inhabit? One writer expresses the latter view this way: "The *nature* of cognitive processing is uniquely determined within its context, and . . . it cannot be studied in isolation without destroying its defining properties." Again, let us call up the waitress as an example. Are the memory strategies that she uses to remember orders supported and directed by the structure and conventions of the restaurant, and are they thus best analyzed and understood in that setting? Or are these strategies more abstract and, therefore, transferable and effective in the supermarket, the classroom, or the church social?

I've summarized and simplified the strong views of these positions, but in actual practice many scholars would locate themselves somewhere between the two. The reader interested in a fuller discussion can consult the sources I cite under "cognition" in the notes (see page 230) or, for a much briefer treatment pertinent to this book, can read the methods sections of two of my earlier articles: " 'Our Hands Will Know': The Development of Tactile Diagnostic Skill—Teaching, Learning, and Situated Cognition in a Physical Therapy Program" in the journal *Anthropology and Education* (vol. 30, no. 2, 1999, pp. 133–160) and "The Working Life of a Waitress" in *Mind, Culture, and Activity* (vol. 8, no. 1, 2001, pp. 3–27).

I don't believe that the basic argument I'm making about cognition and common work depends, finally, on holding one of these positions rather than another. People along the continua could support it, though the laboratory-oriented psychologist would want to devise experiments to test the claims I make from more naturalistic studies.

Although I conduct studies of a particular kind, my basic orientation toward issues of cognition tends toward the eclectic and synthetic. Each theory and each methodology shines a particular kind of light on a remarkably complex cognitive and social reality, and each, I think, helps us make partial sense of the swirling whole. Particularly with a topic like the one in this book—one that is not much studied—I needed to range wide, synthesize as best as I could, trying to be mindful of and honor the tensions among these various research traditions, but seek correspondence where possible.

␣

When at a job site or in a classroom, I observed people at work, writing notes on their activity and, when permissible, taking photographs of the task at hand. Once I got a sense of the rhythms of the work—its moments of less intense focus and its pauses—I would begin asking questions about what people were doing and why, trying to gain an understanding of their behavior and the thinking that directed it. As they got more familiar with me and I with them and their work, I was able to ask increasingly specific questions, probing the reasons for using one implement rather than another, for a particular positioning of the body, for the benefits of this procedure over that one. I wondered aloud how they knew what to do, given the materials and constraints of the present task, what they had in mind to do next, how they knew something was wrong. (In instructional settings, the answers to such questions sometimes emerged naturally in exchanges between student and teacher or among peers assisting one another.) Over time, the exchanges became more conversational, and frequently people on their own began explaining what they were doing and what their thinking was for doing it, a kind of modified think-aloud procedure, long used in studies of problem solving.

In some cases, I was able to conduct follow-up interviews—which I tape-recorded—after class or when the workday was over. These interviews provided the opportunity to inquire about a person's biography and work history, motives, and short- and long-term goals. These interviews also enabled me to ask further questions about the work I had observed earlier, using descriptive passages from my notes, or photographs if I had them, to ground us in specifics.

Some settings afforded additional materials that aided me in exploring practice: videotapes of a student's performance, audiotapes of a collaborative discussion of a task, CD-ROM presentations of a procedure. These provided further means for me to explore people's thinking, learning, and knowledge of a field.

Any method is subject to biases and distortions. And, of course, my presence at a site could have influenced things in all sorts of ways, just as my style as an interviewer could affect what is and isn't said. One thing I did to check myself was to have the primary participants read what I had written about them and their work. Did I get the technical details right? Did I accurately render their sense of the task?

I also sought to validate or revise my findings by seeking further perspectives and multiple sources of information on the material I observed and recorded. I would, for example, present vignettes from my notes and my photographs to other skilled practitioners—to other plumbers or hairstylists or surgeons—and invite their analysis. I did the same with psychologists or anthropologists who study cognition. And in the few cases where cognitive research had been done on the phenomena I was studying—for example, on the memory of waiters and waitresses or the mathematics used by carpenters—I was able to incorporate that research into my writing.

During the time of these studies, I was reading technical and social histories of the work in question, trying to gain an understanding of how it developed, both in its techniques and norms of practice and in the way it came to define itself and be defined by the various occupational categories our society provides. I wanted a sense of the antecedents to the work I was observing.

And there are research literatures in a range of disciplines—from biological anthropology to education—that, while not directly concerned with the kinds of work before me, were certainly relevant. Examples would include studies of the evolution of tool use; studies of attention, memory, mental imagery, problem solving, and the timing and rhythm of behavior; sociological studies of work and emotion; studies of identity development; historical studies of apprenticeship; and so on. These literatures provided rich knowledge and perspective, helping me consider more carefully and with more appreciation a novice's refinement in the swing of a hammer, or the role of emotion in remembering a customer's order, or the interrelation of manual skill and one's sense of self.

Finally, let me say a word about my use of family material. There certainly are arguments against it, arguments concerning bias and threats to objectivity. True enough. But as some feminist social scientists would argue, personal history can provide a valuable way of knowing that extends beyond one's own immediate circumstances. Given my background, I understand things about social stratification that all the reading in the world couldn't provide. Or I have a sense of the complicated and contradictory set of attitudes someone like my mother could have toward hard physical work. I find significant value, as well, in combining personal material with scholarship, matching it, each providing a check on the other. For example, as I was reading historian David Montgomery's extraordinary chapter on "The Common Laborer" (in *The Fall of the House of Labor*), I kept thinking of my grandfather Tony Meraglio. As vivid as Montgomery's writing is, my knowledge of Tony—the stories I heard, the photograph on my desk—all brought a further depth of understanding to the historian's portrayal. Conversely, the context Montgomery provides, the macro view of social and economic forces, brings Tony to fuller life. He's not only a cluster of family stories but a man located in a time and a place. The table of labor statistics and the narrative of a life are, clearly, quite different ways of representing the world, but they also can complement and enhance each other.

All of the foregoing perspectives contributed to a sharper focus on the particulars of cognition and behavior. They encouraged, as well, consideration of broader social and institutional phenomena: The way occupation gets linked to definitions of mind. The educational traditions that relegate practices typical of physical work to a curricular (and thus, career) path quite separate from the high-status course of study. The tendency of social science, segmenting human activity as it does into disciplinary domains, to reduce inadvertently the complexity of work—tool use is dealt with anthropologically or historically, skill is addressed in a few areas of psychology or, in a different way, in economics, and questions of work and identity are raised in sociology. If I have been successful, *The Mind at Work* functions as a corrective to that segmentation. Perhaps we can arrive at a synthesis whereby we consider skill, emotion, and identity on the same page. Or think about tool use and values simultaneously. Or shuttle back and forth between the close particulars of the way work gets done and larger social concerns about justice and opportunity, viewing mental and physical operations through the lens of democratic theory.

ACKNOWLEDGMENTS

This project ran about six years and involved so many people. There were all those I observed or interviewed for each chapter, and the reader is introduced to a number of them along the way. Then there were the folks who read what I had written, some of whom were the subjects of the book, some who work in the various occupations covered, and some who bring expertise in the disciplines I use. It would have been impossible to write this book without them.

At its earliest stages, Marion Maneker, then at Viking Penguin, urged the project forward, and, at the end, Wendy Wolf signed *The Mind at Work* and provided superb editorial guidance. Writers crave, but rarely find, Wendy's blend of advocacy, wit, and nimble toughmindedness.

There was a point in the development of the manuscript when Andy Hrycyna, a talented editor at Beacon Press, read several chapters and assured me that there was a book here. His incisive feedback was as timely as could be. And Joyce Seltzer, my editor for *Lives on the Boundary* who is now at Harvard University Press, intervened with her typically deft advice to remedy a clumsy introduction. Thanks, Joyce.

Some of the material in this book appeared in different form in professional and scholarly publications, and the editors of each had a hand in refining my ideas and my language: Sandra Reeves and Ihsan Taylor, *Education Week*; Drew Lindsay and Blake Rodman, *Teacher Magazine*; Susan Florio-Ruane, *Anthropology and Education Quarterly*; Michael Cole, *Mind, Culture, and Activity*; Cindy O'Donnell-Allen, *NCRLL Newsletter*; Anne DiPardo and Melanie Sperling, *Research in the Teaching of English*.

John Wright has been my agent for fifteen years. He has provided strong counsel and warm friendship. Here's to the next fifteen, John.

As the book went through production, Hilary Redmon provided close and thoughtful editorial counsel. Carla Bolte's design work was both elegant and playful. And Bruce Giffords smoothly managed things while Maureen Clark's expert copyediting refined the text.

I have received generous and sustaining support from the Spencer Foundation. In particular, I want to thank the program officers who made things happen along the way: Terri Pigott, Katherine Lacey, and Mark Rigdon. They provided emotional as well as monetary resources—and terrific feedback as well. I also want to acknowledge Kim Wright for her good cheer and thoughtful reading. Pat Graham was president of the foundation during the period of my grants, and I thank her for her continued belief in my work.

At several key points in the project, the Committee on Research of the UCLA Academic Senate provided small grants that made a big difference. And, at the end, a grant from the University of California Institute for Labor and Employment provided support that enabled me to finish the book. Particular gratitude is due director Ruth Milkman.

I benefited immensely from a series of thoughtful and engaged research assistants; from beginning to end, they were: Lisa Hardimon, Brendesha Tynes, Michelle Renee, Katherine Masyn, Elizabeth Rivera, and Artineh Samkian. They provided so much help and good talk, and they made a huge contribution to this project. I also want to thank those who have typed and typed again the many revisions of this thing: Emily Chang, Hillary Hai, Traimy Hai, Rosemary Kim, and Rona Pau. What a fine and patient group.

I learned more than a few sentences of acknowledgment can express from those who have been reading sections of this book over the years, talking to me about it, recommending sources and revisions, then reading some more. How do I render the intelligence and sensibility they brought to bear? Deborah Appleman, Ellen Cushman, Kris Gutierrez, Michael Hendrickson, Deborah Hicks, Glynda Hull, Michael Katz, Ken Lincoln, Lisa Moore, Deborah Stipek.

During the first stages of the project, a number of people provided warm encouragement and valuable ideas: Hector Alvarez, Michelle Ballif, David Bartholomae, Lynn Beck, Lauren Benjamin, David Bensman, John Bransford, Kristin Crosland, Steve Duarte, Joan Feinberg, Linda Flower, Tim Flower, Richard Foy, Ed Frankel, Chris Fritsch, Ronald Gallimore, Ruth Glendinning, Allen Graubard, Jennifer Gross, Cathie Gum, Rogers Hall, Roy Herweck, Paula Hidalgo, Elham Kazemi, Ron Klemp, Arthur Kovacs, Jon Losk, Jennifer Lundmark, Dan Miller, Carmel Myers, Na'ilah Nasir, Kim Padilla, Bill Sandoval, Geoffrey Saxe, Janelle Scott, James Stigler, John Warnock, Tilly Warnock, Mavourneen (Roberts) Wilcox, Janet Zandy, Danielle Zawodny-Wetzel.

At pivitol points in the middle and, especially, toward the conclusion of this book, I tapped colleagues and friends to read entire drafts of chapters and, in some cases, the whole manuscript. Their responses—detailed and generous—shaped *The Mind at Work*. They are: Arif Amlani, Ben Bagdikian, Susan Carlile, Jim Daniels, Benjamin DeMott, Noel Enyedy, Frederick Erickson, Manuel Espinoza, Jan Frodesen, Julie Gainsburg, Maxine Greene, Marlene Griffith, Norton Grubb, Charles Healy, Amina Humphrey, Andrea Lunsford, Julie Lindquist, Yolanda Majors, Karen McClafferty Jarsky, Joan McFarland, Deborah Meier, Michael Merrill, Ruth Milkman, Ted Mitchell, Michael Seltzer, Richard Shavelson, Jessica Siegel, David Stern, David Tyack, Ash Vasudeva, Lynn Waldorf, Noreen Webb, Buzz Wilms, Steve Witte.

And sometimes, especially as a long project is reaching its end and you are so out of gas, sometimes it's just a conversation over dinner or a few key phone calls that give you the boost and the fresh take on things to move forward. So, thanks to Tina Christie, Nick Coles, Yasmin Damshenas, Dean Jamison, Peter McLaren, Danny Solorzano, Sandy Taut, Elliot Washor.

Finally, Jack McFarland, who taught me high school English, read the manuscript and, just as he did a jillion years ago, gave me the most helpful feedback, his penciled script running along the border of the page.

In addition to those acknowledged above and in the chapters themselves, there were many people who provided various kinds of assistance in specific settings or with specific topics. I'll list them by chapter, and I thank them for the detail and direction they provided.

Introduction: Donna Clay, Mickey Marell.

The Working Life of a Waitress: Helen Astin, Patricia Baquedano-Lopez, Deborah Brandt, Katherine Broughton, Jane Danielewicz, Sandra Harding, Celina Haro, Patricia McDonough, Giuliana Santini, Brooke Totman, Angie Truman.

Styling Hair: Nancy Barden, Vanessa Christensen, Stacy Cunningham, Debbie Fox, Jolena James, Anna Mae Meraglio, Shandra Murray, Gail Rackliffe, Deborah Sheldon, Brooke Totman, Sharon Vidal, Caroline Walthour, Susan Wenck, Kevin Wilmore, Leah Wilmore.

The Intelligence of Plumbing: Marty Hoeffel, Deborah Maceyko, Felix Sandoval, Megan Sandoval.

A Vocabulary of Carpentry: Tarek Azzam, Fred Eberhart, Megan Franke, Al Halferty, Jeff Hendrick, Julie Mack, Morgan Mcpherson, Jo Anne Mitchell, Faye Peitzman, Scott Pfetzing, Jody Priselac, Dave Severn, Tim Sullivan, Terry Tsotse, Rae Jeane Williams.

Reflective Technique: Electrical Wiring and Construction: Terry Cunningham, Gavin Lawrence, Tommi Lenard, Bobby McNeel.

Two Lives: A Welder and a Foreman: Sherry Dundee, Connie Giglio, Dominic Giglio, Mariam Meraglio, Robert Richards.

Rethinking Hand and Brain: Dean Anselmo, Letitia Bridges, Nicole Christensen, Jeff Conisarow, Rosie Cushman Hubert, Tim Gilleran, Chester Griffiths, Greg Hallert, Darryl Hiyama, Julie Martinovich, Reed Metzger, Laura Miller, Cindy Moore, Philip Nivatpumin, Richard Reznick, Sydney Risser, Julie Scira, Vipal Soni, Graham Waring, LuAnn Wilkerson, Lishan Workeneh.

Hand and Brain in School: The Paradox of Vocational Education: Jolly Enciso, Jeannie Oakes, Lynn Olson, Larry Rosenstock, Ted Sizer, Adria Steinberg.

Conclusion: Earl Krug, Sandy Krug.

Finally, a tip of the hat to Tommi Lenard, elegant craftsman, who passed away as this book was moving into print.

NOTES

Introduction

PAGE

xv Mario Cuomo, *More Than Words: The Speeches of Mario Cuomo* (New York: St. Martin's Press, 1993), p. 30.

xv **testaments to physical work . . . rather than on the thought it requires:** I don't mean to suggest that the writers of the testaments themselves would necessarily deny the intelligence of working people. Rather I am interested in the standard story lines and conventions we tend to rely on when producing such testaments. For some recent anthologies that include a wider array of tributes, see Patricia Bell-Scott et al., eds., *Double Stitch: Black Women Write about Mothers and Daughters* (New York: HarperCollins, 1991); C. L. Barney Dews and Carolyn Leste Law, eds., *This Fine Place So Far from Home: Voices of Academics from the Working Class* (Philadelphia: Temple University Press, 1995); Michelle M. Tokarczyk and Elizabeth A. Fay, eds., *Working Class Women in the Academy: Laborers in the Knowledge Factory* (Amherst: University of Massachusetts Press, 1993); Janet Zandy, ed., *What We Hold in Common: An Introduction to Working Class Studies* (New York: Feminist Press, 2001).

xix **symbolic analysis** and **knowledge work:** See, for example, Robert Reich, *The Work of Nations: Preparing Ourselves for 21st Century Capitalism* (London: Simon and Schuster, 1991), and Peter Drucker, "The Next Society" and following pieces, in *The Economist*, November 3, 2001, pp. 3–20.

xix **historical amnesia:** See, for example, Jeff Madrick, "Enron, the Media and the New Economy," *The Nation*, April 1, 2002, pp. 17–20, and Clark Kerr et al., *Industrialism and Industrial Man* (Cambridge, MA: Harvard University Press, 1960).

xx Steven Peter Vallas, "Comments and Observations on the Nature of Work," in *The Nature of Work: Sociological Perspectives*, ed. Kai Erikson and Steven Peter Vallas (New Haven, CT: Yale University Press, 1990), p. 348.

xx–xxi John P. Hoerr, *And the Wolf Finally Came: The Decline of the American Steel Industry* (Pittsburgh: University of Pittsburgh Press, 1988), p. 273.

xxi **post–Revolutionary War mechanics:** See Alfred F. Young, "Revolutionary

Mechanics," in *Working for Democracy: American Workers from the Revolution to the Present*, ed. Paul Buhle and Alan Dawley (Urbana and Chicago: University of Illinois Press, 1985), pp. 1–9.

xxii Barbara Ehrenreich, *Nickel and Dimed: On (Not) Getting By in America* (New York: Metropolitan Books/Henry Holt, 2001).

xxii **cognition:** For a representative sample of sources, see Lawrence W. Barsalou, *Cognitive Psychology: An Overview for Cognitive Scientists* (Hillsdale, NJ: Lawrence Erlbaum Associates, 1992); Seth Chaiklin and Jean Lave, eds., *Understanding Practice: Perspectives on Activity and Context* (Cambridge: Cambridge University Press, 1993); Michael Cole, *Cultural Psychology: A Once and Future Discipline* (Cambridge, MA: The Belknap Press of Harvard University Press, 1996); K. Anders Ericsson and Jacqui Smith, eds., *Toward a General Theory of Expertise: Prospects and Limits* (Cambridge: Cambridge University Press, 1991); Howard Gardner, *The Mind's New Science: A History of the Cognitive Revolution* (New York: Basic Books, 1985); Kathleen R. Gibson and Tim Ingold, eds., *Tools, Language and Cognition in Human Evolution* (Cambridge: Cambridge University Press, 1993); Robert Glaser, "On the Nature of Expertise," in *Human Memory and Cognitive Capabilities: Mechanisms and Performances*, F. Klix and H. Hagendorf, eds. (Amsterdam: Elsevier Science Publishers, 1986), 915–28.; Robert Glaser, "Education and Thinking: The Role of Knowledge," *American Psychologist* 39.2 (February 1984): 93–104; James G. Greeno, "The Situativity of Knowing, Learning, and Research," *American Psychologist* 53 (January 1998): 5–26; Jean Lave and Etienne Wenger, *Situated Learning: Legitimate Peripheral Participation* (Cambridge: Cambridge University Press, 1991); Barbara Rogoff and Jean Lave, eds., *Everyday Cognition: Its Development in Social Context* (Cambridge, MA: Harvard University Press, 1984); Jan D. Sinnott, ed., *Everyday Problem Solving: Theory and Applications* (New York: Praeger, 1989); Edward E. Smith and Daniel N. Osherson, eds., *An Invitation to Cognitive Science*, vol. 3, *Thinking* (Cambridge, MA: MIT Press, 1995); L. S. Vygotsky, *Mind and Society: The Development of Higher Psychological Processes* (Cambridge, MA: Harvard University Press, 1978); James V. Wertsch, *Mind as Action* (New York: Oxford University Press, 1998); Robert A. Wilson and Frank C. Keil, eds., *The MIT Encyclopedia of the Cognitive Sciences* (Cambridge, MA: MIT Press, 1999).

xxiii–xxv **intelligence:** For a representative sample of sources, see Ian J. Deary, *Intelligence: A Very Short Introduction* (Oxford: Oxford University Press, 2001); Howard Gardner, *Frames of Mind: The Theory of Multiple Intelligences* (New York: Basic Books, 1983); Jean Khalfa, ed., *What Is Intelligence?* (Cambridge: Cambridge University Press, 1994); Ulric Neisser et al., "Intelligence: Knowns and Unknowns," *American Psychologist* 51, no. 2 (February 1996): 77–101; Robert J. Sternberg, ed., *Handbook of Intelligence* (Cambridge: Cambridge University Press, 2000); Robert J. Sternberg and Richard K. Wagner, eds., *Practical Intelligence: Nature and Origins of Com-*

petence in the Everyday World (Cambridge: Cambridge University Press, 1986); Robert J. Sternberg et al., *Practical Intelligence in Everyday Life* (Cambridge: Cambridge University Press, 2000); Robert M. Thorndike with David F. Lohman, *A Century of Ability Testing* (Chicago: Riverside Publishing Company, 1990); Leila Zenderland, *Measuring Minds: Henry Herbert Goddard and the Origins of American Intelligence Testing* (Cambridge: Cambridge University Press, 1998).

xxv–xxvi **skill:** For a representative sample of sources, see Robin Barrow, "Skill Talk," *Journal of Philosophy of Education* 21, no. 2 (1987): 187–95; Charles N. Darrah, *Learning and Work: An Exploration in Industrial Ethnography* (New York: Garland Publishing, 1996); Theodore Lewis, "Toward the 21st Century: Retrospect, Prospect for American Vocationalism," Information Series No. 373 (Columbus, OH: ERIC Clearinghouse on Adult, Career and Vocational Education, 1998); David Montgomery, *The Fall of the House of Labor* (Cambridge: Cambridge University Press, 1987); Carroll Pursell, *The Machine in America: A Social History of Technology* (Baltimore: Johns Hopkins University Press, 1995); Edward W. Stevens Jr., *The Grammar of the Machine: Technical Literacy and Early Industrial Expansion in the United States* (New Haven, CT: Yale University Press, 1995).

xxv *American Heritage Dictionary,* 3rd ed. (Boston and New York: Houghton Mifflin, 1993), p. 1277.

xxvi–xxvii **work:** For a representative sample of sources, see Herbert Applebaum, *The Concept of Work: Ancient, Medieval, and Modern* (Albany: State University of New York Press, 1992); Erikson and Vallas, *The Nature of Work*; Richard H. Hall, *Dimensions of Work* (Beverly Hills: Sage Publications, 1986); Michael Keith Honey, *Black Workers Remember: An Oral History of Segregation, Unionism, and the Freedom Struggle* (Berkeley and Los Angeles: University of California Press, 1999); Patrick Joyce, *The Historical Meanings of Work* (Cambridge: Cambridge University Press, 1987); Ken C. Kusterer, *Know-How on the Job: The Important Working Knowledge of "Unskilled" Workers* (Boulder, CO: Westview Press, 1978); Daniel T. Rodgers, *The Work Ethic in Industrial America, 1850–1920* (Chicago: University of Chicago Press, 1974); Ellen Israel Rosen, *Bitter Choices: Blue-Collar Women In and Out of Work* (Chicago: University of Chicago Press, 1987); Studs Terkel, *Working* (New York: Ballantine Books, 1972).

xxvi Everett Cherrington Hughes, *Men and Their Work* (Glencoe, IL: Free Press, 1958), p. 42.

xxviii–xxix Barbara Garson, *All the Livelong Day: The Meaning and Demeaning of Routine Work* (1975; repr., New York: Penguin Books, 1994), p. ix. The phrase "electronic sweatshop" also comes from Barbara Garson: *The Electronic Sweatshop: How Computers Are Transforming the Office of the Future into the Factory of the Past* (New York: Simon and Schuster, 1988).

xxix **A common theme:** For an incisive discussion of class consciousness and the worker, see Gordon Marshall, "Some Remarks on the Study of Working-Class Consciousness," *Politics and Society* 12, no. 3 (1983): 263–301.

xxix **There is also research:** See Melvin L. Kohn, "Unresolved Issues in the Relationship between Work and Personality," in Erikson and Vallas, *The Nature of Work*, pp. 36–68.

xxxiv **Some critics:** See, for example, Malcolm Gladwell, "The Talent Myth," *The New Yorker*, July 22, 2002, pp. 28–33, and David Elkind, *The Hurried Child: Growing Up Too Fast Too Soon* (Reading, MA: Addison-Wesley, 1981; repr., Reading, MA: Addison-Wesley, 2001).

Chapter 1: *The Working Life of a Waitress*

1 Let me explain the use of people's names. Where students and novices are concerned—a situation where competence is still developing—I use pseudonyms to protect their identities. Otherwise, I use the actual names of the people I studied and/or interviewed. I do this with their permission. Sometimes I incorporate what I learned from the people I observed but do not use their names so that the reader can move through the narrative more easily, following relatively few characters. I do, however, thank these people in the acknowledgments.

For a selection of background material on interviewing and the use of oral reports and life history, see Daniel Bertaux, ed., *Biography and Society: The Life History Approach in the Social Sciences* (Newbury Park, CA: Sage Publications, 1981); Trevor Lummis, *Listening to History: The Authenticity of Oral Evidence* (London: Hutchinson, 1987); Elliot G. Mishler, *Storylines: Craftartists' Narratives of Identity* (Cambridge, MA: Harvard University Press, 1999); Max Van Manen, *Researching Lived Experience: Human Science for an Action Sensitive Pedagogy* (Albany: State University of New York Press, 1990).

For a selection of background material on waitressing, see Dorothy Sue Cobble, *Dishing It Out: Waitresses and Their Unions in the Twentieth Century* (Urbana and Chicago: University of Illinois Press, 1991); Frances Donovan, *The Woman Who Waits* (Boston: Gorham, 1920); Leon Elder and Lin Rolens, *Waitress: America's Unsung Heroine* (Santa Barbara, CA: Capra, 1985); Arlie Russell Hochschild, *The Managed Heart: Commercialization of Human Feeling* (Berkeley and Los Angeles: University of California Press, 1983); Greta Pauff Paules, *Dishing It Out: Power and Resistance among Waitresses in a New Jersey Restaurant* (Philadelphia: Temple University Press, 1991); Lydia A. Salisch and Emily G. Palmer, *An Analysis of the Waitress Trade* (Sacramento: California State Department of Education, 1932); James P. Spradley and Brenda J. Mann, *The Cocktail Waitress: Woman's Work in a Man's World* (New York: John Wiley and Sons, 1975); Amy E. Tanner, "Glimpses at the Mind of a Waitress," *American Journal of Sociology* 13 (July/May 1907/1908): 48–55; William Foote Whyte, *Human Relations in the Restaurant Industry* (New York: McGraw-Hill, 1948).

2 **"the least skilled":** Paul D. Montagna, *Occupations and Society: Toward a Sociology of the Labor Market* (New York: John Wiley and Sons, 1977), p. 372.

3 **"rendered invisible"**: Cobble, *Dishing It Out*, p. 120.

6 **restaurant is a structured environment**: For a cognitive psychological perspective on this structure, see Roger C. Schank and Robert P. Ableson, *Scripts, Plans, Goals and Understanding: An Inquiry into Human Knowledge Structures* (Hillsdale, NJ: Erlbaum, 1977); see especially chapter 3, "Scripts."

9 **"You learn a walk"**: Elder and Rolens, *Waitress*, pp. 19–20.

10 **small body of psychological research**: See, for example, King Beach, "Becoming a Bartender: The Role of External Memory Cues in a Work-directed Educational Activity," *Applied Cognitive Psychology* 7 (1993): 191–204; K. Anders Ericsson and Peter G. Polson, "A Cognitive Analysis of Exceptional Memory for Restaurant Orders," in *The Nature of Expertise*, ed. Michelene T. H. Chi, Robert Glaser, and Marcia J. Farr (Hillsdale, NJ: Lawrence Erlbaum Associates, 1988), pp. 23–70; and Joy Stevens, "An Observational Study of Skilled Memory in Waitresses," *Applied Cognitive Psychology* 7 (1993): 205–17. For a discussion of "short-term" or "working" memory, see Alan D. Baddeley, *Working Memory* (Oxford: Oxford University Press, 1986), and John Jonides, "Working Memory and Thinking," in *An Invitation to Cognitive Science*, vol. 3, *Thinking*, ed. Edward E. Smith and Daniel N. Osherson (Cambridge, MA: MIT Press, 1995), pp. 215–65.

14 **Attention is described**: See, for example, David LaBerge, *Attentional Processing: The Brain's Art of Mindfulness* (Cambridge, MA: Harvard University Press, 1995), and Raja Parasuraman, *The Attentive Brain* (Cambridge, MA: MIT Press, 1998).

14 **"the purpose of allowing"**: Parasuraman, *Attentive Brain*, p. 6.

15 LaBerge, *Attentional Processing*.

18 **"flow" experience**: Mihalyi Csikszentmihalyi and Jeanne Nakamura, "Emerging Goals and the Self-Regulation of Behavior," in *Perspectives on Behavioral Self-Regulation*, ed. Robert S. Wyer Jr. (Mahwah, NJ: Lawrence Erlbaum Associates, 1999), p. 113.

19 **"Eating is the most intimate act"**: Elder and Rolens, *Waitress*, p. 16.

19 **"hungers of many kinds"**: Cobble, *Dishing It Out*, p. 2.

19 Donovan, *Woman Who Waits*.

19 **"[D]ishes are placed"**: Salisch and Palmer, *Analysis of the Waitress Trade*, pp. 47–48.

20 **"emotional labor"**: Hochschild, *Managed Heart*.

21 **stereotypic gender scripts**: See, for example, Elaine J. Hall, "Smiling, Deferring, and Flirting: Doing Gender by Giving 'Good Service,' " *Work and Occupations* 20, no. 4 (November 1993): 452–71; Patti A. Giuffre and Christine L. Williams, "Boundary Lines: Labeling Sexual Harassment in Restaurants," *Gender and Society* 8, no. 3 (September 1994): 378–401.

21 **There is actually a fair-sized social-psychological literature**: See, for example, Suellen R. Butler and William E. Snizek, "The Waitress-Diner Relationship: A Multimethod Approach to the Study of Subordinate Influence," *Sociology of Work and Occupations* 3 (1976): 209–22; April H. Crusco and

Christopher G. Wetzel, "The Midas Touch: The Effects of Interpersonal Touch on Restaurant Tipping," *Personality and Social Psychology Bulletin* 10 (1984): 512–17; Michael Lynn and Kirby Mynier, "Effects of Server Posture on Restaurant Tipping," *Journal of Applied Social Psychology* 23 (1993): 678–85; and Kathi L. Tidd and Joan S. Lockard, "Monitary Significance of the Affiliative Smile: A Case for Reciprocal Altruism," *Bulletin of the Psychonomic Society* 11 (1978): 344–46.

22 "tip in every spirit imaginable": Elder and Rolens, *Waitress*, p. 19.

22 Paules, *Dishing It Out*, p. 37.

22 "[P]lay the people and the tips will follow": Elder and Rolens, *Waitress*, p. 64.

23 the waitress as a private entrepreneur: Paules, *Dishing It Out*.

23 if tipping were outlawed: In fact, in some other countries people do not normally tip in the restaurant, so this discussion of tipping is culture-specific.

28 "How else can I learn about people?": Studs Terkel, *Working* (New York: Ballantine Books, 1972), p. 390.

29 "the restraints put upon [them]": Donovan, *Woman Who Waits*, p. 145.

29 Given the recent studies . . . stereotyped gender roles: See the first note for page 21.

29 "set up new standards for herself": Donovan, *Woman Who Waits*, p. 145.

Chapter 2: Styling Hair

31 For a selection of background material on hairdressing, see Ingrid Banks, *Hair Matters: Beauty, Power and Black Women's Consciousness* (New York: New York University Press, 2000); Wendy Cooper, *Hair: Sex, Society, Symbolism* (New York: Stein and Day, 1971); Michele A. Eayrs, "Time, Trust and Hazard: Hairdressers' Symbolic Roles," *Symbolic Interaction* 16, no. 1 (1993): 19–37; Juliette Harris and Pamela Johnson, eds., *Tenderheaded: A Comb-Bending Collection of Hair Stories* (New York: Pocket Books, 2001); Marybeth Janssen et al., *Milady's Standard System of Salon Skills: Hairdressing: A Student Course Book* (Albany: Milady Publishing, 1999); Jean Keyes, *A History of Women's Hairstyles, 1500–1965* (London: Methuen and Co., 1967); Yolanda J. Majors, "Shoptalk: Teaching and Learning in an African American Hair Salon," in *Mind, Culture, and Activity* (forthcoming); Marilyn S. Notkin, "Situational Learning in a School with Clients," in *Learning to Work*, ed. Blanche Geer (Beverly Hills: Sage Publications, 1972), pp. 49–58; Noliwe M. Rooks, *Hair Raising: Beauty, Culture, and African American Women* (New Brunswick, NJ: Rutgers University Press, 1996); Diane Simon, *Hair: Public, Political, Extremely Personal* (New York: St. Martin's Press, 2000); Anthony Synnott, "Shame and Glory: A Sociology of Hair," *British Journal of Sociology* 38, no. 1 (March 1987): 381–413.

32 planning style: See, for example, John R. Hayes, *The Complete Problem Solver*, 2nd ed. (Hillsdale, NJ: Lawrence Erlbaum Associates, 1989), pp.

58–62; Barbara Hayes-Roth and Frederick Hayes-Roth, "Cognitive Processes in Planning," *Cognitive Science* 3 (1979): 275–310.

34 **statistics on hairdressers and cosmetologists:** U.S. Department of Labor, Bureau of Labor Statistics, "Annual Averages." Washington, DC, 2000.

41 **"I want to *create* coiffures":** quoted in Cooper, *Hair*, p. 168.

42 **Right now on my desk:** Cooper, *Hair*, p.121; Heinrich Lindlar, *Loreley-Report, Heinrich Heine und die Rheinlied-Romantik* (Köln-Rheinkassal: Verlag Dohr, 1999); Richard Lovelace, "Song to Amarantha, That She Would Dishevel Her Hair," in *The Poems of Richard Lovelace*, vol. 2, ed. C. H. Wilkinson (Oxford: Oxford University Press, 1925), pp. 18–19; Raymond Firth, *Symbols Public and Private* (London: George Allen and Unwin, 1973); "Hair: In African Art and Culture," May 26 through August 19, 2001, California African American Museum Guide.

42 **to reword Freud:** The allusion is to Freud's dictum reminding us not to overinterpret: "Sometimes," he said, "a cigar is just a cigar."

48 Lanita Jacobs-Huey, "Becoming Cosmetologists: Language Socialization in an African American Beauty College" (PhD diss., UCLA, 1999).

49 Louise Kapp Howe, *Pink Collar Workers: Inside the World of Women's Work* (New York: G. P. Putnam's Sons, 1977).

50 Debra Gimlin, "Pamela's Place: Power and Negotiation in the Hair Salon," *Gender and Society* 10, no. 5 (October 1996): 505–26.

51 **community mental health researchers:** Alan R. Wiesenfeld and Herbert M. Weis, "Hairdressers and Helping: Influencing the Behavior of Informal Caregivers," *Professional Psychology* 10 (December 1979): 786–92.

53 Gary Alan Fine, "Occupational Aesthetics: How Trade School Students Learn to Cook," *Urban Life* 14, no. 1 (April 1985): 3–31; Gary Alan Fine, *Kitchens: The Culture of Restaurant Work* (Berkeley and Los Angeles: University of California Press, 1995).

Chapter 3: *The Intelligence of Plumbing*

56 For a selection of background material on plumbing, see Ellen Lupton and J. Abbott Miller, *The Bathroom, the Kitchen, and the Aesthetics of Waste: A Process of Elimination* (Cambridge, MA: MIT List Visual Arts Center, 1992); Nancy M. Morris and William B. Rouse, "Review and Evaluation of Empirical Research in Troubleshooting," *Human Factors* 27, no. 5 (1985): 503–30; National Center for Construction Education and Research, *Construction Technology, Trainee Guide*, vol. 1 (Upper Saddle River, NJ: Prentice Hall, 2002), modules 02105-00, 02106-00, 02110-00; Maureen Ogle, *All the Modern Conveniences: American Household Plumbing, 1840–1890* (Baltimore: Johns Hopkins University Press, 1996); David Owen, *The Walls around Us: The Thinking Person's Guide to How a House Works* (New York: Vintage Books, 1991).

57 **The emphasis in much of what:** See chapter 8 for a fuller discussion.

60 Geoffrey Canada, *Fist, Stick, Knife, Gun: A Personal History of Violence in America* (Boston: Beacon Press, 1995), p. 25.

62 **There is a long tradition:** See, for example, Berenice M. Fisher, *Industrial Education: American Ideals and Institutions* (Madison: University of Wisconsin Press, 1967).

Chapter 4: A Vocabulary of Carpentry

67 For a selection of background material on carpentry, see John L. Feirer, *Cabinetmaking and Millwork*, 2nd ed. (Peoria, IL: Bennett Publishing Company, 1982); Gilbert Hutchings et al., *Working with Wood* (New York: Glencoe/Macmillan/McGraw-Hill, 1985); L. A. Koltun, *The Cabinetmaker's Art in Ontario, 1850–1900* (Ottawa, ON: National Museum of Canada, 1979); Henry C. Mercer, *Ancient Carpenter's Tools* (Doylestown, PA: The Bucks County Historical Society, 1960); Wendy Lesley Millroy, *An Ethnographic Study of the Mathematical Ideas of a Group of Carpenters* (Reston, VA: The National Council of Teachers of Mathematics Inc., 1992); Bob Reckman, "Carpentry: The Craft and Trade," in *Case Studies on the Labor Process*, ed. Andrew Zimbalist (New York: Monthly Review Press, 1979), pp. 73–102; W. J. Rorabaugh, *The Craft Apprentice: From Franklin to the Machine Age in America* (New York: Oxford University Press, 1986); Jeff Taylor, *Tools of the Trade: The Art and Craft of Carpentry* (San Francisco: Chronicle Books, 1996); Edwin Tunis, *Colonial Craftsmen: And the Beginnings of American Industry* (Baltimore: Johns Hopkins University Press, 1965); Gwendolyn Wright, *Building the Dream: A Social History of Housing in America* (Cambridge, MA: MIT Press, 1981).

67 **From the Renaissance through the nineteenth century:** See Eugene S. Ferguson, *Engineering and the Mind's Eye* (Cambridge, MA: MIT Press, 1992).

71–72 **"Focalization, concentration of consciousness":** William James, quoted in David LaBerge, *Attentional Processing: The Brain's Art of Mindfulness* (Cambridge, MA: Harvard University Press, 1995), pp. 19–20.

72 D. N. Perkins, *The Mind's Best Work* (Cambridge, MA: Harvard University Press, 1981), p. 274.

72 **"Use the eyes to test straightness":** Gustaf Larsson, *Elementary Sloyd and Whittling* (New York: Silver, Burdett and Company, 1906), p. 71.

73 **disciplined perception:** See Reed Stevens and Rogers Hall, "Disciplined Perception: Learning to See in Technoscience," in *Talking Mathematics in School: Studies of Teaching and Learning*, ed. Magdalene Lampert and Merrie L. Blunk (Cambridge: Cambridge University Press, 1998), pp. 107–49. See also Charles Goodwin, "Professional Vision," *American Anthropologist* 96, no. 3 (September 1994): 606–33.

77 Douglas Harper, *Working Knowledge* (Chicago: University of Chicago Press, 1987), p. 54.

78 **"Skilled performances [are] conceptually embedded":** Charles M. Keller and

Janet D. Keller, *Cognition and Tool Use: The Blacksmith at Work* (Cambridge: Cambridge University Press, 1996), p. 174.

79 Richard Gregory, "Seeing Intelligence," in *What Is Intelligence?* ed. Jean Khalfa (Cambridge: Cambridge University Press, 1994), pp. 13–26, p. 14.

79 Taylor, *Tools of the Trade*, p. 8.

81 **"funds of knowledge":** See, for example, James B. Greenberg, "Funds of Knowledge: Historical Constitution, Social Distribution, and Transmission" (paper presented at the annual meeting of the Society for Applied Anthropology, Santa Fe, NM, April 1989), and Luis C. Moll and Norma González, "Teachers as Social Scientists: Learning about Culture from Household Research," in *Race, Ethnicity and Multiculturalism: Policy and Research*, ed. Peter M. Hall (New York: Garland Publishing, 1997), pp. 89–114.

82 Taylor, *Tools of the Trade*, p. 5.

83 **"build the skill into the machine":** L. T. C. Rolt, *Tools for the Job: A Short History of Machine Tools* (London: B. T. Batsford, 1965), p. 13.

85 Susan Eisenberg, *Pioneering: Poems from the Construction Site* (Ithaca, NY: ILR Press, 1998), p. 18.

90 **There are other ways these skills can be learned:** For a good discussion of the differences and trade-offs between learning in school versus a work setting, see Howard S. Becker, "A School Is a Lousy Place to Learn Anything In," in *Learning to Work*, ed. Blanche Geer (Beverly Hills: Sage Publications, 1972), pp. 89–109. See also Frank Achtenhagen and W. Norton Grubb, "Vocational and Occupational Education: Pedagogical Complexity, Institutional Diversity," in *Handbook of Research on Teaching*, 4th ed., ed. Virginia Richardson (Washington, DC: American Educational Research Association, 2001), pp. 604–39.

90 **a long line of psychological studies:** See, for example, Lawrence W. Barsalou, *Cognitive Psychology: An Overview for Cognitive Scientists* (Hillsdale, NJ: Lawrence Erlbaum Associates, 1992); K. Anders Ericsson and Jacqui Smith, eds., *Toward a General Theory of Expertise: Prospects and Limits* (Cambridge: Cambridge University Press, 1991); and Janet L. Starkes and Fran Allard, eds., *Cognitive Issues in Motor Expertise* (Amsterdam: North-Holland, 1993).

94 **research literature on mental imagery:** See, for example, Stephen M. Kosslyn, "Mental Imagery," in *An Invitation to Cognitive Science*, vol. 2, *Visual Cognition*, ed., Stephen M. Kosslyn and Daniel N. Osherson (Cambridge, MA: MIT Press, 1995), pp. 267–96.

94 **nineteenth-century shipbuilder:** quoted in Daniel Calhoun, *The Intelligence of a People* (Princeton, NJ: Princeton University Press, 1973), p. 238.

96 Frank R. Wilson, *The Hand: How Its Use Shapes the Brain, Language, and Human Culture* (New York: Pantheon Books, 1998), p. 207.

96 **There is a small but growing research literature on mathematics in the workplace:** See, for example, Rogers Hall and Reed Stevens, "Making Space: A

Comparison of Mathematical Work in School and Professional Design Practices," in *The Cultures of Computing*, ed. Susan Leigh Star (Oxford: Blackwell Publishers, 1995); Jean Lave, "Cognitive Consequences of Traditional Apprenticeship Training in West Africa," *Anthropology and Education Quarterly* 8, no. 3 (1977): 177–80.

97 **matched earlier studies:** See Millroy, *Ethnographic Study*. But see also Analúcia P. Schliemann, "Mathematics among Carpentry Apprentices: Implications for School Teaching," in *Mathematics for All: Problems of Cultural Selectivity and Unequal Distribution of Mathematical Education and Future Perspectives on Mathematics Teaching for the Majority* (paper presented at the 5th International Congress on Mathematical Education, Adelaide, Australia, August 24–29, 1984, UNESCO Division of Science, Technical, and Environmental Education).

97 Sam Maloof, *Sam Maloof Woodworker* (Tokyo: Kodansha International, 1983), p. 55.

98 **"Tools are instruments . . .":** Larsson, *Elementary Sloyd*, p. 12.

99 Marge Piercy, "To Be of Use," *The Art of Blessing the Day: Poems with a Jewish Theme* (New York: Alfred A. Knopf, 1999), p. 73.

Chapter 5: Reflective Technique

100 For a selection of background material on electrical wiring, see David E. Nye, *Electrifying America: Social Meanings of a New Technology* (Cambridge, MA: MIT Press, 1990); National Center for Construction Education and Research, *Electrical Level One, Trainee Guide, 2000 Revision* (Upper Saddle River, NJ: Prentice Hall, 2000); David Owen, *The Walls around Us: The Thinking Person's Guide to How a House Works* (New York: Vintage Books, 1991).

100 Plato, *The Republic of Plato*, trans. Francis Macdonald Cornford (Oxford: Oxford University Press, 1945), p. 203.

100 Aristotle, *Politics, VI*, trans. H. Rackham (Cambridge, MA: Harvard University Press; London: William Heinemann, 1972), p. 503.

101 Plutarch quoted in Alison Burford, *Craftsmen in Greek and Roman Society* (London: Thames and Hudson, 1972), p. 12. For a discussion of the connection between the Greeks' social order and their views on work, see Herbert Applebaum, "Part One: The Concept of Work in Ancient Greece and Ancient Rome," in *The Concept of Work: Ancient, Medieval, and Modern* (Albany: State University of New York Press, 1992), pp. 3–175; Maurice Godelier, "Work and Its Representations: A Research Proposal," *History Workshop* 10 (1980): 164–74; Ellen Meiksins Wood and Neal Wood, *Class Ideology and Ancient Political Theory: Socrates, Plato, and Aristotle in Social Context* (New York: Oxford University Press, 1978).

103 Lawrence J. Ouellet, *Pedal to the Metal: The Work Lives of Truckers* (Philadelphia: Temple University Press, 1994).

103 **the codes of physical work:** For a treatment of these issues, see Michèle

Lamont, *The Dignity of Working Men: Morality and the Boundaries of Race, Class, and Immigration* (New York: Russell Sage Foundation; Cambridge, MA: Harvard University Press, 2000); Julie Lindquist, *A Place to Stand: Politics and Persuasion in a Working-Class Bar* (Oxford: Oxford University Press, 2002); Paul Willis, "Shop Floor Culture, Masculinity and the Wage Form," in *Working-Class Culture: Studies in History and Theory,* ed. John Clarke, Chas Critcher, and Richard Johnson (London: Hutchinson, 1979), pp. 185–282.

107 Tracy Kidder, *House* (New York: Avon Books, 1985), p. 140.

108 Leo Tolstoy, "What Is Art?" in *Aesthetics,* ed. Susan Feagin and Patrick Mayhard (Oxford: Oxford University Press, 1997), pp. 166–71, p. 167.

109 D. H. Lawrence, "Making Pictures," in *The Creative Process,* ed. Brewster Ghiselin (Berkeley and Los Angeles: University of California Press; New York: Mentor, 1952), pp. 68–73, p. 69.

110 **Canadian Inuit:** Pamela R. Stern, "Learning to Be Smart: An Exploration of the Culture of Intelligence in a Canadian Inuit Community," *American Anthropologist* 101, no. 3 (1999): 502–14.

112 **Some historians have noted:** See, for example, E. P. Thompson, "Time, Work-Discipline and Industrial Capitalism," *Past and Present* 38 (1967): 56–97. But see also Richard Whipp, " 'A Time to Every Purpose': An Essay on Time and Work," in *The Historical Meanings of Work,* ed. Patrick Joyce (Cambridge: Cambridge University Press, 1987), pp. 210–36.

115 Douglas Steere, *Work and Contemplation* (New York: Harper and Brothers, 1957), p. 32.

Chapter 6: Two Lives

116 For a selection of background material on welding, see Margaretta Jolly, ed., *Dear Laughing Motorbyke: Letters from Women Welders of the Second World War* (London: Scarlet Press, 1997); Richard D. Simonson, *The History of Welding* (Morton Grove, IL: Monticello Books, 1969); U.S. Department of the Interior Bureau of Reclamation, *Welding Manual* (Denver, CO, and Washington, DC: U.S. Government Printing Office, 1953); "Welder," in *Women and Work: In Their Own Words,* ed. Maureen R. Michelson (Troutdale, OR: New Sage Press, 1994), pp. 102–3.

116 For a selection of background material on auto assembly, see Stanley Aronowitz, "Lordstown: Disruption on the Assembly Line," in *False Promises: The Shaping of American Working Class Consciousness* (New York: McGraw-Hill, 1973), pp. 21–50; Doug Reynolds, "We Exploit Tools, Not Men: The Speed-Up and Militance at General Motors, 1930–1941," in *Work, Recreation, and Culture: Essays in American Labor History,* ed. Martin Henry Blatt and Martha K. Norkunas (New York: Garland Publishing, 1996), pp. 233–52; Robert Blauner, *Alienation and Freedom: The Factory Worker and His Industry* (Chicago: University of Chicago Press, 1964); Ely Chinoy, *Automobile Workers and the American Dream,* 2nd ed. (Urbana

and Chicago: University of Illinois Press, 1992); Ed Cray, *Chrome Colossus: General Motors and Its Times* (New York: McGraw-Hill, 1980); Kathryn Marie Dudley, *The End of the Line: Lost Jobs, New Lives in Postindustrial America* (Chicago: University of Chicago Press, 1994); Burleigh B. Gardner and William F. Whyte, "The Man in the Middle: Position and Problems of the Foreman," special issue *Applied Anthropology: Problems of Human Organization* 4, no. 2 (Spring 1945); Barbara Garson, "Luddites in Lordstown," *Harper's Magazine*, June 1972, pp. 68–73; John H. Goldthorpe, "Attitudes and Behaviour of Car Assembly Workers: A Deviant Case and a Theoretical Critique," *The British Journal of Sociology* 17 (1966): 227–44; Ruth Milkman, *Farewell to the Factory: Auto Workers in the Late Twentieth Century* (Berkeley and Los Angeles: University of California Press, 1997); Gene Richard, "On the Assembly Line," *Atlantic Monthly*, April 1937, pp. 424–28; Fritz J. Roethlisberger, "The Foreman: Master and Victim of Double Talk," *Harvard Business Review* 23 (1944–45): 283–98; Patricia Cayo Sexton, "The Auto Assembly Line: An Inside View," *Harper's Magazine*, June 1962, pp. 54–57; Sumner H. Slichter et al., "The Changing Position of Foremen in American Industry," *Advance Management* 10, no. 4 (December 1945): 155–61; Wessel Smitter, *F.O.B. Detroit* (New York: Harper and Brothers, 1938); Harvey Swados, *On the Line* (Boston: Little, Brown, 1957); Charles R. Walker and Robert H. Guest, *The Man on the Assembly Line* (Cambridge, MA: Harvard University Press, 1952); Charles R. Walker et al., *The Foreman on the Assembly Line* (Cambridge, MA: Harvard University Press, 1956).

118 **injury of occupational exclusion:** For a brief and useful discussion of gender and work, particularly as the occupational landscape has been changing, see Linda McDowell, "Work/Workplaces," in *Gender, Identity, and Place: Understanding Feminist Geographies* (Minneapolis: University of Minnesota Press, 1999), pp. 123–47.

124 Alfred North Whitehead, *The Aims of Education and Other Essays* (New York: Free Press, 1929; repr. 1967), pp. 49–50.

128–29 **In a sociological study:** Walker et al., *Foreman on the Assembly Line*.

130 **In that midcentury study:** ibid.

132 Aronowitz, *False Promises*.

134 **problem finding:** Jacob W. Getzels and Mihaly Csikszentmihalyi, *The Creative Vision: A Longitudinal Study of Problem Finding in Art* (New York: John Wiley and Sons, 1976).

134 Eugene Ferguson, *Engineering and the Mind's Eye* (Cambridge, MA: MIT Press, 1992).

135 Swados, *On the Line*; Ben Hamper, *Rivethead: Tales from the Assembly Line* (New York: Warner Books, 1986).

137 Ramiro González, "Un 'Canario' Quiere Cantar," *La Opinion*, February 13, 2001. Thanks to Manuel Espinoza for translating.

137 John Kotre, *Outliving the Self: Generativity and the Interpretation of Lives* (Baltimore: Johns Hopkins University Press, 1984).

139 **An ongoing debate in social analyses:** See, for example, Ken C. Kusterer, *Know-How on the Job: The Important Working Knowledge of "Unskilled" Workers* (Boulder, CO: Westview Press, 1978), especially chap. 9,
pp. 187–94.

Chapter 7: Rethinking Hand and Brain

142–46 Frederick Winslow Taylor, *The Principles of Scientific Management*
(1911; repr. New York: W. W. Norton, 1967). Schmidt is discussed on
pages 44–62.

144 **a number of critics:** Socialist and novelist Upton Sinclair, for example,
wrote a letter in response to *The Principles of Scientific Management* when
it was published in *The American Magazine*. Sinclair's letter is dated February 26, 1911, and is reprinted in Frank Barkley Copley, *Frederick W. Taylor: Father of Scientific Management* (New York: American Society of
Mechanical Engineers, 1923), pp. 50–51. For a more recent and comprehensive critique of Taylor, see Harry Braverman, *Labor and Monopoly
Capital: The Degradation of Work in the Twentieth Century* (1974; repr., New
York: Monthly Review Press, 1998), pp. 59–85. After writing the section
on Schmidt, I found that Barbara Garson had a similar take on his encounter with Taylor; see Barbara Garson, *All the Livelong Day: The Meaning and Demeaning of Routine Work* (1975; repr. New York: Penguin Books,
1994).

144 **huge increase of manual laborers:** See David Montgomery, *The Fall of the
House of Labor: The Workplace, the State, and American Labor Activism,
1865–1925* (Cambridge: Cambridge University Press, 1987), pp. 58–111.

144 **"The key to industrial growth"** ibid., pp. 49–50.

144 **"The hard work of America":** quoted in Daniel T. Rodgers, *The Work Ethic
in Industrial America, 1850–1920* (Chicago: University of Chicago Press,
1974), p. 171.

145 Thomas Bell, *Out of This Furnace: A Novel of Immigrant Labor in America*
(Pittsburgh: University of Pittsburgh Press, 1976).

145 **sociologists and social reformers visited mill towns:** See, for example, Mar-
garet F. Byington, *Homestead: The Households of a Mill Town* (New York:
Russell Sage Foundation, 1910; Pittsburgh: University of Pittsburgh
Press, 1974).

145 **adventurous academics and journalists:** See, for example, Walter A. Wyck-
off, *The Workers: An Experiment in Reality* (New York: Charles Scribner's
Sons, 1898).

145 **give workers back their heads:** William Serrin, *Homestead: The Glory and
Tragedy of an American Steel Town* (New York: Vintage Books, 1993),
p. 421.

146 **rich in fraternal organizations:** See, for example, Milton Cantor, "Social
Lodges and Fraternal Associations and the Maintenance of Urban Community," in *Work, Recreation, and Culture: Essays in American Labor History,*

ed. Martin Henry Blatt and Martha K. Norkunas (New York: Garland Publishing, 1996), pp. 101–23.

147 **MIT Commission:** Michael L. Dertouzos et al., *Made in America: Regaining the Productive Edge* (Cambridge, MA: MIT Press, 1989), p. 72.

147 Barbara Ehrenreich, *Nickel and Dimed: On (Not) Getting By in America* (New York: Metropolitan Books/Henry Holt, 2001), p. 100.

147 Amy Tanner, "Glimpses at the Mind of a Waitress," *American Journal of Sociology* 13 (July 1907–May 1908): 48–55, 54.

148 Rogers Hall, "The Organization and Development of Discursive Practices for 'Having a Theory,' " *Discourse Processes* 27, no. 2 (1999): 187–218, 215.

149 For a selection of background material on surgery, see Thomas N. Bonner, *Becoming a Physician: Medical Education in Great Britain, France, Germany, and the United States, 1750–1945* (New York: Oxford University Press, 1995); D. Michael Elnicki et al., "Interpretive and Procedural Skills of the Internal Medicine Clerkship: Performance and Supervision," *Southern Medical Journal* 89, no. 6 (June 1996): 603–8; David A. Evans and Vimla L. Patel, eds., *Cognitive Science in Medicine: Biomedical Modeling* (Cambridge, MA: MIT Press, 1989); Ward O. Griffen Jr., "Medical Education: A Continuum in Disarray," *American Journal of Surgery* 154 (September 1987): 255–60; Mark Kramer, *Invasive Procedures: A Year in the World of Two Surgeons* (New York: Penguin Books, 1979); Harold I. Lief and Renee C. Fox, "Training for 'Detached Concern' in Medical Students," in *The Psychological Basis of Medical Practice*, ed. Harold I. Lief et al. (New York: Hoeber Medical Division/Harper and Row, 1963), pp. 12–35; Carol M. Mangione, "How Medical School Did and Did Not Prepare Me for Graduate Medical Education," *Journal of Clinical Education of Medical Students* 61, no. 9 (September 1986, part 2): 3–10; Max D. Miller, "Education, Training, and Proficiency of Procedural Skills," *Primary Care*, 24, no. 2 (June 1997), pp. 231–40; Don K. Nakayama and Andrei Steiber, "Surgery Interns' Experience with Surgical Procedures as Medical Students," *American Journal of Surgery* 159 (March 1990): 341–44; William A. Nolen, *The Making of a Surgeon* (New York: Random House, 1968); Stanley J. Reiser, *Medicine and the Reign of Technology* (Cambridge: Cambridge University Press, 1978); Richard Reznick et al., "Testing Technical Skill via an Innovative 'Bench Station' Examination," *American Journal of Surgery* 173 (March 1997): 226–30; Donn Weinholtz and Janine Edwards, with consulting medical editor Laura M. Mumford, *Teaching during Rounds: A Handbook for Attending Physicians and Residents* (Baltimore: Johns Hopkins University Press, 1992).

151 **procedural . . . declarative knowledge:** See, for example, John R. Anderson, *The Architecture of Cognition* (Cambridge, MA: Harvard University Press, 1983).

152 For a selection of background material on physical therapy, see: Joseph P. Farrell, "In Search of Clinical Excellence," *Journal of Orthopedic and Sports Physical Therapy* 24, no. 3 (September 1996): 115–21; Ruth Grant,

ed., *Physical Therapy of the Cervical and Thoracic Spine*, 2nd ed. (New York: Churchill Livingstone, 1994); Gail M. Jensen et al., "The Novice versus the Experienced Clinician: Insights into the Work of the Physical Therapist," *Physical Therapy* 70, no. 5 (May 1990): 314–23; G. D. Maitland, *Vertebral Manipulation*, 5th ed. (Oxford: Butterworth-Heinemann, 1986); Rosemary M. Scully and Marylou R. Barnes, eds., *Physical Therapy* (Philadelphia: J. B. Lippincott, 1989); Katherine F. Shepard and Gail M. Jensen, eds., *Handbook of Teaching for Physical Therapists* (Boston: Butterworth-Heinemann, 1997).

154 **Jeff Taylor:** See the note for page 82.

156 **"a practical-minded obsession":** Malcolm Gladwell, "The Physical Genius," *The New Yorker*, Aug. 2, 1994, p. 60.

156 Charles L. Bosk, *Forgive and Remember: Managing Medical Failure* (Chicago: University of Chicago Press, 1979).

158 Lee Shulman, "Knowledge and Teaching: Foundations of the New Reform," *Harvard Educational Review* 57.1 (February 1987): 1–22.

159–60 **on average, the surgeon will earn:** See U.S. Department of Labor, Bureau of Labor Statistics, Occupational Employment Statistics, "2000 National Occupational Employment and Wage Estimates" (Washington, DC, 2000).

160 Jeff Taylor, *Tools of the Trade: The Art and Craft of Carpentry* (San Francisco: Chronicle Books, 1996), p. 13.

160 **"itself a cultural boundary":** Montgomery, *Fall of the House of Labor*, p. 181.

160 **boilermakers:** ibid., p. 197.

160 **In an attempt to settle:** See "Report of Proceedings of the Thirty-sixth Annual Convention of the American Federation of Labor" (Baltimore, MD, November 13–25, 1916; Washington, DC: Law Reporter Printing Company, 1916).

161 **one historian of the field:** Richard D. Simonson, *The History of Welding* (Morton Grove, IL: Monticello Books, 1969), p. 102. Newer occupational classification systems, like the one from the U.S. Department of Labor listed below, go beyond the simple nonskilled/semiskilled/skilled scheme, though that older scheme still has influence in the culture and in some job settings.

161 **Department of Labor's Standard Occupational Classification System:** See the Occupational Information Network (O*NET) and O*NET OnLine, U.S. Department of Labor.

161 **But these analyses can also diminish:** See, for example, Helena Znanieck Lopata et al., "Job Complexity as Perceived by Workers and Experts," *Work and Occupations* 12, no. 4 (Nov. 1985), pp. 395–415. The study relies on earlier occupational classification schemes but is still instructive.

163 **"Boys, the family luck":** John Strohmeyer, *Crisis in Bethlehem: Big Steel's Struggle to Survive* (Bethesda, MD: Adler and Adler, 1986), p. 11.

164 Richard Hofstadter, *Anti-Intellectualism in American Life* (New York: Knopf, 1963).

Chapter 8: Hand and Brain in School

167 For a selection of background material on vocational education, see Frank Achtenhagen and W. Norton Grubb, "Vocational and Occupational Education: Pedagogical Complexity, Institutional Diversity," in *Handbook of Research on Teaching*, 4th ed., ed. Virginia Richardson (Washington, DC: American Educational Research Association, 2001), pp. 604–39; Melvin L. Barlow, *History of Industrial Education in the United States* (Peoria, IL: Chas. A. Bennett Co., 1967); Sue E. Berryman and Thomas R. Bailey, *The Double Helix of Education and the Economy* (New York: Teacher's College Press, 1992); Anthony P. Carnevale and Donna M. Desrochers, "The Missing Middle: Aligning Education and the Knowledge Economy," Office of Vocational and Adult Education, U.S. Department of Education, April 2002, www.ed.gov/@/offices/list/ovae/pi/hs/commisspap.html; Berenice M. Fisher, *Industrial Education: American Ideals and Institutions* (Madison: University of Wisconsin Press, 1967); Kenneth Gray, "The Baccalaureate Game: Is It Right for All Teens?" *Phi Delta Kappan* (April 1996): 528–34; W. Norton Grubb, ed., *Education through Occupations in American High Schools*, vols. 1 and 2 (New York: Teacher's College Press, 1995); Stephen F. Hamilton and Mary A. Hamilton, "Building Strong School-to-Work Systems: Illustrations of Key Components," U.S. Department of Education and U.S. Department of Labor, Cornell Youth and Work Program: Preparing Youth for the Future, n.d.; Harvey Kantor and David B. Tyack, eds., *Work, Youth, and Schooling: Historical Perspectives on Vocationalism in American Education* (Stanford, CA: Stanford University Press, 1982); Joe L. Kincheloe, *Toil and Trouble: Good Work, Smart Workers, and Integration of Academic and Vocational Education* (New York: Peter Lang, 1995); Herbert M. Kliebard, *Schooled to Work: Vocationalism and the American Curriculum, 1876–1946* (New York: Teacher's College Press, 1999); Marvin Lazerson and W. Norton Grubb, *American Education and Vocationalism: A Documentary History, 1870–1970* (New York: Teacher's College Press, 1974); Theodore Lewis, "Toward the 21st Century: Retrospect, Prospect for American Vocationalism," Information Series No. 373 (Columbus, OH: ERIC Clearinghouse on Adult, Career, and Vocational Education, 1998); Richard J. Murnane and Frank Levy, *Teaching the New Basic Skills: Principles for Educating Children to Thrive in a Changing Economy* (New York: Free Press, 1996); Jeannie Oakes et al., *Educational Matchmaking: Academic and Vocational Tracking in Comprehensive High Schools*, (report prepared for the National Center for Research in Vocational Education [Santa Monica, CA: Rand], n.d.); Lynn Olson, *The School to Work Revolution: How Employers and Educators Are Joining Forces to Prepare Tomorrow's Skilled Workforce* (Reading, MA: Addison-Wesley, 1997); James E. Rosenbaum, "Beyond Empty Promises: Policies to Improve Transitions into College and Jobs," Office of Vocational and Adult Educa-

tion, U.S. Department of Education, April 2002, www.rand.org/publica-tions/R/R4189.pdf; Larry Rosenstock, "The Walls Come Down: The Over-due Reunification of Vocational and Academic Education," *Phi Delta Kappan* (February 1991): 434–36; Adria Steinberg, *Real Learning, Real Work: School-to-Work as High School Reform* (New York: Routledge, 1998); *Vocational-Technical Education: Major Reforms and Debates: 1917–Present* (report prepared for the Office of Vocational and Adult Education, U.S. Department of Education, 1993); Dan Walters, "Vocational Education Struggles to Survive College-Oriented Politics," *Sacramento Bee*, May 24, 2002; "What Work Requires of Schools: A Scans Report for America 2000," (report prepared for the Secretary's Commission on Achieving Necessary Skills, U.S. Department of Labor, June 1991); Arthur G. Wirth, *Education in the Technological Society: The Vocational-Liberal Studies Contro-versy in the Early Twentieth Century* (Scranton, PA: Intext Educational Pub-lishers, 1980); Michael E. Wonacott, "Benefits of Vocational Education: Myths and Realities No. 8" (from the Educational Resources Information Center OnLine, http://ericacve.org/docgen.asp?t61=mr&ID=96); Susan Yonezawa, Amy Stuart Wells, and Irene Serna, "Choosing Tracks: 'Free-dom of Choice' in Detracking Schools," *American Educational Research Jour-nal 39*, no. 1 (spring 2002): 37–67; Michael Young, "Bridging the Academic/ Vocational Divide: Two Nordic Case Studies," *European Journal of Educa-tion 28*, no. 2 (1993): 209–14.

167 **There was some social-class mixing:** See Carl F. Kaestle, *Pillars of the Repub-lic: Common Schools and American Society: 1780–1860* (New York: Hill and Wang, 1983), p. 121.

168 **by 1890:** See Thomas James and David Tyack, "Learning from Past Ef-forts to Reform the High School," *Phi Delta Kappan* (February 1983): 400–406.

168 W. Norton Grubb and Marvin Lazerson, *The Education Gospel and the Vo-cational Roles of Schooling* (Cambridge, MA: Harvard University Press, 2004).

169 **there remain patterns of inequality:** See Samuel Roundfield Lucas, *Tracking Inequality: Stratification and Mobility in American High Schools* (New York: Teacher's College Press, 1999).

169–70 **recent historical analysis:** *Vocational-Technical Education: Major Reforms and Debates, 1917–Present* (report prepared for the Office of Vocational and Adult Education, U.S. Department of Education, 1993), p. 7.

170ff. **history of VocEd:** This history is drawn from the following sources listed in the background material on VocEd; see pages 244–45: Barlow, Fisher, Kantor and Tyack, Kliebard, Lazerson and Grubb (1974), and Wirth.

170 **"Throw in the fire":** Calvin M. Woodward quoted in Kliebard, *Schooled to Work*, p. 1.

171 **Consider these remarks:** John Balzar, "Craftmanship as a Door to Artisan-ship," *Los Angeles Times*, Commentary, April 10, 2002, p. B13.

172 **observation made by those who study curriculum reform:** See, for example, David K. Cohen and Barbara Neufield, "The Failure of High Schools and the Progress of Education," *Daedalus* 110 (Summer 1981): 69–89; and David Tyack and Larry Cuban, *Tinkering toward Utopia: A Century of Public School Reform* (Cambridge, MA: Harvard University Press, 1995).

172 **the president of Harvard:** Charles W. Eliot, "Industrial Education as an Essential Factor in Our National Prosperity," *Proceedings of the National Society for the Promotion of Industrial Education, Bulletin No. 5* (April 1908), pp. 9–14, pp. 12–13.

174 **Social predestination:** John Dewey, *Democracy and Education* (New York: Macmillan, 1916; repr. New York: Free Press, 1944), p. 317.

175 **One Depression-era survey:** cited in Kliebard, *Schooled to Work,* p. 227.

175 A. B. Hollingshead, *Elmstown's Youth: The Impact of Social Classes on Adolescents* (New York: John Wiley and Sons, 1949).

175 Jeannie Oakes, *Keeping Track: How Schools Structure Inequality* (New Haven, CT: Yale University Press, 1985).

176 **more European than American:** The irony here is that in some European countries—Germany is a good example—vocational education, though a separate system, is more substantial and respected than VocEd is in the United States. The reasons are complex, but have to do with different cultural traditions and attitudes involving work, and with different governing arrangements among the state, business, education, and labor. See, for example, Grubb and Lazerson, *Education Gospel.*

177 The sampling of journals included *American Vocational Journal, Vocational Education Journal, VocEd,* and *Techniques.* The years ranged from 1971 to 2001.

181 W. Norton Grubb, "The New Vocationalism: What It Is, What It Could Be," *Phi Delta Kappan* (April 1996): 535–46.

182 **a visionary faculty:** for example, "High Tech High" in San Diego, California, http://www.hightechhigh.org, and "The Met" in Providence, Rhode Island, www.bigpicture.org.

182 Theodore Lewis, "Vocational Education as General Education," *Curriculum Inquiry* 28, no. 3 (1998): 283–309, p. 291. See also his "Valid Knowledge and the Problem of Practical Arts Curricula," *Curriculum Inquiry* 23, no. 2 (1993): 175–202.

184 **manager of a Motorola plant:** quoted in William Greider, *One World, Ready or Not: The Manic Logic of Global Capitalism* (New York: Touchstone, 1997), p.84.

184 **What else but human consciousness:** For a discussion of reductive notions of technology, see David F. Noble, *Forces of Production: A Social History of Industrial Automation* (New York: Oxford University Press, 1986).

187 **One influential early-twentieth-century superintendent:** Frank Spaulding, who is discussed and quoted in Raymond E. Callahan, *Education and the Cult of Efficiency: A Study of the Social Forces That Have Shaped the Admin-*

istration of the Public Schools (Chicago: University of Chicago Press, 1962), pp. 67–79.

187 Horace Mann, "Fifth Report, for 1841," in *Life and Works of Horace Mann*, vol. 3, *Annual Reports of the Secretary of the Board of Education of Massachusetts for the Years 1839–1844* (Boston: Lee and Shepard Publishers, 1867; repr. 1891), pp. 92–128.

188 **to quote one research team:** Karen M. McClafferty et al., "What Is a College Culture? Facilitating College Preparation through Organizational Change" (paper presented at the annual conference of the American Educational Research Association, New Orleans, LA, April 1–5, 2002), p. 1.

190 Richard Sennett and Jonathan Cobb, *The Hidden Injuries of Class* (New York: W. W. Norton, 1972), p. 179.

192 **research supports this:** See, for example, David Stern et al., *Career Academies: Partnerships for Reconstructing American High Schools* (San Francisco: Jossey Bass, 1992).

193 **"How can a culture be created":** Robert P. Moses et al., "The Algebra Project: Organizing in the Spirit of Ella," *Harvard Educational Review* 59, no. 4 (November 1989): 423–43, p. 428.

Conclusion

195 **"The scream of the engine":** U. J. Jones, quoted in *A History of Blair County, Pennsylvania*, vol. 1, ed. Tarring S. Davis with associate editor Lucile Shenk (Harrisburg: National Historical Association, 1931), p. 255.

196 **waitressing . . . projected for growth:** cited in Michael B. Katz, *The Price of Citizenship: Redefining the American Welfare State* (New York: Metropolitan Books, 2001), pp. 350–51.

196–97 **"The habit of work":** Frances Fox Piven and Richard A. Cloward, *Poor People's Movements: Why They Succeed, How They Fail* (New York: Vintage Books, 1979), p. 47.

197 **Many have commented on the continued tendency toward de-skilling:** See, for example, Harry Braverman, *Labor and Monopoly Capital: The Degradation of Work in the Twentieth Century* (1974; repr. New York: Monthly Review Press, 1998), and Barbara Garson, *All the Livelong Day: The Meaning and Demeaning of Routine Work* (1975; repr. New York: Penguin Books, 1994).

197 **There is an extensive philosophical and sociological literature:** See, for example, Herbert Applebaum, *The Concept of Work: Ancient, Medieval, and Modern* (Albany: State University of New York Press, 1992).

199 Howard Gardner, *Frames of Mind: The Theory of Multiple Intelligences* (New York: Basic Books, 1983), p. 208.

199 Frank R. Wilson, *The Hand: How Its Use Shapes the Brain, Language, and Human Culture* (New York: Pantheon, 1998), p. 307.

201 Reg Theriault, *How to Tell When You're Tired: A Brief Examination of Work* (New York: W. W. Norton, 1995), p. 133.

203 "social behavior is intelligent": John F. Kihlstrom and Nancy Cantor, "Social Intelligence," in *Handbook of Intelligence*, ed. Robert J. Sternberg (Cambridge: Cambridge University Press, 2000), pp. 359–79, p. 368.

205 Lower-order mathematics: Lynn Arthur Steen and Susan L. Forman, "Mathematics for Work and Life," in *Prospects for School Mathematics*, ed. Iris M. Carl (Reston, VA: National Council of Teachers of Mathematics, 1995), pp. 219–340, p. 221.

206ff. workplace literacy: There is a fair amount of research done on workplace literacy. See, for example, William A. Diehl and Larry Mikulecky, "The Nature of Reading at Work," *Journal of Reading* 24, no. 3 (December 1980): 221–28; Glynda Hull, ed., *Changing Work, Changing Workers: Critical Perspectives on Language, Literacy, and Skills* (Albany: State University of New York Press, 1997); Evelyn Jacob, "Literacy Skills and Production Line Work," in *Becoming a Worker*, ed. Kathryn M. Borman and Jane Reisman (Norwood, NJ: Ablex Publishing Corporation, 1986), pp. 176–200; Thomas G. Sticht and Larry Mikulecky, "Job-Related Basic Skills: Cases and Conclusions," Information Series No. 285 (ERIC Clearinghouse on Adult, Career and Vocational Education, Columbus, OH: The National Center for Research on Vocational Education, 1984).

209 "Fewer than 10 percent of front-line American workers": "Learning a Living: A Blueprint for High Performance: A Scans Report for America 2000," U.S. Department of Labor, April 1992, p. 12.

209 Since the early 1980s: For a good overview, see Richard J. Murnane and Frank Levy, *Teaching the New Basic Skills: Principles for Educating Children to Thrive in a Changing Economy* (New York: Free Press, 1996).

210 There is a genuine debate among economists: See Philip Moss and Chris Tilly, *Stories Employers Tell: Race, Skill and Hiring in America* (New York: Russell Sage Foundation, 2001); Gordon Lafer, *The Job Training Charade* (Ithaca, NY, and London: Cornell University Press, 2002).

210 And there are some well-documented cases: See, for example, Wellford Wilms, *Restoring Prosperity: How Workers and Managers Are Forging a New Culture of Cooperation* (New York: Times Business, 1996).

211 Glynda Hull, "What's in a Label?: Complicating Notions of the Skills-Poor Worker," *Written Communication* 16, no. 4 (1999): 379–411. For another account that involves the effects of institutional assumptions and ideologies on the organization of work, see Frances Julia Riemer, *Working at the Margins: Moving Off Welfare in America* (Albany: State University of New York Press, 2001).

212 Daniel Calhoun, *The Intelligence of a People* (Princeton, NJ: Princeton University Press, 1973), p. ix.

213 As an ideal, democracy assumes: For background material to this discussion of democracy, see John Dewey, *Democracy and Education* (1916; repr., New York: Free Press, 1966); Amy Gutmann, *Democratic Education* (Princeton, NJ: Princeton University Press, 1987); Joseph F. Kett, *The Pursuit of Knowledge under Difficulties: From Self-Improvement to Adult Educa-*

tion in America, 1750–1990 (Stanford, CA: Stanford University Press, 1994); Michael Walzer, *Spheres of Justice: A Defense of Pluralism and Equality* (New York: Basic Books, 1983); Rush Welter, *Popular Education and Democratic Thought in America* (New York: Columbia University Press, 1962).

214 **eugenics and IQ:** Stephen Jay Gould, *The Mismeasure of Man* (New York: W. W. Norton, 1981); Leon J. Kamin, *The Science and Politics of IQ* (Potomac, MD: Lawrence Erlbaum, 1974); Leila Zenderland, *Measuring Minds: Henry Herbert Goddard and the Origins of American Intelligence Testing* (Cambridge: Cambridge University Press, 1998).

215 Richard J. Herrnstein and Charles Murray, *The Bell Curve: Intelligence and Class Structure in American Life* (New York: Free Press, 1994). For a sympathetic but trenchant review of *The Bell Curve*, see James J. Heckman, "Cracked Bell," *Reason Magazine* 26, no. 10 (March 1995): 49–56.

215 **as a number of firsthand accounts . . . would certify:** See, for example, Vera John-Steiner, *Notebooks of the Mind: Explorations of Thinking* (New York: Oxford University Press, 1997).

215 Albert Borgmann, *Technology and the Character of Contemporary Life: A Philosophical Inquiry* (Chicago: University of Chicago Press, 1984), p. 89.

Afterword

217 **involved and contentious discussions:** See citations under "cognition," page 230.

218 **One writer:** Colleen M. Seifert, "Situated Cognition and Learning," in *The MIT Encyclopedia of the Cognitive Sciences*, ed. Robert A. Wilson and Frank C. Keil (Cambridge, MA: MIT Press, 1999), pp. 767–69, p. 767.

219 **Each theory . . . shines a . . . light:** For a compatible, though distinct, view, see James G. Greeno et al., "The Situativity of Knowing, Learning, and Research," *American Psychologist* 53, no. 1 (1998): 5–26. See also John R. Anderson et al., "Perspectives on Learning, Thinking, and Activity," *Educational Researcher* (May 2000): 11–13.

221 **as some feminist social scientists:** See, for example, Anna Neumann and Penelope L. Peterson, eds., *Women, Research, and Autobiography in Education* (New York: Teachers College Press, 1997).